PRAISE for *The 5 Habits to Mine Your Gold*

This book is an inspiration. Thank you for doing such a service to humanity.

Amanda Allen, 3 x CrossFit Games World title winner, Australia

I have learned from Matt that habits are those somewhat hidden little creatures that are either building or blocking your success. The 5 Habits to Mine Your Gold shines a brilliant spotlight on the discovery journey from where you are now to reaching your full potential. Whether you are just starting out or wanting to recalibrate, use this as your GPS.

Stephen C. Lewis, Principal, AB Bernstein Global Wealth Management, USA

I met Matt 12 years ago in a 'Fearless Referrals' coaching program he led for Financial Advisors. To this day, that experience has influenced and informed nearly every aspect of my mindset, communication style, and drive to win. 'The 5 Habits to Mine Your Gold' is an impressive, heart-felt treatise in which Matt goes deep into his own psyche to develop a methodology that unlocks one's own potential to drive success. Matt brings a level of accessibility that is rare in books that "coach", to build a successful mindset within a succinct and executable plan of action. I recommend this book to anyone looking to unlock the potential within themselves to achieve measurable and sustainable success.

Vern Montross, Western Division Managing Director at City National Rochdale, USA

The 5 Habits to Mine Your Gold really spoke to me. As a divorce lawyer with partners and our own practice, the process and goal of moving forward, getting better, finding purpose is always at the forefront of my mind. As a result, I have been reading business development, marketing, and self-help improvement literature for more than 20 years. I usually will find something helpful, but then forget the advice after a month or two. Matt's book is different because as Matt explains the ups and downs of his own career, you can see his purpose revealed in a way I have never heard or read anyone else explain and in a way that is so relatable. His story and advice provides encouragement and hope to one to keep moving forward, but with sustainable and practical advice to make the journey a successful one. Thanks for a great book!

Nanette McCarthy, Principal Partner, GMR Family Law, USA.

What type of person do you want to be? What's your purpose, and how do you overcome those daily obstacles that get in the way of you "mining your gold"? This book provides a perfect blend of storytelling (on Matt's own journey), academic insight, process, and habits, that truly make you pause and reflect on your own situation and empower you to take action. If you want to achieve results not just in work, but in life, this book is for you and give some great pointers along the way. Brilliant work Matt.

Paul Golledge, Head of Division, Marketing, St. James's Place, UK.

*"I heard about Matt through a good friend. He told me that Matt helped him to reach Top of the Table, and here our coaching relationship started to grow. Matt was next to me for the past three years. In addition, he has powerfully impacted all attendees of the Beirut Life Insurance Seminars. Matt helped me to find out my real fear - despite all the success I've achieved – is the **Fear of Success**. In this book Matt urges us all to "Pull the Weeds Fast!" I recommend this book to every agent, manager, and for every person looking for success. Thank you, MATT!*

Naji Haddad, Financial Planner, BLIS founder, MDRT Region Chair Middle East, Africa, and South Asia.

All of us hear some brilliant ideas from time-to-time which sound so exciting but are truly difficult to apply. Matt's book, on the contrary, is full of ideas put in simple form which are easy to implement. This is a proven practical guide written by someone who has been coaching top professionals in the life insurance business for over 20 years that could help anyone aspiring to be their best.

Svetlana Pitlin, Senior Finance Advisor-Expert, Allianz, Lithuania

It's precisely the kind of book one needs no matter which part of life's journey you are on. I learned from this book, that we should be a writer of our life and a reader of our mind. The more you get to know yourself, the less you need approval of others. It's a must read for all my new recruits. Thank you, Matt.

Manmohan Abdullah, CEO, Life Specialist Financial Planners, Senior District Director with AIA, Malaysia

The transformation process through which you achieve success would not be so difficult if you had a great guide. Well, now you have it! Love your vulnerabilities: they will lead you to those powerful habits that will make great changes in your professional and personal life! The 5 Habits to Mine Your Own Gold is the definitive book on **how to take action** *and create small but powerful habits. This book gives you a beautiful perspective on how to motivate yourself to achieve your big life goals.*

Ana-Daniela Morosanu, Senior Expert Unit Manager, Metropolitan Life, Romania

Another simple strategy to achieve success from Matt Anderson. I have personally known and worked with Matt for over 10 years and his passion to help people succeed again shines through in this book. The "pulling up weeds" section in particular helps people analyse what is holding them back and the need to push through comfort zones. A must read.

Andy Gilbert, Executive Business Partnering Manager, St. James's Place, U.K.

Matt brings his authenticity and passion for helping people to get unstuck and do the actions that lead to however you define success. He gives tangible ways to accomplish what you want in life through love and "choosing your hard"! Why not do the hard work and achieve what you want in life!

Melissa Masitto, Vice President, Sales and Marketing, Hyatt Hotels Corporation

Matt's very personal story and journey has led to him creating some great habits to help you 'mine your own gold'. One of the areas which hit home to me was around 'Pulling the Weeds Fast' – how often do we stop ourselves from achieving something? 'Oh, that's too risky' or 'am I really up to this?' and these self-limiting beliefs end up stopping us from making the most of ourselves. Linked to this is making sure we create an environment around us which enables us to 'shine', whether colleagues, friends, or family and if we don't have this support, make it a goal to find people who will have your back. Thank you, Matt for building and sharing these habits which will undoubtedly resonate with many people and help them be the best they can be.

Lesley Cameron, Head of Practice Development, St. James's Place (Hong Kong) Limited

I love this book! Matt reminds us that we are all living on a gold mine—ourselves! He provides the tools we need to look inward, mine our own gold, and live a life of authentic happiness and abundance.

Joe Brocato, author of *HIT IT OFF: 21 Rules for Mastering the Art and Science of Relationships in Life and Business*

Life is short. When we were kids, we lived in the theta brain state. We played in a land of imagination where anything could happen, and time moved slowly. Where once we dreamed the impossible dreams, the narrative changes quickly as we move into adulthood and realize, dreams are only dreams without action. Matt shares his knowledge and opens the reader's eyes to the possibilities and potential we all have if we set simple habits into place. A little passion, persistence, and a solid plan are the steppingstones for real results. Ready to set a foundation for success? Read this book.

Sue Hitzmann, Founder, Chief Creative Officer, MELT Method, USA

THE
5 HABITS
TO MINE YOUR
GOLD

Matt Anderson

ISBN 978-1-66789-297-9

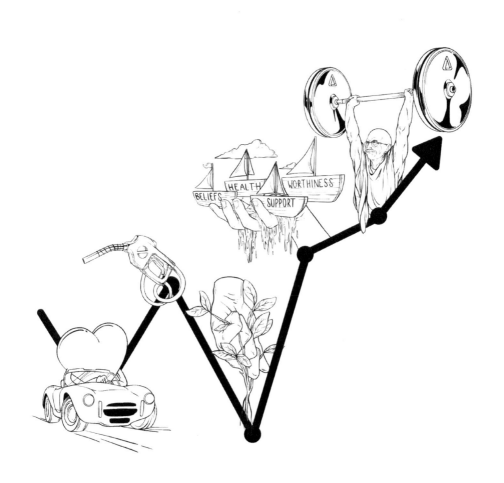

To Erica

"The mother of all fears: Fear that we will succeed.
That we can access the powers we secretly know we possess.
That we can become the person we sense in our hearts we truly are...
We fear this because if it's true, then we become estranged from all we know...

But here's the trick: we wind up in space, but not alone.

Instead, we are tapped into an unquenchable, undepletable, inexhaustible source of wisdom, consciousness, and companionship."

Steven Pressfield, *The War of Art*

CONTENTS

ACKNOWLEDGEMENTS

Thirty years ago, when I was working my first year as director of two special needs camps in the Wisconsin Dells, a woman I'd met in a hot tub and dated once (you can't make this stuff up, can you?) sent me a book she'd read in college called *The One Minute Manager*. I found it so helpful that I really didn't want to give it her back! Funnily, looking back, that was the first non-fiction book I recall reading for pleasure. It was so helpful, it led to a lifelong habit of seeking information from others on ways to grow and make a more positive difference. Two years after that I read *The 7 Habits of Highly Effective People*, then a friend bought me Deepak Chopra's *7 Spiritual Laws of Success* for my birthday …and 30 years later here is my contribution.

Many, many great minds have helped me along the way. If I start mentioning influential thinkers, I won't stop. But I must give special credit to three people. First, Fiona Harrold, because chancing across her book, *Be Your Own Life Coach,* at a Waterstones in Leamington Spa definitely changed my life in 2002 and prompted me to train as a coach.

Four years later I stumbled on Robert Holden's book *Success Intelligence* on a bookshelf at Foyles, my favorite bookshop in the world on Charing Cross Road in London. His ability to shift my paradigms about the success I was chasing (and that most people continue to chase) was profoundly meaningful to me – and I really needed this message over and over!

More recently in 2020, John James, a client of mine from Seattle, kept recommending a book called *Tiny Habits*. At his third attempt, I bought it and was bowled over because the author had created a simple formula on how to change effectively. For the first time in my life I researched whether this author (BJ Fogg) had a course where I could certify to teach his process. Why? Because it was that good and it took him 20 years to develop – 20 more years I certainly didn't have. I am certified as a Tiny Habits coach and it has proved incredibly helpful. Thanks BJ and thanks John!

While it was the emotional pain from my upbringing that most influenced me to want to learn what I've learned so far and share in this book, my parents deserve a lot of credit for valuing and supporting my education from the age of 7 at King Henry VIII in Coventry and then later at Warwick University. They cared deeply for me in their own way, and I am desperately sad my father died at 58 and never got to meet his daughter-in-law or grandchildren. He would have been a kind and devoted grandad.

I am sure I've learned an enormous amount from most of the many hundreds of clients I've coached over the past 20 years. I am sure the frequent reinforcement of their lessons has built a pivotal foundation to much of what you're holding in your hands. Thank you to repeat clients/friends/referral sources/high achievers Steve Lewis, Asvin Chauhan, John Nichols, Dave Altman, Dave Bentson, Michael Kloster, John Brewer, Faten Noueihed, and all the great work Naji Haddad does for the people of Lebanon, the Beirut Life Insurance Seminars, and the (currently) less heralded sales professionals of Asia, Africa, and Eastern Europe.

To my pioneer clients from my Breakthrough Bound program: Brian Dixon, Nanette McCarthy, Bob Hart, and Colleen Bertrand – thanks for being early adopters!

For your support and encouragement over the past decade, I'd like to thank my many friends at Alliance Bernstein (including Don Braun, Rachelle Neumann, and Helaine Teperman), City National Rochdale (especially Vern Montross and Marina Rivkind) and St. James's Place Wealth Management (especially Andy Gilbert, Paul Golledge, and Lesley Cameron). You have helped me help many people at your companies and help me support my family.

A very special thank you to my maestro editor Lisa Buntrock. Your insights and suggestions have helped shape this book into being my truer voice and something that makes a whole lot more sense! Thank you also for your powerful friendship and support over the years. And to Dinni Astriani: a big thank you for the inspiring artwork and all the help you've provided my business over the past 4-5 years. We all need a support team, and you have both provided this for me.

Lastly, I saved the best for last. A huge thank you to my wife, Erica, for your patience and support over many years and in many ways understanding how important this book is to me to live my purpose. Izzy and Cal my amazing children: a thank you from the bottom of my heart for doing your best to understand me "working on my book again". All three of you are the reason I do what I do, and you are my everything. If I do die before this book is 'discovered' as great art, that's why I create and encourage you all to create too. Your art lives forever.

All artwork courtesy of Dinni Astriani. Hire her. She's great - astrianidinni@gmail.com

Photography courtesy of Vicky Wager.

INTRODUCTION

I wrote this book to help set you free:

It sets you free from what you don't know that you need to know if you want to mine your gold = be, do and have what you most want in life.

It sets you free from the mental shackles that have held you back.

It set you free by providing a recipe and action plan to follow to mine your gold.

I believe you were born with a vein of gold inside you, and you know you were too. You can *sense* it. Yes, there are perhaps plenty of times when you doubt this and doubt yourself, but every once in a while, it whispers to you. It sends you unexpected messages that you could do something remarkable. You remember moments of greatness. (You've come up with great ideas before). The thought stays with you: I'm special. It gives you the hope to achieve more, it encourages you to learn more, and it helps you stay in the game.

Proof of its existence arrives every year on New Year's Day when you almost always wake up with a renewed sense that '*this* year' better things are possible. *This* can be the year that you get that breakthrough with your health, your business, your finances, or with a key relationship.

You know you can.

You can become free to do what you want when you want. You can live a purposeful life, be loving, bold, learn and grow. You can spend your life serving and inspiring.

Your vein of gold has gifted you certain skills and strengths. It's provided self-belief at times that you didn't think you had it, given you accolades and praise you can't fully explain and has saved your backside on many occasions. It's gifted you a level of confidence at times that you couldn't comprehend or articulate to anyone, including yourself.

It is a vein of riches. And you *know* it's there. You can *feel* it. It is your gold mine.

Sometimes. All too often, your vein of gold lies dormant. Like a brilliant shining moon that's hidden behind thick clouds, you treat it as if it's invisible and all too often it lies untapped. Often you experience the intuition that it's there for you only to dismiss it with the next thought: "Oh, that'll never happen to me."

But wait: How do you feel about that? How much would you like to source your gold and bring it to the surface so that you can shine. Yes, YOU. Shone even to your fullest – whatever that means for you? You don't have to wait until New Year's Day to make a change.

The purpose of this book is to help you reveal your gold mine. Yes, it helps to understand what obstacles are out there so you don't unwittingly repeat the same mistakes, but what really matters is to focus on all the things you can build on.

It is not an easy journey – let's not be naïve – everyone would mine their gold if it were as accessible as fast-food. But you CAN handle all your situations in more empowered ways from now on one step at a time. Life will test you along the way and force you to take steps back: these tests are all completely normal and part of everyone's journey (despite the surface 'perfection' you might see in public). Your journey is not likely to be a constant upward trajectory with no valleys. That's rarely how real-life works. And you are on a legitimate quest to source your own gold, source it your way and nobody can talk you out of it anymore – including you!

I too wake up on New Year's Day feeling like almost all the other seven billion people on the planet: much more is possible. I remember my mother telling me when I was five years old that I could do whatever I wanted to in life. I always wanted to believe that the skies are the limit. I always wanted to keep that dream alive.

My passion for this same quest to bring my own gold to the surface and to help others with it comes, perhaps not surprisingly, from my upbringing.

I grew up with an unhappy, rather critical mother and a workaholic, emotionally distant father. They married as a product of their generation (I assume). My dad was a Cambridge University graduate and had the brains and my mother (also bright) had the looks. Long after my dad died, my mum told me that marrying him was the biggest regret of her life. My sister and I got to reap the outcomes of this joyless marriage.

Even though my Scottish grandfather Jim assured my mum on her wedding day that she'd never have to work a day in her life, my dad wasn't motivated by money or climbing a corporate ladder and discovered he enjoyed teaching and research. Since his college lecturer income wasn't high, my mother also taught full-time and did all the cooking and housework. Her dreams of being an actress were quickly quashed by my father. They both gave up on love and, to avoid each other, they both buried themselves in evening hobbies or work.

My mother was also a talented storyteller. It was her gold mine. Growing up, she would entertain me and my sister, Caroline, with stories about the naughtiest birds on the planet: Fred and Mo. She would take everyday situations and stretch them to the point where you would think: "Oh no, they're going to get into so much trouble," and you would hold your breath waiting for them to get caught or escape their demise. She was a primary school teacher and parents would arrive outside her classroom early to pick up their children and stand outside the open window so they could listen to her stories. I remember frequently exhorting her to write down her stories, but she would always talk herself out of it. I knew she was talented; she knew she had that vein of gold, but she would talk herself out of it.

I still remember being 14 and walking into the dining room expecting to see her writing one school holiday and, when I saw that she wasn't writing, I heard her repeat for the umpteenth time: "There's no money in children's books!" (Later the irony of hearing this so many times was not lost on me when I learned that I was one year younger than, and had grown up in the same country as, billionaire children's author JK Rowling. I suppose that's why there have been books in more recent years about how talent is not enough). But it was really hard to grow up seeing talent go unexpressed and live with my mum's big unhappy emotions.

The deepest reason I'm writing this book is because I felt powerless as a child to make a difference for her career path or her happiness. I tried to do things as a child that I thought would please her, but once I moved towards my teenage years that backfired badly. I needed to do my own thing and, maybe, I could already tell that nothing I did was going to make her happy anyway.

The pain and cumulative effect of growing up with a highly emotional person who felt unable to do what she really wanted to in life and being directly impacted by that every day is certainly one factor that drives me so deeply to write this book. While it's too late to help my mother, I can help you get in action to be, do and have more in life. I feel like I have been determined to learn how to mine your own inner gold and teach it to others my whole life. Only since putting this book together has it helped me be fully aware of what has driven me all these years and fully understand my passion for helping people get from where they are to where they want to be. *But it's only part of the story.*

Second, growing up I was led to believe that dreams were a fool's errand and should not be pursued. Looking back, I can see that this makes perfect sense because the adults I was surrounded by - parents, family, and teachers – had often not felt like they could pursue theirs! My dad did seem to enjoy his work, but he was silent when it came to lofty goals and encouragement, and he gave up on finding a soul mate. Nor was I was encouraged to aim high.

Except for the messages I got from my mother as a very small boy that I could be, do and have anything I wanted in life, I was raised by default to graft through school and adult life to get a sensible, well-paid professional job, and do more or less the same things all the other grown-ups in my world did (why?) and avoid poverty. Conforming like this repelled me entirely as a teenager, but not having much confidence to try a lot of things, I worked fairly hard in school and kept to my music, reading and chasing girls (to mixed results)!

My parents did do their best to care for me and my sister with the skills that they had (as I think all parents do); we never had to worry about basic needs, education and reading were priceless values they shared with us along with the arts: theatre, concerts, film, and art. We never went without annual holidays. Having been a parent myself now I realize these are significant contributions which have left a powerful legacy for which I'm really grateful. The awkward part was the absence of love they had for each other.

In my family, people with wealth were deeply resented and criticized as either crooks, mavericks, show-offs or merely as 'other worldly'. Nobody talked about self-made people with respect for how hard they worked, how creative and tenacious they were or how bold they were to put themselves out there. Some of it was the non-entrepreneurial culture of the time and post-war fear. Much of this was sour grapes and ignorance but I didn't know that, and it hardwired my thinking with some very unhelpful mindsets about what was possible for me and about money and 'success' (however you define it) that took a long time to shift (yes, ouch).

The third factor that drives me to write this book to help you mine your gold is that I was heavily criticized as a child. This

created such a huge mountain for me to climb that so often I would get discouraged and was sure I would never get far. At some point, that criticism turned into learned self-talk – self-abuse. My heart goes out to everyone who has had similar experiences growing up, whether it came from parents, teachers, or other adults and how undermining this is. My mother didn't know a different way to be; she'd learned it from her equally unhappy mother. She brought her frustrations home and took them out on everyone else. My dad wasn't critical, but he was silent. He never intervened or stood up for us and struggled with his own confidence. Neither of them was a source of support for each other either. My schoolteachers were also part of a culture where public criticism was normal, acceptable, and frequent.

So often I lacked the confidence to try things or to step up and go first. So often I expected someone else to be better than me. So often I expected to be put down for a choice I made. **I had no idea that unhappy, bitter people don't look in their own mirror; they find solace in picking on others to deflect from their own failings.** This caused me to doubt myself at every turn for many, many years and took so much time to turn around. *I share this in case you can relate and because I really want to impart what I've learned over the past thirty years to help you walk a much shorter path. You have gold to mine!*

Yet despite my decades of trying to crack the nut of how to source my own gold and help others do the same, I don't think I would be writing this book if I hadn't hit an all-time low just a few years ago.

I had spent all my adult life trying to make a positive difference in the lives of others using the best skills and knowledge I had at that time. After university and because of a summer job I'd loved, my first 'proper' job was as the director of two special needs camps. It was rewarding work to hire and develop college students and provide a great time to people with disabilities of all ages, but it was lonely work at the 'top'. Then I spent a few years as a schoolteacher and kids improv comedy coach before training as a personal coach in 2002.

When I first read about coaching in an inspiring book that changed my life – Fiona Harrold's *Be Your Own Life Coach* – I couldn't believe there was a vocation that did exactly what I needed and wanted to do with my skills and passions: help people get from where they are to where they want to go. Those first few months being self-employed were both exhilarating and terrifying for me. I tried an entire life upheaval by starting my coach training from a Motel 6 room in Albuquerque after I left England and moved to New Mexico. Fiona Harrold had motivated me to address my unhappiness head on and her words encouraged me to live somewhere I'd always wanted to live – by the mountains – and in stark contrast to growing up in the rather rainy UK to somewhere with 300 days of sunshine.

For nearly twenty years I embarked on a journey that took me from being single and living in a rented apartment with no furniture but a desk in one of the three poorest states in the USA to travelling much of the globe, writing a popular business book about how to get more referral business, speaking to audiences as large as 2000, coaching hundreds and hundreds of people – many dozens of them to seven-figure incomes, getting married and having twins and moving to one of the wealthiest neighborhoods in the wealthiest country in the world.

It was a very gratifying, fast-paced journey throughout which I worked very hard and (foolishly) paused very seldom to enjoy. I was very driven to make something of my life and help as many people as I could. My decline came gradually after several banner years because only about 15% of the people I coached would follow through on my referral process and get excellent results.

I found this *deeply* distressing as I learned that I didn't know how to help the 85% who resisted or didn't follow through on the process I taught. I tried to motivate them more; that didn't work because motivation is an inside job. I seemed to want it more than them. I told clients to set more exciting goals. That didn't seem to help either. I told clients to believe in themselves more. Telling people this doesn't work. Telling people they need more self-discipline doesn't work either!

What built up inside me was a mounting and quite crippling fear of failure as many of my clients did not follow through consistently on the sales process I had created. Rightly or wrongly, I took responsibility for their lack of follow through. This became more than I could bear – **lots of people paying me good money, most of them not remotely getting the results possible and me not knowing how to help them**. **It left me feeling a lot of pain and *feeling powerless again*** - just like I had with my mother. I was the child again who couldn't help. I threw myself into trying everything I knew how to help my clients, but I didn't understand the obstacles and how to overcome them; my frustration simmered then boiled. This went on for SIX YEARS.

It was exacerbated personally from self-induced pressure to make more money as fatherhood approached. I wanted to be an even bigger achiever and provider when the season in my life also called for me to parent new-born twins and attempt to work together with an equally challenged and wildly stressed-out wife. I wanted to tell my overworked, underappreciated doctor-wife: "You don't need to work anymore." Not only could I not do this, but I was going backwards professionally and further away from being able to do this. I hated this powerlessness. And I'm sure I also had my own demons around fear of success to face further too.

For six years I felt totally lost. There is no photo of me during this period with an authentic smile on my face. To this day, I squirm at the thought of looking at pictures from this period because it was so painful, which is particularly sad since it was my children's early years. Living on old fumes professionally and feeling impotent to contribute financially at home, it was a dark time full of self-loathing. It's a miracle I didn't give up. I came very close, signing up to work at an insurance company on commission sales for a couple of months. But I couldn't fully let go and put my heart into something that wasn't my purpose.

Margaret Atwood describes this fog: "When you're in the middle of a story it isn't a story at all, but only a confusion; a dark roaring, a blindness, a wreckage of shattered glass and splintered wood; like a house in a whirlwind, or else a boat crushed by the icebergs or swept over the rapids, and all aboard powerless to stop it." That's how I felt for a painfully long time. Every morning I remember walking down the stairs feeling like a failure.

My vein of gold got buried as I mostly gave up on my dreams and took over the mantle of critic to pile it on myself. I just couldn't understand what the problem was. I tried to put on a brave face and grind through the weeks. My ego also made me feel like a fraud. On the increasingly infrequent occasions when I did have a speaking engagement, it felt disingenuous to tell audiences and clients about what was possible when I knew that most of them would not achieve this and that I had lost the plot.

I set myself up to fail because I had unrealistic expectations. I didn't understand that if you give people a proven process, most of them still won't follow through on it.

Firstly, there are quite a lot of things we don't know and need to understand better (hence this book) - about how we get in our own way, about how our subconscious and conscious minds work, and how to source more motivation and change effectively.

Second, I didn't understand that most people's biggest problem isn't a knowing problem.

Most people's biggest problem is they have a *consistent doing problem*.

I was still feeling responsible for and blaming myself for other people NOT doing the push-ups they needed to do. I was beating myself up because I thought I should be able to help them follow through successfully and I couldn't.

I was (rightly) not satisfied with the assumption that only a small percentage had the 'drive' to follow through and make big things happen when *everyone* I worked with expressed the desire to grow. **There had to be solutions for the rest of us. Everyone has their vein of gold.** What was going on?

For several years I would half-heartedly pick up yet another book seeking better answers to my dilemma: how do you help people mine their gold even when you give them a recipe that will help them? And how could I get my own mojo back?

On January 1st, 2019 I hit rock bottom because it was a new year for which I felt no optimism and because I've never felt more lost. Looking back, I can now see that part of my 'hero's journey' was this stage: it often feels like rock bottom when you've been working hard on finding solutions to your problem but still don't feel any clearer about solutions. You might be learning a lot, but it all feels foggy and themeless.

I thought I was still trapped in the early stages of my learning journey even though I'd been on it for years. I felt like I was getting nowhere. And this topic - 'getting out of your own way' - traps 85% of people all the time and the other 15% some of the time! It is a meaty topic; it was taking me a long time to get to the end of the tunnel. I thought I'd never get there, and my confidence was non-existent.

The emotional pain that day was so intense I knew I had to do something significant about it. It was unbearable. I couldn't live feeling that way anymore.

Finally, out of necessity, I started asking better questions: How did other people overcome their hardships and go onto remarkable accomplishments? And, more importantly, what lessons did they learn that everyone else could borrow and implement? I had to walk this talk myself and rebuild my self-respect and help others wherever I could.

I started a podcast to interview other high achievers on this topic. As I started to hear their responses, what hit me (mostly) was that I'd done enough reading and living over the years such that I *knew* many of the answers already, but I was no longer living many of these principles. For the most part, I too had a consistent *doing* problem!

It was a slow process but bit by bit the momentum started to change. The results started to improve slowly but quite significantly. Even companies I was rather embarrassed to re-approach (because they were disappointed with the *overall* results from the past just as I had been) slowly started to come around as they heard my story and saw ever-better outcomes. They accepted that I had learned some painful lessons, had made some significant changes, and was hell-bent on seeing better results from better methods.

My own life changed gradually too in powerful ways. From all the pain, I started to emerge stronger and more resourceful. I started building up my self-discipline muscle. For me, it took a rise and fall both of which I'd never imagined possible to learn what needed to be learned.

And I want to shorten your learning curve and help you journey from wherever you are today – however challenging things may seem now – to know that many remarkable things are possible when you:

a) Walk down from the stands

b) Get onto the playing field

c) Stay there whether you feel like it or not (but you are allowed half-time breaks and an off season!)

Remember: you've got that vein of gold waiting to be mined! The rewards are immense. Your journey allows you to be true to yourself, to honor the best in you and to live fully from a place of love. Each of us has this gold mine.

"Don't die with your music still inside you," pleaded Wayne Dyer in his later years.

You owe it yourself and everyone who knows you to shine your light, and you give permission for others to do the same. Be that role model to your children and others you care about. Tap your potential and see what astonishing things can become real and help you feel deeply fulfilled. Face your fears. Live from your heart. Honor your soul, see where it can take you and see how it can lift others up too.

As I review what I've learned in this book, it truly has taken me at least thirty *years* of professional learning and life lessons to put this together.

In terms of what's ahead, there are three mistakes we all make when we show up to learn. First, we confuse what we already *know* with what we actually *do*. *Knowing* isn't doing. We all have good knowledge about how to live healthy lives, but how many of us effectively and consistently follow through on all of this?

When you read through this and consider the exercises, try to catch yourself when you say 'Yeah, I know this' and instead ask yourself: **'How well do I apply this?'**

Second, look out for your 'confirmation bias' when you read. This is where you focus your thoughts on what already supports what you know and *fail* to notice all the other ideas that challenge or contradict how you think or what you currently do. You will know what I mean if you've ever re-read a book and been surprised how often you came across something you hadn't picked up on the first time. The wisest minds in human history tell us that we must continue to be willing to change our minds. George Bernard Shaw put it best: *"Progress* is impossible without change and those who cannot change their minds cannot change anything."

Third, one of the hardest areas to learn from is what we *don't know* we don't know. For example, there are things I know I don't know about such as nuclear physics, how a car runs, or how to knit and there are things like this that are also true for you. But as you read, try to be open to things that have *never* crossed your mind.

For example, for many years in my life, I was reluctant to commit to a woman in a relationship and would usually match myself with someone whom I suspected deep down it couldn't possibly work out with long-term. BUT I didn't know why I did that. My thinking felt 'normal'. I would justify my behavior to myself because somehow to me it felt logical. "I like a calm life," I would tell myself and blame my upbringing and the turbulent household that I grew up in. But it didn't resolve anything or ever make me any happier.

Then one day, when I was 42, I was attending a weekend seminar hoping to get a business or money breakthrough and someone told a story about their love life. And it was my story. I couldn't believe it. Then as the person processed their story, they expressed that they had had their heart broken in high school in a deep loving relationship and ever since then they had made near impossible choices in relationships to assure that somehow things couldn't work out. They didn't dare to fully fall in love again. They didn't want to risk experiencing that level of pain again if the relationship ended. As a result, they would choose people that they knew they couldn't love as much because of some significant difference.

It had never occurred to me that I was living with a broken heart and had been behaving the same way. As I heard this story, I felt like a ghost was being exhumed from me and that I now had permission to get on with my life and make a proper commitment. **All those years I didn't know what I didn't know.** If I hadn't exposed myself to that idea, my life would be the same now and I wouldn't have been married for 11 years and have nine-year-old twins. I had resigned myself to thinking 'well, this is just the way it is'. I never understood that when I was hurt at 18, I'd *unwittingly* said to myself: "Never again. This is too painful. Don't put yourself in this position again."

I really urge you to use this book as a 5-habit recipe and a workbook; as a reference tool for different highs and lows and, once you feel more competent in one area, revisit other steps of the book again and again with a journey mindset. Nobody masters all of these topics, and we all need to reinforce various lessons that we couldn't possibly have learned entirely in the years we've been alive so far – or remember them all.

The book is broken up into five habits.

The first habit is to **Let Love Drive**. Tune into your heart and be led by love – what you love to do and who you love. Love can provide you purpose and direction. So can God if you are open to that. Both have inspired many of the greatest minds and leaders in human history. Love doesn't get enough airtime in any of our lives. It is frequently ignored in our homes and places of work and is used too loosely by marketers with ulterior motives. Being a more loving person and practicing acts of love makes life worthwhile and along the way further exposes your vein of gold.

The second habit is to **Fuel Up Often**: to make sure you have enough fuel – motivation – to get the most from mining your gold.

Before you can mine your gold, you need a lot of FUEL. A LOT OF FUEL. Motivation is erratic. Your level of drive is not the same every day, every week. Nobody's is. And you need to be consistent to mine your gold well. You need to show up at the mine on all the days when you really don't feel like it and your brain is doing a remarkable job of convincing you that it is okay for *you* not to show up today. This is most people's biggest challenge. January 1st and 2nd are pretty easy, but February 16th, April 7th, August 10th, November 12th – not so easy; you get the idea.

Your habit to source DEEP levels of fuel will help you show up when life throws you off course, when you're scared, when you don't feel 100%, and when it's raining. Again. Your varied sources of fuel will give you the will to do the work.

Habit 3 is to **Pull the Weeds Fast**! Whether it was my mother not following through on her books or the 85% of my clients not using my referral process enough, there are many ways we get in our own way and fail to do what we say we want to do. Pulling your weeds involves understanding your brain better so your thoughts and feelings do not derail you for long because you re-route them; you filter them out. It involves avoiding doing certain things or behaving in certain ways that sabotage your efforts. Pulling the weeds literally means removing unempowering ways of thinking *and* doing that are going to mess up your ability to mine your gold.

Life can frequently throw unexpected challenges at us. The list can get long, and the world will never really care whether you complete your important tasks. Building the habit to pull the weeds fast makes a huge difference.

The fourth habit is **Elevate Your Control**. There are, fortunately, at least a dozen worthy areas in your life that you have control over that can help you live your best life. From how much you think you deserve success, to what you choose to believe and who you surround yourself with, there are many factors within your control that impact your outcomes. When you're more aware of how you're thinking and behaving, when you're more grateful for all that you do have, when you take care of your physical and mental health and realize you need to ask for what you want, these keys help you raise your game in all areas. The rising tide lifts all boats.

Habit 5 is **Be and Do Your Change *Consistently***. When I looked closely at what the 15% of my clients did right, I was shocked to see only two things: they all shifted how they saw themselves (what type of person do you want to BE?) and all homed in on one power habit for themselves to DO consistently to create the change they wanted.

This sounds straightforward but replicating this and being consistent are not easy – and that's why there are 11 chapters in Step 5. Like the rest of the steps, you don't need them all, but they all add up and make it easier for you to succeed and ever harder to give up on yourself especially when life gets tough.

Lastly, before you jump in, there's no point in fooling yourself: getting great outcomes in any area of life almost always requires a lot of work. I learned a powerful concept from financial advisor Eszylfie Taylor when I sat on a top producer panel with him at the Beirut Life Insurance Seminars in 2022:

CHOOSE YOUR HARD

Being successful is hard. Being a failure is hard.
Being rich is hard. Being poor is hard.
Being married is hard. Being divorced is hard.
Being fit is hard. Being unfit is hard.
CHOOSE YOUR HARD.

I would argue that **being average can be hard too – if it's anything that matters to you.**

Understanding that there is rarely a short cut is important. When you look at a high achiever's routines, they are simply not what average people are willing to do. Consistently. BUT it is enormously empowering to know that you can choose your hard too. Yes, it is hard to be, do and have many of the things you want in life, *but the alternative is just as hard too*. Frankly, it is harder to live with because you know that you could have tried harder. You could have done the work, but you made the many small daily decisions not to.

Knowing there is a hard to choose can be reassuring and make it easier to get out of bed early to exercise (or write your book – what I'm doing right now on the day of this writing!). **"I'm choosing my hard."** It can make it easier to make extra prospecting phone calls or go to additional events to promote your business. "I'm choosing my hard." It can make it easier to go out to meet a new date when your comfort zone would rather you stay at home and watch a movie. "I'm choosing my hard." Gradually these daily decisions can help you to build your self-discipline muscle.

There is no failure on this journey unless you give up forever. *Experiment* with what you do, stay focused on who you want to be and keep taking action after learning from what does and doesn't work. Even though there will be periods of your life when you take steps back, keep moving and you can mine your gold. Let me show you how…

HABIT 1:
LET LOVE DRIVE

Choose
LOVE (of all you can contribute to the world)
Over
Fear (that you're not loveable)

CHAPTER 1

Make Love Your Purpose

There's only been one day in my life when I had children of my own being born (twins). And there was only one moment when I found out that they were going to be born that specific day. And I will never forget the euphoria I felt. Words can't describe how I felt but my spirits were scooped upward on some kind of accelerating emotional thrill ride. "I can't believe it's going to happen!" I said to myself. I was so excited. My own children. I was 46 years old and could recall many occasions in the past when I had resigned myself to never becoming a father. I remember being 25 and telling a few close friends that I wanted to be a dad. If you are a parent, I'm sure you've had your own jubilant emotions that are impossible to put into words.

On July 4th 2022 the hospital they were born in, Highland Park Hospital, that has brought so much joy to so many new parents – where my wife has spent the last fifteen years delivering babies - was filled with dead and dying after a mass shooting incident at a parade that left seven people dead including a synagogue employee who lives in my town, a 76 year-old-man from Mexico visiting family who was sitting in his wheelchair, and two thirty-something parents whose two-year-old son Aidan was found covered in blood walking around town afterwards by police. When his grandfather came to the police station to get him, he said: 'Are Mommy and Daddy coming soon?" It also left 29 wounded. My children were eight at the time. Up the road from us there is now a mother and father whose eight-year-old boy is paralyzed from the waist down.

The 22-year-old who committed the murders was clearly at the opposite end of love. I am reminded of something Nelson Mandela wrote in a letter to Makhaya Ntini (the first black South African to play for his country), on his 100th cricket test appearance: "No one is born hating another person because of the color of his skin, or his background, or his religion. People must learn to hate, and if they can learn to hate, they can be taught to love, for love comes more naturally to the human heart than its opposite."

I was still so profoundly disturbed by what happened that the following day I felt shaky and uncomfortable dropping my daughter off for a sailing lesson a few miles down the road. I stayed with her for longer than I needed to and afterwards sat on a bench nearby not quite sure what to do with myself. Then I thought: "Why am I worrying about working? I need to grieve."

When I asked myself the question: "What's real?" almost immediately the word "love" came to me. Instead of watching the endless horror on the TV that day, I sat tight at home on police-recommended lock down with my children, and we watched two Harry Potter movies. Perhaps not coincidentally, it is the love from Harry's parents that protects him from his nemesis, Lord Voldemort. It is his fight for good versus evil that brings additional support and miracles to his aid.

In a world where evil acts exist and where some people in power enable this evil, it becomes ever clearer that what our world demands of us all is to be a force for love – to create that ripple effect to the best of our ability. And to be more conscious that we don't even unwittingly support people, causes or organizations that cause harm to others and deny them their freedom and happiness. And that we don't shrink to those who manipulate us with fear tactics.

We can't *over-estimate* what impact we can have during our fleeting time on Earth. Even the Roman Emperor Marcus Aurelius, the most powerful person on the planet in his time, knew full well that his impact and existence was very brief and that he would soon be forgotten and return to the soil upon his death: "Life is a small thing, and small the cranny of the earth in which we live it; small too even the longest fame thereafter, which is itself subject to a succession of little men who will quickly die, and have no knowledge even of themselves, let alone of those long dead." Nonetheless, he was taught that the *key to life* was to be free of passion but *full of love.*

Desmond Tutu said, "Do your little bit of good where you are; it's those little bits of good put together that overwhelm the world."

While we are here, we owe it to everyone to do our best to make the biggest positive difference we are capable of and to prove the power of love is real.

It is time to untap the gold inside us and let it shine. Love can do this. When you let love drive, you can mine your gold.

Love is something we share with others. In his book *Love*, Leo Buscaglia says that one of the greatest miracles to being human is that you can share as much love as possible and never lose any of it. It's NOT like sharing a piece of pie where it all ends up eaten. Share love because you're fortunate enough to have it to share. After all, you can't give what you don't have.

For too long, love has been removed from our agendas and trivialized as fanciful and impractical. This is so warped because much of the best of what we do is driven deep down by a desire to love and be more loved – to be seen and receive recognition, admiration.

Many of those who achieve greatness were inspired by love (and did not all achieve 'fame' in their lifetime) – do the same!

The Beatles, one of the most influential bands of all time, sang: "All You Need is Love."

Mozart declared: "Neither a lofty degree of intelligence nor imagination nor both together go to the making of genius. **Love, love, love – that is the soul of genius."**

Isabel Allende wrote: "When love exists, nothing else matters, not life's predicaments, not the fury of the years, not a physical winding down or scarcity of opportunity."

Lady Gaga was interviewed in 2010 saying: "I want my fans to love themselves. It's almost like I want to hypnotize them so when they hear my music, they love themselves instantly."

Van Gogh believed: "It is good to love many things, for therein lies strength, and whosoever loves much performs much, and can accomplish much, and what is done with love is well done." He also said: "There is nothing more truly artistic than to love people."

Many leaders were motivated by love to step up - do the same!

"Darkness cannot drive out darkness: only light can do that. Hate cannot drive out hate: only love can do that." –Martin Luther King Jr.

"Love is the vital essence that pervades and permeates, from the center to the circumference, the graduating circles of all thought and action. Love is the talisman of human weal and woe - the open sesame to every soul." - Elizabeth Cady Stanton

"It takes courage to love, but pain through love is the purifying fire which those who love generously know. We all know people who are so much afraid of pain that they shut themselves up like clams in a shell and, giving out nothing, receive nothing and therefore shrink until life is a mere living death." - Eleanor Roosevelt

Kofi Annan said in a Nobel lecture in 2001: "We can love what we are, without hating what — and who — we are not. We can thrive in our own tradition, even as we learn from others, and come to respect their teachings."

It's time that you tune into your own heart more deeply and honor what's inside it and live a richer life. Don't risk waiting any longer before the world you live in numbs you further into just existing as a physical body hoping things don't get any worse.

I'm not trying to be Pollyanna here. There is plenty of adversity to play against in life. What happened three miles from me on that July 4th was an immediate example. This is why we all need to step up and more proactively create a bigger ripple effect. Leonardo da Vinci observed this too: "Love shows itself more in adversity than prosperity; as light does which shines most where the place is darkest." Have you had such a wake-up call?

You can decide which team to play for and, if you focus on who you love and on sharing love with others, you can look yourself in the mirror each day with a clear conscience and it can provide the fuel you need to make great things happen.

Embrace More Love in Your Life

After the mass shooting near my home on July 4th, it woke me up to the fact that I couldn't stand idly by to learned hatred and darkness in our society. It made me want to counter such darkness by being a more loving person and learning more about how to do this (since it was never talked about at home or school). I started a program called *Choosing Love Over Fear* designed to make actionable a loving practice each week and then process with a small group. Candidly, I needed it as much as anyone else.

It seems bizarre that any of us needs more reasons to be more loving, but unfortunately as we all age, we can become jaded to the subject. It's easy to get to a point where maybe we are content with some love in our life (typically restricted to a very small handful of close relatives and friends) and assume that this is all there is.

But this misses *so much…*

Love is infinite and deep and **the more love you share, the richer your life will be**. It will help you enormously in mining your gold and becoming more of the person you really want to be. Why would you not want that?

What can you DO to ride the wave of love and cause a bigger ripple effect?

Psychologist Eric Fromm, a German Jew who fled the Nazis, explained that "Love...requires discipline, concentration, patience, faith, and the overcoming of narcissism. It isn't a feeling, it is a practice." Yes, love is a verb. The useful word for us all is "practice".

Why make love your purpose and let love drive you to breakthroughs?

The Divine Dozen: 12 Benefits to Being More Loving:

1. You love yourself more
2. You stop judging yourself all the time
3. You live more of your one life in the present
4. You don't have to be perfect anymore to be loved and neither do you expect this from others
5. You become more selfless
6. You can choose love over fear
7. You avoid feeling separate
8. You develop healthier inter-dependency
9. You live increasingly in a state of gratitude
10. You learn to forgive yourself and others
11. Where there is great love, there are always miracles
12. Your search for meaning ends: love is your purpose!

1. You love yourself more.

Loving yourself is the start. Then you can love others and be loved.

The first thing to *know* is this: You are lovable. It's really *remembering* that you are loveable – as you were as a new-born baby. We are more than a body, a self-image, and a story. A Benedictine nun called Macrina Wiederkehr created this prayer: "O God, help me to believe the truth about myself no matter how beautiful it is!"

The first thing to *do* is this: Decide to be a truly loving presence in your life and everyone else's. This helps you know love (not try to 'find' it) because love is your true nature. It's already inside you.

The challenge with being an achiever type is it can be unhealthy if you're always trying to prove something because deep down you don't feel good enough. In his book *Loveability*, Robert Holden warns: **"You keep trying to change yourself into something better, but nothing really changes because you haven't stopped telling yourself: 'I am not loveable'."**

To rekindle these fires, Holden suggests that you journal with these sentence starters:

If I really loved myself, I would…

One way I could love myself more is…

He notes that feeling some resistance to these statements is common and "is an expression of the basic fear 'I am not loveable.' This fear deserves your compassion. It is a call for love."

This fear is not the real you though: A Course in Miracles states: **"The ego does not love you. It is unaware of who you are."**

Shortly into the Pandemic, my son (then 7) started getting angry with the world. A year ago, he was diagnosed with ADHD and as being on the autism spectrum and since then he takes it very personally when other kids call him 'weird'. One week I started telling my (then) 8-year-old son he was lovable. I put my hand on his heart. It wasn't long before he was telling me he was lovable. I replied: "This is the most important thing for you to know in life. Many grown-ups don't believe they are lovable, and it causes them a lot of problems."

Meditation can be an act of loving yourself. "It helps me turn off the airwaves in my head – I spend too much time worrying and second guessing," said Kristin, a lawyer in my *Choosing Love Over Fear* program. At first, I couldn't quite connect how quieting worry related to being a more loving person, so I asked her what she meant. "Everything I need I already have," she said, explaining that by turning down the volume on her ego voice jabbering away, she could pay attention to the love she already had inside her - her Unconditioned Self that was born as love.

"The quality of your relationship with yourself determines the quality of your relationship with everything else." Robert Holden points out that this applies to our food choices, exercise, relationship to money, emotional well-being, the pace you set for your life, the time you make for yourself, and how lovable you feel, spiritual wellbeing, relationship to God, your creativity and how happy you are. He adds: *"Your capacity to love yourself also influences how much you let yourself be loved by others."*

Everything starts with knowing you are loveable. The better you feel about yourself, the better you treat others. This knock-on effect can only help you mine your gold.

2. You stop judging yourself all the time

"Oh, my friend,
All that you see of me
Is just a shell,
And the rest belongs to love." - Rumi.

"I judge myself constantly," commented one of my banker clients the other day in my program. The managing director of a law firm described how shocked she was that a *mentor* of hers in the Los

Angeles legal world considered herself a "fraud and failure" most of the time!

On one level, it's remarkable that some people can sustain high performance levels even though they are being so hard on themselves. But who wants to live like this long-term – or now? We think it drives us to achieve more. While there is a place for feedback and improvement since none of us is perfect, achiever types typically beat themselves up far too much. It is a fool's errand, a miserable existence and hard to mine your goal when your foot is slammed on the brake! How do you get it go away?

The Dalai Lama tells us that: *"Love is the absence of judgment."* Mother Teresa concurred that: "If you judge people, you have no time to love them."

If you look yourself in the mirror and don't feel good, understand that you are looking at your judgements, not the real you. Well, your ego is judging you. It declares: 'I am not loveable.' It's like you're putting yourself in a courtroom to be judged all your waking hours.

Your Real Self does not judge you. Can you imagine the pleasure of not judging yourself all day long? Positively remind yourself: "I'm okay today. I've got this. I'm doing my best."

Greek playwright Sophocles hit the nail on the head when he wrote:

"One word frees us of all the weight and pain of life, that word is love."

Practice self-acceptance: this is the ABSENCE of judgement. When you judge, there is always another model of perfection to strive for in vain because the ego is never the whole you.

Don't believe your judgements. What can you see if you loved this person instead? You will focus on their positive traits and notice those instead. Fuel that fire.

The ego judge is hardest on you when something in your life goes badly: you are the first to blame yourself. This is when you most need grace or forgiveness to appear. A UK sales manager in my group found himself in the emergency room with a blood clot in his lungs between sessions: "I was angry at myself because I'm so health conscious. I was saying 'why me?' I am much healthier than most people my age." His sister helped defuse his judgement by reminding him that all the work he'd done with his health would help him recover quickly. And it did.

Silence in court! What can you do to be less judgmental and not sabotage your mining efforts?

a) Pick a 15-minute slot and make no judgements about yourself

b) Pick a mealtime and try to see another person with your heart, not your (judging) eyes – the way you see a baby as a person only made of love

c) Try a loving kindness meditation where you focus loving thoughts in turn on yourself, then a loved one, then a stranger, followed by someone you are not fond of, then lastly the whole world.

d) Strike up a conversation with a stranger, ask an open-ended question and be curious about this person without making a judgement.

e) Remind yourself: "I'm okay today. I got this. I'm doing my best."

f) When you do catch yourself being judgmental, say to yourself: "Cancel." One of my clients added: "Let it go. I'm loveable."

g) Take five minutes and talk to yourself the same way you'd talk to a close friend. S/he would notice every-thing you're doing right. Look at yourself through the eyes of love. Irish priest and poet John O'Donohue wrote: "Your soul longs to draw you into love for your-self. When you enter your soul's affection, the torment in your life ceases."

It's really hard to mine your gold when your ego is in your ear dump-ing doubt and criticism. Perhaps the best thing you can do to reduce being judgmental is to catch your harshest judge: the ego voice inside you that says you don't deserve something because you hav-en't worked hard enough on something yet or haven't yet achieved the lofty goal you set. Be gracious to yourself anyway. You don't need a reason to love yourself. You are already loveable.

Robert Holden concludes: "When you stop judging yourself, the habit of gratuitously judging others will also stop. **The more you love yourself, the more people feel loved by you**. It's how reality works." This too is great momentum to leverage on your journey.

3. You live more of your one life in the present

> "To love is to be present. If you are not there,
> how can you love?" - Thich Nhat Hanh

(The entire next chapter – chapter 2 – is on this supreme benefit)

4. You don't have to be perfect anymore to be loved and neither do you expect this from others.

Even gold mines aren't perfect.

"God's not measuring us," commented Andrea in my program. "Love isn't a meritocracy. I don't have to contribute value to be loved." She expressed how hard this can be when so much around us is based on measures, Key Performance Indicators and 'progress'.

"You don't love someone because they're perfect, you love them in spite of the fact that they're not," explains author Jodi Picoult. We all need to learn that real love has no conditions. Leo Tolstoy said: "When you love someone, you love the person as they are, and not as you'd like them to be."

It goes beyond us and towards unconditional love. When you can learn to love others without conditions, you also let yourself be loved without conditions. Think about how freeing this is. No more pretending to be perfect! You can be your natural flawed self who is carrying some extra weight, debt or an incomplete plan; no perfect conditions are required for you to keep taking steps to mine your gold.

Love has NO conditions.

Love does not need a reason as there are no conditions to love. **Unconditional love for others becomes possible when we are willing to practice unconditional love for ourselves.**

Practice Unconditional love

Unconditional love is not about having one special relationship. **"The goal of love is not just to love one person; it is to love everyone,"** writes Robert Holden. I admit this is a big concept when you first think about it, but as our love for one person increases, our love for others increases too. *Love is not a pie with just a few small slices*, and when we treat a relationship that way, Holden believes that it "leads to dependency, possessiveness, jealousy, neurosis, and ten thousand other forms of fear."

Your journey to mining your gold is going to be messy. It's going to look like a stock market history, not a single straight line of continued perfect growth. And through all this you are still

lovable and capable of being loving. Let love drive and be free to pursue your imperfect loves now.

5. You become more selfless

We are only a part of the equation: "Love is the whole thing. We are only pieces," wrote 13th-century Persian poet, Rumi. Robert Holden adds: "In love, the real desire is not about what I want *from you*; it's about what I want *for you*." This is what can help you mine your gold. When you are focused on serving others selflessly rather than satisfying your ego, it becomes a positive magnet that attracts people to support you and your causes.

First, practice compassion and smiling - as Mother Teresa believed - *"The smile is the beginning of love."*

Second, treat everyone with unconditional positive regard.

See the potential in everyone. When you expect this, they will almost all rise to the occasion.

Third, make your livelihood your cause, passion, or purpose. Let that be your medium to selflessly serve as best you can. Life will be far more fulfilling and it will attract stronger advocates.

Lastly, if you can muster the courage, tell people you love them. Look them in the eye and mean it when you say it. When it is meant truly, your soul sees the soul of another. If that's too much of a stretch (and I don't find this one easy), at least try to let people feel your caring nature.

The key to knowing if you love someone and if someone loves you: you both want each other to be happy. When you make the success of others your fuel, mining your gold gets to be an easier two-way street.

6. You can choose love over fear

"Oh, how a quiet love can drown out every fear." - Jessica Katoff.

Fear dictates so much in your life whether you realize it or not. It limits you personally and has a big impact on your business and professional life. It stops you asking for what you really want and trying to reach your full potential. **Fear can stop you mining your gold. Fear is debilitating.**

A Course in Miracles teaches that there are only two basic states of mind: love and fear. Love is your Unconditioned Self (the one you are born with) and **fear is your ego**. Love is natural and fear is learned. On many occasions throughout the day, you are choosing between love or fear.

<u>**There is only one real fear**</u> (other than a rare fear for your physical safety) and that is**:**

"I am not loveable."

This was an epiphany for me. For decades, I've read and worried about fears of failure and fears of success. What I've found is that when you stack these topics together, mining your gold can feel like an insurmountable mountain to climb in life - especially because fear of success can be a foggy topic masked and compounded by worthiness challenges. But if at the end of the day, there's only ONE fear and only ONE choice:

If you are lovable, you can pursue what you love without fear of what happens.

If you are not loveable, you will be afraid to even try.

Only your ego, your insecure self-image, is going to get scared about what might happen. **Remember that your ego is not the real you; it's just an image.** Yes, you will still experience failure, frustration, and disappointment *at times*, but if you can see that you're still lovable, it doesn't have to feel so crushing or feel like a permanent label.

You can face your fear/s by coming from a place of love instead.
Say to yourself: "I'm taking this step because…
*I love to help others,
*I love my family and want to support them better
*I love to make a difference in the world…"

Tell yourself: **"It won't always work out perfectly, but it doesn't mean I have to live in fear or call myself a failure. It doesn't mean I'm not lovable. I CHOOSE (to let) LOVE (drive) – not fear - and I can mine my gold more easily now."**

7. You avoid feeling separate

Psychologist Erich Fromm believed that *all* our problems were caused by one basic problem: separateness and that the need to overcome this was our deepest need. Have you ever felt alone? That there was no one you could talk to about the path you were walking on? It's a really scary and undermining experience that will deeply derail your efforts to be, do and have what you most want in life.

The downhill slope begins when first (subconsciously) we feel unlovable, then we feel that others don't love us, and thirdly we make up the story that the world doesn't care about us. All fearful thoughts. On a micro level, it stalls your progress and spirals your emotions, and taken to the furthest extreme, it is what can drive some people to acts of violence like the shooter on July 4th. Fromm knew plenty about this as a Jew who fled Nazi Germany.

The GOOD NEWS: **Matter and spirit are one** (see chapter 11, Understand Your Garden, for more on this). Only the ego separates them. Start to notice the inter-connectedness in your world. Notice how much you depend on others to feel more bonded. Who made the book you're reading? What is it made out of? Who made the chair you're sitting on? Who farmed the food you most recently ate? Who delivered it to your supermarket or your door? Who hired you to do the work you're doing? How did you meet them? We are so wired to think independently yet look around you.

Did you make any of the things surrounding you: the buildings, the cars, the roads, the trees, the flowers? Who designed the lamp in the corner? It's one reason why it's wise to surround yourself with things and people you love – let love drive, not fear. You know you're not going to get far on your journey alone. Notice where you're connected to others and build on that to achieve more success on your mining path.

Author Caroline Myss said, *"The cause of your suffering is you do not love enough."* In other words, if you want to stop feeling the pain of separation and to feel ever better, be a more loving person and absorb the inter-connectedness to all things. Be the change you want to see. It's be-do-have.

8. You develop a healthier inter-dependency

For many people who have been raised flying the flag that extols the virtues of independence, healthy inter-dependence does not come easily, and it's not always clear-cut which path is best. I've had this challenge throughout my life. We live in a culture of do-it-yourselfers who think they can figure everything out on their own.

There are other hurdles to inter-dependence: "There's a constant tension between personal authenticity and belonging," said Ann during my class. "For a child it might be the fear of having to trade off some authenticity out of fear that s/he will feel isolated within their family. For me, I'm divorced raising three kids. When I'm closer with my ex, it's better for the kids, but I'd prefer it be more separate."

"In 29 years of marriage, there's never been a day when my wife and I haven't checked in," Derek shared in my *Choosing Love Over Fear* class. This impressive example of synergy in a marriage highlights the benefits of real collaboration rather than two independent-minded people getting tasks done on their own and calling it teamwork. Stephen Covey referred to these relationships as "married singles."

Nancy explained that she was pleased with how she was managing a newer law associate at her Seattle firm: "We hired him during the Pandemic. He was very rigid and protective of himself. I've tried to be a better listener now, more curious about him, and letting go of my old expectations that he has to build his practice the same way I did twenty years ago. So much has changed since then. I'm open to his questions." Her being more interested (loving) in him and flexible to how he gets things done has built new trust. "It's become an easier relationship now."

How much truth can you speak in your relationships? How well can you work together for the greater good? It's not easy and there can be multiple dynamics at play: "My relationship with my mother has always been a struggle because she steps on boundaries and is such a Debbie Downer," Nancy admitted to my group. "A psychiatrist once asked me: why is it your job to make your mom happy? I thought it was!"

It is not healthy inter-dependence when someone makes you feel guilty for wanting to be yourself or everything in your world must fit with theirs. Try to choose love over fear.

How can you practice healthier inter-dependence that comes from a place of love and where everyone wins (it's going to help you mine your gold faster!)? Ask for help, be open to inspiration, cooperate/collaborate with others on more projects, ask others how they think something should be done, and gradually build out your team (all sources of strength and inspiration – see Habit 4, Key 10 for more on Elevate Your Support Team).

9. You live increasingly in a state of gratitude

When you pay more attention to who you love and what you love, you start to feel better and more grateful for what you have versus what you don't have. Lynne Twist summarizes it in her book *The Soul of Money*: "What you appreciate appreciates." **Feeling grateful accelerates good things happening to your mining efforts!**

(For more on the impact of gratitude, see Habit 4: Key 5)

10. You learn to forgive yourself and others

> *"We forgive so as to set ourselves free. Forgiveness*
> *helps us to see beyond our masks to who we truly are. It*
> *shows us that who we really are has nothing to do with*
> *what happened to us in the past."* – Robert Holden

I don't hear people talk about forgiveness, do you? Nor do I read about it in books. Have we forgotten how to do it and how valuable it can be? It may well be a practice to bring back into your life or a question to add to a monthly review (see Habit 4, Key 3). One thought leader who does talk about it is Robert Holden in his book *Loveability*. He describes three steps, the first of which is to forgive yourself for ever believing you're unlovable.

To keep your momentum to mine your gold, it's important to know that there's nothing wrong with your true self and to let go of past albatross emotions!

The second step in forgiving a grievance is to let yourself grieve. One of my past clients lived in a country whose currency went through a devaluation and his $200,000 book of business dropped in value to $10,000. Many of his clients no longer trusted him or his insurance company and for three years he fought to persuade his clients not to live uninsured. He changed but not in a way that felt good: "I had to be so aggressive with people who otherwise were running huge risks not to have their health and lives insured."

He truly had to mourn the loss of most of his livelihood to support his family and, out of loyalty to his past clients, chase them to keep them protected financially even though he couldn't make a living on what this paid him. I urged him to grieve over this loss and then to start a 'second' business with a new group of clients who could afford to pay him and to focus ever more time on them.

The third step is to let the grieving go, so it doesn't chain you to the past. Make the inner shift of walking from the past to the present. You will often be tempted to hold onto the grievance a bit longer. Holden calls this "miserable righteousness". It is folly; it is also pure negative energy which is never going to help you progress (the purpose of this book, remember?). He reminds us that:

a) The love that created you (God) holds no grievances.

b) Grievances are made of fear; you are hurting yourself to gain some revenge.

c) Grievances are not a solution. You have to let go. The anger does not change the past. Being guilty forever heals nothing and trying to make others guilty gives you no peace.

d) Grievances hold you back; they show up in your present. The story stays the same. Holden cautions us: "The purpose of your life is not to carry a grievance." Move in the direction of love.

e) Grievances don't make you happy. Make love more important than your grievances, your ego, and your past.

Who do you need to forgive for past grief? Start with forgiving yourself, then let forgiving thoughts towards others filter down from your brain. I realize this is not easy and I hope you realize that it may well be an area you need to address.

When you let love drive, you focus on positive factors in your life that can move you forward. Yesterday (as I write this), Blake, one of my clients, told me that he'd been spotlighted at his firm's weekly sales team meeting.

In front of everybody, his manager asked him why his business development activity had been higher than anyone else's for the past few months (and he has only been there for a few months). Blake's first response was: "That's just my work ethic; I always work like this. That's how I'm driven." Then he felt a need to elaborate (perhaps because he was concerned that the others would feel judged by him as having a 'better' work ethic). He told everyone that his father had died from a brain tumor when he was six and that he had promised his mother that he would take care of her. "That's what drives me."

Make your purpose far greater than any grievance - just like Blake has done. Some people live their lives unable to forgive a parent who died when they were young. The resentment interferes with the rest of their lives as they blame that parent for not being there at times when undoubtedly, they wished they had been. Yes, feeling this way is understandable and everyone deserves empathy.

But if you want to mine your gold, return to the above steps: grieve, let it go, and focus on what you can control - fulfilling your own potential. Since none of us goes through life without bruises, scars, and injuries, learning how to forgive is part of this process. Unshackle yourself and make your love your purpose.

11. "Where there is great love, there are always miracles." - Willa Cather.

Two years before the end of World War Two, Simon Wiesenthal arranged for his wife, Cyla, to be smuggled by the underground to Warsaw. Tragically, sometime later, he heard that she had been killed in a Nazi firestorm that had torched her street. Meanwhile, Cyla was told that her husband had committed suicide to avoid torture by the

Gestapo in June 1944 (such was the reputation of the sadist he was turned over to, he did try to kill himself three times but failed!).

During the Holocaust, Wiesenthal experienced every imaginable atrocity and 89 of his relatives were murdered including his mother. After all he had witnessed, it will not surprise you to hear that by 1945 he had little religious faith left and certainly no belief that something miraculously good could happen to him.

Yet what happened after the war was a remarkable chain of events for Wiesenthal and his wife to discover that each other was still alive and to reunite:

"If my letter hadn't reached Dr Biener the day before, if Cyla's train hadn't been delayed, if she hadn't gone for a walk, if she hadn't met Landek, if Dr. Biener hadn't been home, then the two women would have gone back to the station and continued their journey to Russia. Cyla might have wound up anywhere in the Soviet Union and it would have taken years to find her again, let alone get her out of there."

A Course in Miracles says that "miracles occur naturally as expressions of love." These miracles can only happen if each of us believes our voices can cumulatively make a ripple effect difference even in our own small part of the world: I believe it is our duty to hold stock in what Jimi Hendrix said: "When the power of love overcomes the love of power the world will know peace." Wiesenthal sought peace in the world by making his purpose in life to hunt down Nazi war criminals. After the war, he helped to bring over 1100 Nazis to justice including Adolf Eichmann and Josef Mengele.

Miracles happen; we're just not paying attention. I don't think we take the time to trace back how some of the great things in our life materialized. And when we do, it becomes clearer just how many quirky things contributed to that miracle happening or could have sent it in a very different direction.

We tend to thoughtlessly dismiss our better outcomes as "timing", "luck", or justify them by thinking that life somehow owed us something good after various other things had not worked out. When you live from your heart and are driven by love - and can avoid making *too many* silly mistakes - that's an enormously positive force for good. It doesn't mean only good things will happen, but it raises your odds and makes your life more enjoyable. It's infinitely better than all the alternatives.

When you let love drive, not everything has to come from the hard grind and strategic planning meetings. Wiesenthal's biographer, Alan Levy explains that he came to believe in miracles after he reunited with his wife**. If Simon Wiesenthal believed in miracles after all the horrors he went through, you can too, and it will elevate your ability to be, do and have what you most want in life.**

What brings you joy? What do you love to do? What's the most fun/meaningful thing you could do right now? Think about what you used to love doing as a child and a teenager. Are there ways you can ease some of those things back – even in smaller doses?

Who do you love spending time with? At least ask: 'who do I really enjoy spending time with?' Who makes you feel good? Share that love.

Make miracles natural expressions of your love. Pray and ask what miracles you should perform. Do anything that opens you up to acknowledge that sometimes, astonishing things happen, AND they can happen to you.

12. Your search for meaning ends: LOVE IS YOUR PURPOSE!

"The salvation of man is through love and in love." – Victor Frankl

Victor Frankl was a psychiatrist who had plenty of reasons not to hold much stock in love. According to Wikipedia: "In 1942, just nine months after his marriage, Frankl and his family were sent to the Theresienstadt concentration camp. His father died there of star-vation and pneumonia. In 1944, Frankl and the surviving members of his family were transported to Auschwitz, where his mother and brother were murdered in the gas chambers. His wife died later of typhus in Bergen-Belsen. Frankl spent three years in four concentra-tion camps."

Yet despite years of tragedy that would destroy most people – prob-ably because of these experiences – he learned what matters most. He was the founder of logotherapy, a school of psychotherapy that describes *a search for life's meaning as the central human motiva-tional force*, and what was his conclusion? **That love is our purpose: love brings us the most meaning in life.**

Not happy customers, better burgers, or speedy delivery. Something nobler. And it compels us to look in the mirror, no?

(And isn't it curious that I share two deeply profound lessons learned from two people on two consecutive points who endured similar nightmares during the Holocaust? In other words, if we are wise, we learn what matters most from people who, like the Winston Churchill quote, went through hell and kept going – hopefully so we don't have to learn these lessons??? Their wisdom was brutally learned: **believe in miracles and make love your purpose**.)

While few of us have experienced such trauma, it doesn't mean we can't have the same drive and passion behind our purpose. The truth is, the more you have of these things, the easier it is for you to keep going on your path to mining your gold. This is the deeper meaning for you whatever your past experiences.

What used to hold me back was thinking that I lacked the trauma in my life that people like Blake, Victor Frankl, and Simon Wiesenthal had endured - **that my comparatively comfortable middle-class upbringing somehow denied me enough drive to aim for the heavens. Don't make the same mistake I did**. Use everything from your past to make meaning to be, do and have what you want in life and put love first. This is precisely where love appears for your mining mission. Forget trauma metrics and who has had it worse!

Love has been too clinically separated from 'purpose' and from business mission statements.

What can you do to be more loving and make it your purpose?

It will help you enjoy the riches of your gold mine.

Start small. Actions that move you in the right direction include performing acts of kindness - doing things with no agenda whatsoever other than to be more loving is a great place to start. Listen to your heart and work in a way that shares love.

I am embarrassed to say that outside my home, performing acts of kindness just for the sake of them were rarely top of mind. After over twenty years of self-employment, most of my actions were steered towards taking care of paying clients or communicating with prospects where, sure, I had an ulterior motive because I wanted to do business with them!

The idea of simply communicating with others to be a more loving person was rarely on my list except unwittingly as a person trying to be as useful as possible. What I've learned is that the practical application of coming from a place of love is **thoughtfulness** - showing you genuinely care about someone as a human being and (in business) not simply as a potential revenue source. The only way you can be more **thoughtful** is to give yourself time to think - to be *full* of *thought*.

Sometimes your act of kindness might be staying around longer in the conversation such that others can tell you're truly concerned about them: "My 11-year-old son opened up to me about his hopes and fears," commented one of my class participants, "he said he doesn't feel safe living in New York anymore."

In a different way, Ann in my class wisely connected love to presence and purpose: "When you're present, you see the opportunity to do something kind and loving."

At times, this degree of thoughtfulness means being more conscious about when you are going to think about an important topic. I have to schedule this sometimes otherwise it doesn't happen. I know this might sound absurd – schedule the time to think? But to hope you will either remember or give your brain the time and space to do it is often not something you can be sure will happen. Most of our days simply race by with too many interruptions and unexpected events.

One useful idea is this: when you realize you have a topic that needs thought, think about when you have commute time, running/biking time, or walking time (even with your dog) and decide to use that time to give it the contemplation it deserves.

Give an unexpected gift: *everyone* loves getting a gift when it's *not* their birthday or a specific holiday. And the feeling you get is rich too. Author John Updike observed this: "We are most alive when we're in love."

Make love your purpose and increase your momentum through acts of kindness. You will find over time that they come more automatically. Your identity changes such that **you become an increasingly loving person. Let love guide you to mine your gold. Everything gets easier when decisions come from your heart.**

The real purpose to embrace more love is to know love - not to find it. It's to recognize that you are made of love and are deeply loveable. You make it your purpose, your fuel.

Curiously, my children were born at Highland Park Hospital on a day (September 11th) that in the USA is associated with tragedy from the terrorist attacks in 2001. Yet they have come along to bring a great deal of joy to many (well, most of the time!!) and they already make a big positive contribution to many of the people they touch in their lives.

Let me finish with this: Two people influenced me to include this chapter in my book and ultimately to start with this topic. One was my spokesperson for love, author Robert Holden, who found his path in life after his father's death to alcoholism: *"Love is the ultimate coach. Do what you love, let love guide you and let love inspire you."* The second person was the young man so filled with hate for himself and the world that his only solution was to murder innocent locals on that July 4th morning. His actions made it clear to me that I needed to speak up and do more for love since I cannot influence the politicians and lobbyists in the United States who enable his actions and refuse to listen to their conscience.

Hecato, the Greek Stoic philosopher, gave us the solution in 100 BC to how we elevate the world we are living in: *"I can teach you a love potion made without any drugs, herbs, or special spell—if you would be loved, love."*

Make love your purpose. Go forth and mine your gold.

Let love drive!

CHAPTER 2

Live in the PRESENT

"Enjoy yourself, it's later than you think
Enjoy yourself, while you're still in the pink
The years go by, as quickly as you wink
Enjoy yourself, enjoy yourself
It's later than you think" – The Specials, *Enjoy
Yourself (It's Later Than You Think)*

Until he was almost thirty, Eckhart Tolle described his life as "a state of almost continuous anxiety interspersed with periods of suicidal depression." On one particular evening of darkness and despair, Tolle suddenly had this realization that he was talking to himself *and* listening at the same time. His inner-talk was: "I cannot live with myself" and this led him to ask whether there was one or two of him – the I and the 'myself'. He then thought: "Maybe only one of them is real."

It led that evening to an intense physical and spiritual experience after which he fell asleep. When he awoke, his life (and all his thinking) had changed forever and for many months he lived in a state of pure joy marveling at the miracle of life.

The biggest lesson Tolle shares in his book *The Power of Now* is this: **stop identifying with your mind and live in the present moment.**

The benefit to being present is that you can feel whole and complete NOW – not at some uncertain point in the future that's only possible if you achieve a, b, and c.

You measure this by how much peace of mind you feel now – how much joy, ease, and lightness you feel. This is the joy of being – something that can be felt but never understood mentally.

Focusing on the present makes it easier to mine your gold because your brain isn't dwelling on the past or the future over which you have no control.

What's the problem?

"I feel stupid beating myself up about things," reflected Paul, one of the students in my Choosing Love Over Fear class. "I know I'm re-living something from the past instead of just living in the present and getting on with life." The rest of us allowed a little silence in our Zoom meeting fully aware that we all did the same thing.

Being present seems really challenging. "I think the phone is a big distraction in our house," said Tom rather sadly. I remember my parents used to do this thing they called *relaxing*. They would purposely do nothing but unwind. They would read the newspaper, play relaxing classical music, or sit in the garden and just soak up the view and the sound of the birds. Yes, this a poor attempt at humor but the concept has been mostly absent in my life for as long as I can remember. There are so many more interruptions and distractions with mobile devices and all the people we know as well as internet access to anything that's on your mind. We lose our presence because we are so often wondering what new message, email, comment, or call might be waiting for us. What also suffers is quality time – one of the ways some people feel most loved. It leads to most of us having an adversarial relationship with time.

There's also the pace of our lives today. Mike, another student in my class, commented that there's often this question buzzing around in his head asking during the day: "What else should I be doing right now – or could I be doing?" This can be an incessant distraction. Being at home now – especially after our Pandemic experiences – has even further reduced our separation from work duties. It is easy to feel like there is always work to be done.

Michelle said it was hard to be present when she was "tired, hungry, or hadn't meditated." There's almost always a nagging sense that you should be doing something else for someone else, so it's easy to put off your own needs and easy to give yourself a guilt trip when you do. Then she added: "And I stop being present when I get sucked into my kids' upsets or rattled by other people's emotions and end up carrying their burdens."

"I avoid being present when I'm feeling uncomfortable. I will listen to a podcast, read a book, or watch television to put my mind somewhere else and avoid confronting what's bothering me," admitted Nancy. "And when my youngest son throws a tantrum, I don't want to be present for that either."

A benefit to being present is you can set aside negative emotions and consciously take more loving actions which can boost your momentum to your gold mining.

Once you stop rejecting yourself in the present because of past pain, you can get on with being a loving person today and get on with mining your gold. Martin Luther King also learned this the hard way: "I have decided to stick to love; hate is too great a burden to bear."

What can you do about this?

1. Catch yourself dwelling on the past or future

Tolle describes most thinking as a "sickness". What he calls the "tormentor" in our heads (our ego) is what sucks us of positive energy and fuels problems. We have become enslaved puppets to our thinking, our minds, and our emotions. He believes that over 80% of our thinking is "repetitive and useless" and often dysfunctional and negative. (If you want to test this out, do nothing for the next 60 seconds and just listen to the all the random, sometimes ridiculous thoughts that go through your head).

As you start to WITNESS your thoughts, you can get increasing separation from them. Don't take your thoughts so seriously. Smile at the voice in your head. It is not the real you. Keep reminding yourself: *They are just thoughts*. This is the same process high performers use to filter out self-doubt and the inner critic voice that sometimes tells you that you're not good enough and can talk you out of doing things that are good for you that you don't feel like doing.

2. Feel a sense of connectedness to everything

You may recall from the last chapter, Erich Fromm believed our biggest problem was feeling separate from everything. Eckhart Tolle goes one step further: **true joy comes from two things: an awareness that everything is connected *and* being "intensely conscious of the present moment."** This ties beautifully to the Divine Dozen benefits to being more loving.

3. Stop "looking outside for scraps of pleasure, validation or love" and tune into your best internal self

If you are responsible for bringing in business and you are having a day when things seem slow, try your best to *stop* seeking external validation and acknowledge yourself for what you you're doing right. Remind yourself of the good within you.

When you don't feel connected to others or the world around you, you see yourself as separate from everything – and your ego kicks in. Ego and your mind thrive in the past and future and try to avoid being in the present. Yet you can't do anything about the past or the future.

4. Let go of past baggage

Part of the solution to being present and, therefore, focused on mining your gold, is also about 'letting go' of past emotional baggage – rather like forgiveness - so you don't become a puppet to these hot topics in the future. This is not easy (especially with meaty topics like parents); it IS a learnable skill. It starts with self-awareness: what are some things that can trigger you to slide? A challenging family member? When business is slow? When you compare yourself to certain people? Some topics can almost always set you off. Talking these things through with a therapist can be helpful too. Former Navy SEAL Mark Divine calls these his monthly mental tune-up.

None of us wants to live the rest of our lives reacting automatically to these things like a Pavlovian dog. Addressing this is a PROCESS. The pain you feel comes from old thoughts that need letting go. Another reason to release this mental pain is because it can turn into a physical symptom in your body if it remains repressed. I've been there myself: Me not dealing with past anger brought on acid reflux in my 40's.

When you worry, are anxious or you feel psychological fear, your mind is thinking about something that MIGHT happen in the future. When you identify with your mind like this, your ego is running your life. But if you stay in the present moment, you can cope much better. You can get on with mining your gold.

A key part to the egoic mind is a deep-seated feeling of LACK: that you're never good enough. And it thrives on feeding you these thoughts. Remember that if love is your purpose and you can live in this moment, it's easier to progress and not be influenced by negative thoughts or a negative environment. For more on how to address worthiness, see Habit 4, Pillar 3.

5. Work on the present: Eckhart Tolle's 'Three ways to do everything'

The more you let it sink in that all you can ever do productively is live in the present, the happier you will be and easier you will find it to mine your gold.

Even if you've had a really frustrating week with little positive validation to your efforts, pause for a moment. Those frustrations are in the *past* (even if they've left a 'legacy'). What can you control about them *now*? This moment and then the next, right? Focus on what you can control. **Eventually this circle of influence will grow. It will probably take longer than you want it to but do outstanding work and your circle *will* grow.**

Why do we obsess about the past and future rather than the present moment? Because the past gives you an identity and the future holds the promise of salvation and fulfilment. This is not for you: **Living through memory and anticipation is a GUARANTEE FOR UNHAPPINESS** and endless focus on things you can't control.

The only precious thing about time is right now otherwise you miss out on life. The only experiences we **_ever_** have happen in the present, *but the mind can't understand any of this* – and it is excluded from this.

Eckhart Tolle's three ways to do everything:

I didn't expect to find this in Tolle's second book, *A New Earth,* which I was only listening to because it was Oprah Winfrey favorite book at one point. (I admire Oprah for her ferocious desire to learn and grow that never stops just because she's in her 60's. And how she embraces and celebrates older age rather than dread it.)

Tolle argues that there are only three ways to do something, otherwise all you're creating is suffering for yourself and everyone in your life. I believe this is a healthy layer for each of us in how we can focus on the present:

a) **Acceptance:**

There are definitely some things in life that are not fun, but we have to do them: washing our clothes, buying food, cleaning up after pets or young children, and commuting to work. Tolle's point is to accept that the task is necessary and *to be at peace with it*.

Then there are things it's wise to accept since you can't control it: traffic jams, flight delays, inclement weather and your favorite team being inconsistent or playing badly.

If you resent or hate a task, he says stop doing it because it only creates negative energy.

It is part mindset and all awareness – living conscious to the only reality there is – right now. It's a reality that took 13.8 billion years to get here.

Let's say your business is quite new so your funds are limited and there are tasks you have to do because you simply can't afford to outsource them yet. Do all you can to accept this and be okay with it rather than be angry at the world and have that anger affect everyone in your life.

Like attracts like. If you can be at peace, you'll attract better things into your life faster. If you're resentful, it's only going to lead to other negative things and negative people happening.

A couple of years ago, I listened to the stunning life story of Michael Singer (*The Surrender Experiment*). All he wanted to do with his life was live alone in the woods and meditate. But he did not resist opportunities that came along even though none of them were part of his plan. And he did his absolute best when he was asked to do something (read that again!). He ended up becoming CEO of a software company worth hundreds of millions of dollars. And he still lives in the same woods (yes, yes, just in a much nicer house).

Even when he was asked to do tasks that weren't part of his plan, he accepted. More remarkably, later in life he was taken to court by the U.S government. This lawsuit lasted several *years* and would have wrecked most people's mental health. He accepted it and continued to be happy and at peace – even though he had been wrongly accused the whole time and at certain points looked close to jail time.

In 2019 when I interviewed 40 high achievers for my podcast. One of the lessons I was reminded of frequently was an acceptance by these high achievers about what one world champion described to me as doing the "hard yards". She said that no one was born with mental toughness but that you build it like a foundation on your growing ability to keep your word to yourself.

It's an acceptance that reminds me of the Olympic gold medalist who said: "I only have to exercise twice: when I feel like it and when I don't."

"Whatever the present moment contains, accept it as if you had chosen it," urges Eckhart Tolle: "Make it your friend and not your enemy and this will miraculously transform your whole life." Part of this is because pain can only feed on other pain – it spirals, doesn't it? Pain cannot feed on positive emotions. In the same way, success breeds success. It's the key premise from BJ Fogg's research on how to change in *Tiny Habits*: we change best when we feel good, not when we feel bad.

b) Enjoyment

The advice I love is "do your best with every moment". Put that spirit into it - and indeed everything - and enjoy the only moment you have in your life which is right now: the only thing you can control in your life. Fretting over a past event or non-experienced future is totally pointless and completely beyond your control.

British judge Thomas Troward had a chapter in a 1902 book called *Entering into the Spirit of It*. He wrote that: "the more fully we enter into the spirit of all with which we are concerned, the more thoroughly do we become alive…that we are penetrating into the great secret of Life…its Livingness…it is that good thing of which we can never have too much."

This creative principle (the spirit that you put into things) is inside – *inside you*: your outer world is merely a reflection of your inner world. This also includes appreciating the present moment more as the only thing you can control – so get into the spirit of it.

It's the reminder here we all need. Find the spirit of pleasure in what you're doing, and if you can't, accept what you need to do. And if that's not possible, then don't do it.

c) Enthusiasm

"Nothing great was ever achieved without enthusiasm." - Ralph Waldo Emerson

HOW you do things is more important than what you do. I'm sharing this as someone who has spent too much time trying too hard and likely creating strain rather than joy. It reminds me of Richard Branson's "work hard (acceptance), have fun (enjoyment and enthusiasm) and the money will come." Think about it: if you're enjoying yourself, it's far more likely you'll persevere at mining your gold.

Lastly, focusing on a deep love for all that IS - rather like a gratitude habit - can help you feel really alive now. *You can still work on lofty goals*, but the point is to feel complete as a person now not with all these conditions, ifs, and 'someday' thinking.

Good things will come your way from:

a) **Being grateful**
b) **Feeling fulfilled for what you have NOW**

c) Doing your best to enjoy the present.

See Habit 4, Key 5 for more on gratitude.

HOW TO BE MORE PRESENT

Here are some ideas to experiment with. **Remember your 'measure' is how much you feel peace of mind, joy, ease, or lightness.**

Tip: Have an experimental mindset – treat all this in a curious and playful manner and your results will come much quicker. These habits are crafted based on an approach shared in BJ Fogg's outstanding *Tiny Habits* which is explained further in Habit 5 (Chapter 17) of this book:

a) After I (pick a current specific habit e.g., 'put the kids to bed'), I will sit still for 30 seconds and ask myself: "What's going on inside at the moment?" and just feel the energy of my emotions. (No need to analyze. This will get you to be present.)

b) While my son/daughter/partner is talking to me at dinner, I will look at them intently and fully listen.

c) After I click "Join Meeting" before a client meeting, I will write down BE PRESENT on my meeting notes as a reminder.

d) After I think a negative thought from the past, I will ask myself: "How do I solve this problem now?" (This will help you address it in the present or realize it is a pointless old problem that your ego mind is creating for no good reason. Shining light on it will gradually defuse it.)

e) While I am worrying or getting anxious about something in the future, I will ask myself: "What can I do about this now?" and address it or tell myself: "That can wait until tomorrow." (By creating some space, you can start to resolve some of the problems that you can't stop thinking about!)

f) After I complete my first project for the day, I will ask myself: "Am I at ease at this moment?" ("Get the inside right and the outside will fall into place")

g) After I finish dinner and sit down, I will become aware of my breathing.

h) After I grab my keys to walk the dog, I will turn off my phone.

The greatest power comes from taking responsibility for your inner feelings rather than blaming the outside world. Defuse that negative energy!

Tolle concludes: "Many patterns in ordinary unconsciousness...can simply be dropped once you know that you don't want them and don't need them anymore, once you realize that you have a choice, that you are not just a bundle of conditioned reflexes."

Give up WAITING as a state of mind. You will mine your gold sooner from being grateful for what you have NOW and doing your best to enjoy the present.

Let love drive!

CHAPTER 3

Let God Drive

"I have found that whenever you clear your stuff about God, your life shifts. Life gets easier. To be happy, you do not have to religious about God, but you do have to be unafraid of God." -Robert Holden, Shift Happens

"I believe that correct principles are natural laws, and that God the Creator and Father of us all, is the source of them, and also the course of our conscience. I believe that to the degree that people live by this inspired conscience, they will grow to fulfil their natures; to the degree that they do not, they will not rise above the animal plane." - Stephen Covey

Michael Guillen was expected to become a minister like his father and both his grandfathers. His family went to church every *day* in the barrio of East Los Angeles, but despite this influence and being forbidden to dance, watch television, "and a host of other things considered mentally, physically, and spiritually unhealthy," Michael set his heart on becoming a scientist from the age of eight, committed to the world of science – and, by the time he graduated from UCLA with a BS in physics and mathematics, committed to Atheism.

When he went to Cornell for graduate work in physics, he "was more than happy to leave behind the religion I had never really embraced." He became a "scientific monk" who bounced between fields. He studied what the universe was made of, then galaxies and relativity. He subscribed to the adage of all Atheists that seeing is believing.

But then he learned that 95 percent of the entire universe is made of dark matter that is invisible. This forced his worldview to change to include what he could *not* see or prove. Quantum physics is not logical and some of it makes no sense. No scientist fully understands it. In science, the *opposite* of some profound truths are also true! In his book, *Believing is Seeing*, Guillen comments: *"If you insist on limiting your analysis to matters of sense and logic, you risk overlooking the most profound truths about yourself and the universe."* And you risk not mining your gold.

At this point he realized he needed to study three disciplines: physics, astronomy, and mathematics. He sought mathematical explanations in his PhD to explain why galaxies form a remarkable 3D formation in deep space. After this, a surprise encounter at a seminar led to a job as a science reporter for CBS which he did in addition to teaching at Harvard.

His intense curiosity led him to learn that some profound scientific theories are "fundamentally incompatible" and that the more we learn about the universe, the more mysterious it becomes. As he sought to answer life's deepest questions, he studied metaphysical belief systems, including world religions. He voraciously sought contradictions and answers. He noticed that there was plenty about science that was not logical in ways that religion wasn't either. The more he studied and read, the more he saw that scientific and biblical worldviews were alike.

He found that science and mathematics can prove the logical and commonplace but cannot prove everything:

Einstein, the greatest scientist of the 20th century noted that: "The truth of a theory can never be proven."

Kurt Goedel, the greatest mathematician of the 20th century concurred: "Truth is bigger than proof."

Guillen's studies revealed the "enormous improbability" of there being life even on our planet: *"The chance of lambda (a cosmological constant/vital sign) having precisely the value necessary for life… is one in a trillion trillion trillion trillion trillion trillion trillion trillion trillion trillion."*

Studying astronomy also expanded his worldview – how could it not? The observable universe we live in is estimated to be 92 billion light years across. It's estimated that there are roughly 100-200 billion galaxies in the universe and over 100 billion suns in our Milky Way. The world's strongest telescopes have found evidence so far of 4,300 *other worlds* (like ours) but no life forms.

Could there be a God behind such a miracle – since you and I being here is certainly a statistical miracle? He studied light from a biblical perspective (God is light) and quantum mechanical perspective and found them "fundamentally compatible". After twenty years of studying science and world religions, Guillen concluded that: "It's easy for me to be both a scientist and a Christian…**our seminal fate as Homo sapiens sapiens is to be at peace with God**, our creator, in a state of immortality and complete freedom" – even if no worldview can answer every question.

His shift from Atheism was "a slow awakening." Over time, he started to surrender himself body, mind and spirit and let sink in the difference between intellectually believing in something compared to having "a deep, meaningful trust." His surrender was most impacted after *years* of unsuccessfully trying to conceive a child with his wife including multiple attempts through artificial insemination. Their prayers were not answered.

Michael couldn't sleep at night, lost a lot of weight, and became depressed. One afternoon he called a pastor friend who told him to let it all go and to surrender the whole thing over to Jesus. After this conversation, he collapsed onto his bed full of anger and disbelief. But then he had a momentous spiritual experience and was embraced cheek-to-cheek by a giant, translucent figure followed by the deepest sleep he'd had in years. When he awoke, he felt that everything had changed even though it all looked the same. It's an experience not unlike Eckart Tolle's.

"Almost immediately...my life underwent a sea change." At precisely the same moment a few days later he and his wife realized they wanted to adopt a child. They considered it the Holy Spirit talking to them simultaneously. They let God drive. "For the first time in what seemed like forever, Laurel and I felt alive – truly alive!" Within a year they adopted a four-year old boy. "Every time I look into my son's eyes, I see God flashing me a smile that says, 'See, I do keep my promises – if only you'll get out of the way, surrender your will, and give me the chance to do so.'"

Guillen did get out of his own way and found fuel by clearing his stuff about God. This required faith. Gradually, he opened his worldview away from centering only on himself and his feelings (his ego) and instead valuing selflessness and absolute truth. **This too requires faith in things that cannot be seen, proven, or fully imagined.** He urges people to having a service-based worldview that is ever-expansive like our universe and helps you deal with what he calls 'Titanic Moments' when life goes badly south and reveals what you're really made of. "Your worldview is the sum total of what you *believe*." And *believing* is seeing.

Could blocking God be slowing you down on your quest to unlock your best potential?

What if one of the blocks to mining your gold has been your resistance to God? **I'm not talking about a specific religion here (necessarily), but the presence of an infinite intelligence or a universal spirit.**

A big part of my work for over 20 years has been helping people get out of their own way. I've spent 99.9% of that time focused on business strategies and mental hurdles. Sometimes I wonder if that's too small.

Do you think that God puts limits on what *you* can accomplish but not on higher achievers at your firm or in your industry?

I've always been driven to want to make a positive difference with my life, but too often in the past that drive came from a place of 'there's something wrong that has to be fixed'. Can you relate?

I'm not sure how to describe this negative source and negative feeling as it got blended over decades by everything from: childhood pain, to business achievement, goals, fears, business failure, and dozens upon dozens of tips, techniques, and strategies from piles of books and weeks of seminars to spur on my A type activities.

While I could recall plenty of great experiences, too often my journey was not particularly enjoyable. It felt strained by a frequent feeling that something was missing, by trying too hard and a need to fix more. Then one day, after over-doing my workouts for a few months and getting injured, I made a press announcement to my ego: "I can no longer be a team sponsor to this way of being. **Too much fear and not enough love."**

I've had my own issues with God and religion that clearly had such an adverse effect on me as a 10–11-year-old that I unwittingly decided to reject them for several decades. I have definitely had major blocks around a higher power. For me, I needed to separate out religion because it skewed my thinking in unhelpful ways: It was too close of an association to the Coventry Cathedral hierarchy and choirmasters who wouldn't let me leave the choir when I was 11. What I wanted was to embrace the inspiration and higher thinking that comes from God – that is bigger than anything my ego mind can conceive.

I realize that almost everyone has fairly strong opinions on this topic, and I respect that. Here is the message that I wanted to stop resisting so I could be a more loving person who lives ever more from his heart and spirit. What re-sparked it was feeling the presence of evil so close to home when I was confined to my house that July 4th with my family because a killer was on the loose after murdering seven people just up the road from me.

Tune into your own wisdom and take what resonates…

Robert Holden explains in *Shift Happens* that – to him – God is bigger than one religion.

God is universal in spirit and is:
Infinite intelligence
Immeasurable love
Unconditional peace
The creative impulse that supports the highest in everyone

God is bigger than your prospecting problems, your fear, your frustration, your ego, and your self. Yet **your Unconditioned Self has *no limits*. It is your learned ego and self-image that has placed limits and labels on you and your business. Let God drive.**

I spent my whole life putting other people on pedestals because of their impressive achievements. I often treated them as a superior species and that I was just some medium to translate their gospel to anyone that would listen. By being at odds with God and believing my limiting ego, it limited how I saw myself (and possibly how I saw others). I did not know that the source of love was inside me. It's within me, you – within all of us. Your Unconditioned Self allows you to treat everyone as an equal (including that huge prospect and the person emptying your trash outside).

It is NOT your Unconditioned Self – the self you were born with – it is your learned ego and self-image that limits you and chooses from:

*How much success you can expect
How much happiness is acceptable
*How much peace of mind is 'normal'
How much love you deserve
*How much abundance is 'realistic'

Aren't you tired of looking at the prix fixe menu every day?

As Marianne Williamson says:

"Our deepest fear is not that we are inadequate. Our deepest fear is that we are powerful beyond measure. It is our light, not our darkness that most frightens us. We ask ourselves, 'Who am I to be brilliant, gorgeous, talented, fabulous?' Actually, who are you not to be? You are a child of God. Your playing small does not serve the world. There is nothing enlightened about shrinking so that other people won't feel insecure around you. We are all meant to shine, as children do. We were born to make manifest the glory of God that is within us. It's not just in some of us; it's in everyone. And as we let our own light shine, we unconsciously give other people permission to do the same. As we are liberated from our own fear, our presence automatically liberates others."

Nelson Mandela read this when he was inaugurated as South Africa's first president in 1994. Our light is God (however you define God). Darkness is our tiny ego and doing things out of fear. **Fear is the opposite of love**. Have you been tuned into the wrong radio station? Why spend all day in the court room listening to your ego judging you when you can listen to your heart, your Unconditioned Self and to God?

A Course in Miracles tells us that **what we treasure is in our hearts** (which is why you want to make it your purpose). That's what I felt on that July 4th. My treasure was clear. And the fear and the darkness were very clear too. Cowering inside the house felt wrong. Hiding from fear felt wrong.

And the response has to be fighting this darkness not from a place of fear but from a place of love by being more loving, by unconditionally accepting yourself, and by being an instrument of love. I concluded this:

I have a flawed shell but a very healthy spirit. I've made mistakes but these do not define me. I want to be guided by a light that shines all the time. I don't want to be limited by my learned petty ego. And surely neither do you

Take it or leave it but I like these words from *A Course in Miracles* – it's written in Christian language but has a universal message:

I am here only to be truly helpful

I am here to represent Him Who sent me

I do not have to worry about what to say or what to do,

Because He Who sent me will direct me

I am content to be wherever He wishes,

Knowing He goes there with me.

I will be healed as I let Him teach me to heal

Let God do plenty of the driving. Michael Guillen's strongest advice is to "get close to God and become still." It may take time for your destiny to get clearer, but it likely won't be clear if you don't. And as you let your destiny grow with your worldview, all kinds of remarkable things are possible. You can't solve everything on your own so here's a grander solution to consider. The saying goes that when the student is ready, the teacher appears. Drop your self-imposed limits and consider opening up further to some universal guidance and getting more help for you to selflessly mine your own gold.

Lean on Faith

"So many feathers on the eagle. For my eagle, of course, is the symbol of the great spiritual power that I believe carries us all. That supports us when our commitment and determination are put to the test. From which, if we will, we can gain strength and new energy even

when we are at our most exhausted. If we have faith, and if we ask." –
Jane Goodall

On October 26, 1967, the right wing of Commander John McCain's fighter plane was torn off by a surface to air missile during a bombing raid on a recently rebuilt power plant in Hanoi. Witnesses said that his parachute opened so late that had he landed on anything but water, he would have been killed. He was taken to the notorious Hao Lo prison camp dubbed by US troops as 'the Hanoi Hilton' where he spent five years as a prisoner of war – *two years* of them in solitary confinement.

I think you would agree that this is a life experience you cannot understand without having been through it – the sheer mental turmoil it creates. His biographer and thirty-year confidant, Mark Salter writes in *The Luckiest Man: Life with John McCain* that his religious beliefs were a key factor in his ability to survive the ordeal and were "never more potent than during his years in Hanoi. He spoke of religious experiences like they were epiphanies." Later out of solitary, he was appointed chaplain for 'the big room' with 25 other prisoners and "recalled weeping as they all sang 'Silent Night' to end a Christmas service in 1972."

His resilient mindset, fighting spirit, human contact, and visualizing stories from his favorite books and films were all critical factors to enduring all the mental and physical abuse, but he needed help from God to drive.

One of the webcasts I did early on during the Pandemic was on the benefits of religious faith. This idea had been sitting in my mind for many months. In 2019 when I interviewed people for my podcast, I could not ignore the number of high achievers who attributed some of their success to the power of their faith. I wanted to learn more. I Interviewed people from MANY faiths on *multiple* continents to get their perspective.

Even if religion is not your cup of tea, I'd still recommend picking through this because some of the mindsets and actions are really powerful regardless of your spiritual beliefs.

The Divine Dozen Part 2 - Benefits to Faith and Belief That God is Driving

1. **It can be easier to accept a life change:** Sukhi, a financial advisor in the UK, had a conversation with her family after Lock Down started and she exhorted them to follow what I discussed in chapter about presence: **"Accept the situation.** *Don't try to fight it. Let's learn to live in a different way, be kind to each other and get the best out of this."* This is what Eckhart Tolle was talking about in Chapter 2 when life is at its worst.

   At the time, I *really* needed that wisdom myself as I was still upset that the schools would be closed for another eight weeks and felt daunted by having to help out with schooling my children and juggle everything else.

2. **See your life as a gift to God:** A financial advisor in India shared this mindset with me: *"My business is not my entire life, but it is a major part of my life, so leaving my faith out of such a major part of my life would be a huge mistake. In fact, my life's motto is: 'Our life is a gift from God; what we do with that life is our gift to Him,' so what I choose to do in my business is also a part of my gift to God."* This can be reinforced through **reading spiritual text.**

3. **Let God drive:** Michael, the owner of a software development company explained his faith: *"That there is a power greater than me with a plan. I have a part to play but I'm not in the driver's seat. I am not out of control. I look for opportunities to be in partnership with God and find an active place to work. It releases me from feeling responsible for everything."*

4. **Ask for help and see who does and doesn't come into your life as part of God's plan:** I loved this **morning prayer** about prospecting and being of service from Steve, a wealth advisor: *"God put me with the people you want me to be with to do the things you want me to do."* He said it takes the pressure off himself such that he asks about the people who do appear: "What do they need and why did God put them in front of me?"

5. **Live life to the full now:** *"We must make the most out of our time on Earth"*. In the week before this, one of my friends died (aged 48) and one of the people I interviewed was just starting to recover from a three-week battle with Coronavirus. She even said: *"Even when I was really ill, I felt mentally protected."*

6. **Calm:** Your faith, prayer and **meditation** can unburden you of worries and all the things you cannot understand. Anchor, rhythm, gratitude, connection, community, perspective – all these words were used to how people's faith had helped them handle the Lock Down.

7. **It's easier to become a leader:** Jason, an insurance advisor said: *"My faith forces me to be a leader because my clients look to me for guidance."* We all need to step up and show our network what we are made of – whether we feel like it or not.

8. **Service mindset:** *"It reinforces that our mission is not to sell but to seek opportunities to serve."* This priceless comment came from Michael, an extraordinarily successful insurance professional I have known for long enough to know that this is definitely not a "line" but the core of his success. Stephen Covey called this servant leadership.

9. **Compassionate Giver mentality**: *"Most types of faith encourage kindness, caring, loving others, and doing good deeds for others. As you do these things, not only have you helped someone else, but you have also helped yourself. As you become a better*

person, you feel better about yourself, too," added Steve, a professional speaker and author.

10. **You can talk to God with no ego and a quiet inner critic:** *"It helps me not worry what others think because only one opinion matters,"* shared another interviewee. On meditation and prayer, I was told: *"God helps me make key decisions, run my business with integrity and morals and trust my intuition – led by the Holy Spirit."*

11. **Clarity about what matters most:** *"I am clearer about what I'm fighting for and why I am fighting."* Mitch, a Jewish community leader, suggested **reflecting on paper** as a great benefit to achieve clarity and recommended this terrific question: *"**If this were your end, would you be satisfied with your ripple OR is there more work to be done? Not by building a fortune, but by impacting people for good. In what way could you do that?"***

If you'd rather talk to someone than write, **find a spiritual mentor**. Adam, one of my long-time past clients in the UK has sworn by the direction this has given him for years.

12. **In the moment inspiration:** Using **random wisdom insights** from a holy text to answer challenging life questions or for inspiration can also provide a quick uplift or answer. Hukamnama is a Sikh practice that you could easily adapt to your own beliefs or even high-quality personal growth books. When ill with Covid, Sukhi opened a scripture at a random page and received this random message: *"God is with you, there is nothing to worry about."*

My friend Lisa gets her spiritual and immediate inspiration by **spending time in nature** – hiking and skiing with her kids, running trails, rock climbing, and canoeing. For Jason it is **community worship**.

All of these reduce stress, bring peace and pour in all the rewards of faith and an appreciation for God, however you define the universal spirit. I consider God and love to be the same. Either way, when you let God (love) drive too, you can walk taller and stronger and with more confidence to mine your gold.

Let love drive!

HABIT 2:
FUEL UP OFTEN

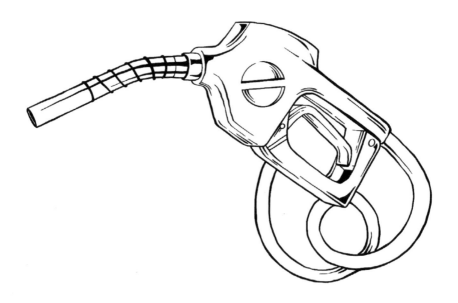

CHAPTER 4

Get a Physical

When I woke up on January 1st 2019, it was the flattest I ever recall feeling emotionally. I couldn't muster one positive thought about the upcoming year. I was alarmed because I couldn't ever recall feeling so hopeless on the first day of a new year before when it's usually almost impossible not to swept up with some optimism for the fresh, new year.

I felt terrible about myself and - after *a lot* of journaling over multiple days - realized that I had lost my self-respect. But it was a long list of traits and bad habits that had spiraled me down over a few years to an all-time low. They had joined the list sporadically over time.

I've been a weak-arsed door mat
I've been unhappy with my marriage for over six years
My wife is too critical, short, and abrasive with me
I've been too scared to do what I really want
I'm physically weak and I don't push myself
I'm not very fit and don't eat enough veggies
I'm not a very patient father and am easily irritated with my children
I've done a TERRIBLE job of saving money for 18 years and have virtually nothing saved for the future
I do not work hard anymore – I've got lazy and unfocused
I've lacked drive and purpose for 8 years
I'm still buying the bullshit my mother taught me about limiting beliefs – that nobody supports me, I'm not good enough and I don't

deserve it
I am not the role model to my children that I want to be

I virtually never take bold action | I am seldom present

I'm intimidated by too many people | I'm too serious

I don't relax | I have reflux

I watch porn | I have tendonitis

I listen to my egoic mind too much
I've not listened to my heart, my soul, or my passion for years
I am a people pleaser who is afraid of confrontation
I seldom express my feelings with my children except anger
and impatience

I have wasted so much time not being true to myself
I've always been waiting to be rescued
I've settled for chump change

Not surprisingly as I look back at this list now, it was the culmination of a long decline for me. I'd experienced some great professional success 6-9 years prior after many years of hard, hard, work, but then I'd hit a wall of burnout and intense frustration. What really pushed me over the edge was feeling like a failure. I'd spent the previous few years speaking on multiple continents yet many of the people I coached did not get the results they (or I) wanted, and I did not know how to help them.

I didn't understand why. I didn't know how to help beyond coaching on my referral system and trying to 'motivate' them (which doesn't last). I was great when the sun was shining, and I knew how to move a client forward who followed through on their action plans. But I was scared when clients hit obstacles because I didn't know what they should do. I felt like a fraud even though my system did work phenomenally well for some people.

Gradually I lost my drive and became overwhelmed by the challenges of parenting for the first time (twins at the age of 46) and trying to juggle marriage and running my business as well. These stressors then put intense pressure on my already-existing flaws and unresolved issues from the past which spiraled into being unable to root out the causes of my misery, to get traction when I did find potential solutions, and climb out of my self-induced hole.

Also on reflection, I think I took other people's lack of results too personally. I couldn't do the push-ups for them, but I felt impotent not having useful strategies to get people into action and out of their own way. That explains why I am so passionate about it now. I had to learn it myself the hard way.

Before you can mine your own gold, you too need to go through this sometimes painful process. You need to do some kind of inventory to see where you truly, currently stand. Each of us can be a master at deceiving ourselves on a day-to-day basis, rationalizing our behavior away even though it's keeping us away from mining our gold.

WHAT TO DO:

Look in the mirror and candidly evaluate your current (imperfect) reality

I tell this humbling, difficult story to say that before diving into change – and while it may be extremely hard – **find out what your current imperfect reality is**. While I'm sharing a time when my reality was at its most ugly – and that's not typical – there are always areas of our life that aren't going as well as we'd like. How much do you weigh and know about your health? On a scale of 1-10 how would you really rate the key relationships in your life? What are the facts about your business or work life today? How clear are you about your personal finances?

Some of this is likely confronting – after all, *everyone* has flaws and problems. But you know it doesn't really serve you to live with your head in the sand all the time. And you will feel better afterwards to face what you've been ignoring or denying anyway. Also remember that your ego is going to love this exercise and that it's not a reflection of your true self.

Look at your present situation. Write down the date and answer these three questions for each area that is important to you:

1. What is the current reality in this area?
2. How do you honestly feel about it?
3. What experiences are you having in this area?
    a) Your key relationships:

Partner:
Children:
Connection with Family members:
Connection with Friends:
Professional/Friend blend:

    b) Your business/vocation:

    c) Your finances:

    d) Your physical health:

    e) Your mental health: Comment on the following or score them on a scale of 1-10:

        i) Your self-belief: How much you believe in yourself is going to impact everything you do. There are degrees of self-belief (it's not all or nothing); it's something that ebbs and flows. Most people find it easier to fall back on a purpose, but you still want to feel like you can come through.

        ii) How confident you feel: Our confidence levels can vary between areas of our life. You may feel confident talking to a current client but less confident talking to a huge prospect who's the biggest opportunity you've ever had.

iii) How much you respect yourself: A great question to ask yourself when you're stuck is: **will I respect myself more if I do this?** Sometimes I admit I often use this one to get me out of bed in the morning!

iv) Your sense of worthiness to achieve your long-term goals: **The degree to which you think you deserve something determines what you choose to pursue in all areas of your life** – can't get much more jugular than that! See Habit 4, Key 1: Elevate Your Worthiness to go deeper.

v) How happy you feel: It's easy to go through life not really grasping that happiness is an inside job and it does not have to depend on outside factors. When you feel most alive, you're putting yourself out there. Sometimes this leads to new problems and challenges, but ships aren't built to stay in the harbor, and neither were you, so how you handle these challenges makes a big difference – and it circles around to your happiness. Stay present.

vi) Degree to which you feel positively challenged: I was talking to Natalie, a client of mine, the other day who told me she changed careers because she was "incredibly bored" working as a banker for celebrities. It's easy to slide into a dull comfort zone but that is not the journey for you – not if you want it to go beyond your living room.

vii) Degree to which you tune into your intuition and trust your gut instinct: It's rare that I hear anyone talk about listening to their intuition. Many people do but mostly unwittingly. It's generally underutilized.

viii) How constructively you deal with anger and other negative emotions: You can only bottle up emotions for so long. While handling frustration isn't something we think of as a fun social engagement that we spend all week looking forward to, it can be an area that we handle so poorly it can do severe damage to our lives.

f)   Sense of spiritual connection:

g)   Adventures/fun/hobbies:

h)   Contribution and giving back:

i)   Living your purpose:

How focused are you on what you do best and love to do (your zone of excellence)?

Where are you making an impact?

Which are your better habits that set you up for long-term success?

Most importantly, how much are you enjoying your journey?

If you want to go deeper:

Tap into greater sources of fuel with these two powerful exercises.

<u>Exercise One:</u> This one helped Tony Robbins turn his life around. Take a large piece of paper and draw a line down the middle. Then make a list.

On the left, write down a list of 'Things That Are No Longer Acceptable'

On the right-hand side, write a list of 'Things I Must Change'

<u>Exercise Two:</u> Answer these questions that I found helpful at my lowest point from David Goggin's book *Can't Hurt Me*:

a) What are the most painful and humiliating experiences you have had?

b) What kind of sewage did you deal with growing up (or in the past x years)?

c) What are the current factors limiting your growth and success?

d) Were you so secure you never pushed yourself?

e) Is someone standing in your way? Are you standing in your own way?

It is worth your time to dig deeper and explore. Shortly before he was sentenced to death, Socrates told the court that: "the unexamined life is not worth living". Self-awareness is pivotal to your personal success yet most of us feel too busy to put in this time.

How can you be true to yourself if you don't really know yourself – if you rarely reflect on who you are, what you want and why you want it? Do you really want to get to your later years in life not really knowing your dreams and drivers? You want to know that you did your best to fulfil your potential rather than 'busy' your way through life.

Looking in the mirror can help source your fuel, so you stay in your race long enough for you to start mining your gold. All the above steps are helpful for sourcing past PAIN. They helped me see better that much of my past pain came from a childhood of being criticized by deeply flawed people and, sadly, believing them – and how irrational that was. It reinforced that I needed to stop giving those people power. I had unwittingly adopted their criticism into my own self-talk (P.S. have you done this too?) and could see now that this wasn't my true self but my learned ego having a field day.

This is a point I'd urge you to read again. Many of the beliefs we have about ourselves that limit us have been learned from authority figures or peers that we erroneously accepted as true. **We didn't realize that hurt people hurt people and they project their own unhappiness, bitterness, and failings onto others to deflect having to look in their own mirror.**

When you're in a real funk, take your motivation wherever you can find it. We all need fuel.

However, for you to enjoy your life, **just having rage at the world as your only source of fuel is unhealthy**. Anger fuels anger. You may accomplish a lot but the cost in other areas of your life will likely be heavy. Fortunately, there are many positive ways to develop fuel so read on!

For now, be clear about where you are so you can craft small steps to move forward and stay in action. This is totally within your control. This can be the hardest thing to confront. Usually there is some relief from facing what's really going on and knowing exactly where you stand. You take your head out the sand. No matter how you feel right now, just stay with me, okay? I've been there too, and you can handle it.

Do an inventory of your reality!

Fuel up often!

CHAPTER 5

Own Everything

What Brian Tracy Told Me About Jack Canfield's #1 Success Principle

I met Brian Tracy about sixteen years ago in Milwaukee in my 'earlier' days. I had bought this VIP ticket so had a chance to talk to him during the break. Feeling nervous and rather intimidated by being face to face with a 'famous' person, I blurted out a completely thoughtless question.

He'd just spent *ninety* minutes talking about the keys to success and I said, "Your life story is remarkable. How did you do it?" He looked slightly exasperated at my broad question as if to say: "Didn't you hear anything I just said?" but, as the consummate professional, he quickly composed himself and replied: "If I had to pick just one thing, it's this: Most people take about a 6/10 responsibility for most areas of their life. If you want to be really successful, you've got to that get to a 9 or a 10."

The mistake I made that day and that I've made a lot since then is that I've assumed *I wasn't 'most people'* and therefore I was *never* a 6/10. That day I reacted to that observation the way I suspect most people do. We say to ourselves: "I'm pretty good ('above average') at most things so I am not 'most people'. I could never be a 6/10 except at things I don't care about."

If you're going to mine your gold successfully, look harder at your results. In which area of your life do you *not* like the outcomes you're getting?

1. Acknowledge areas that are mediocre or not going well from Chapter 4 and decide if you want to change them for the better.

When I hit my all-time low in January 2019, there were too many areas to mention. Even though I felt quite lost, I did commit to change by focusing on a few of them by doing small things I could control. I knew I needed to clean up my own act and stop expecting anyone or anything else to change. I suspected it would be a slow process, but I had to rebuild my self-respect. It's been a transformative journey since then and every week I continue to learn and, more importantly, *experiment* by applying new things that help speed up progress because now I know for sure:

Only you can make these improvements and, if you don't, then things will stay the same. You're hopefully not at such a low point BUT there is an area or two in your life where your results are causing you some grief.

You have three choices: accept the situation (and do nothing), work on changing it, or remove yourself from the situation.

2. Accept that you create every outcome in your life

If there's a result you don't like, it is YOU who created or *allowed* it. Not anyone else. YOU. Until you accept this, the problem will always be 'out there' (in your mind) beyond your control and making you the victim.

This is an easy topic to dismiss because you've heard it before, and it can be hard to stomach. But the reality is that few people live it. They get worn down and ambivalent or accept mediocre outcomes as 'what I'm used to', 'this is just the way it is,' or worse: 'this is just who

I am.' I was alarmed not long ago when I heard my (then eight-year-old) son announce: "I'm not good with change." I thought to myself, "He's labelled himself already?!"

For you, is this really how you want your life to play out if everything continues as it is? **If you're the author of your script, you can write the rest of the script differently.** Fine, it's not as easy as it may sound, but if you stay in the race, you can take more and more steps.

Even if an act of nature or an accident affects you, you may well understandably go through some really challenging transition stages (see Habit 3, Weed 3 - Feeling Beaten After a Setback or Lifequake), but at some point, you will still have one life to make the most of.

"If you want to be really successful in your life, then you have to totally give up blaming, complaining and making excuses. They are all a complete waste of time. None of them move you toward your goals."

This is Jack Canfield's very first principle in *The Success Principles*. The best resource on taking responsibility for everything in your life is in *The Success Principles Workbook* which includes some really helpful exercises that can help you uncover what you blame your lack of success on and how to take ownership for these thoughts.

For example:

"**Instead of blaming** (e.g.) a lack of prospects **for** (e.g.) my slow business growth,

I could do this: (fill in blank) (e.g.) commit to a 20-point daily prospecting system; join a local networking group; organize bi-monthly business events to expand my network; volunteer on a committee to build relationships with like-minded/accomplished people etc.

It also gets you to think through what your biggest complaints are and what you can DO instead of pointlessly complaining about them.

This is surprisingly helpful because unwittingly we have the same revolving thoughts going through our head and too often these are worries and complaints.

You might say to yourself: "that sounds hard." Well, it may not be easy to address, but remember: **If you want to be really successful in your life, then you have to give up:**

| **Blaming** | **Complaining** | **Making excuses** |

When I interviewed MD of Salesman.org and podcast hero Will Barron in 2019, he showed how his mindset had served him: "If I blame myself for everything, I'm in control of my destiny."

Even if this seems unreasonable or too harsh, what it does is help you focus on what you can control versus what you cannot. And that circle of influence grows.

3. **Process through the difficult situation**

Canfield points out that: *"Many of the problems that remain unresolved for us are due to one thing: We don't see that we are part of the problem."*

His workbook contains some incredibly insightful questions to address your most troubling situation such as:

How are you creating it or allowing it to happen?
What are you pretending not to know?
What is the payoff for keeping it like it is?
What is the cost for not changing it?
What would you rather be experiencing?
What actions will you take to create that?
By when will you take that action?

My favorite 'quicker' solution when I'm stuck on something negative is to grab my journal and I write the question: "How do I solve this?"

Sometimes I need to process the frustration or problem first before I feel ready to answer the question (see The Setback Plan in Habit 3, Weed 3 - Feeling Beaten After a Setback or Lifequake also for deeper seated challenges).

The solution to whatever is bothering you is public knowledge: you can find the answers. The real question is whether you want to take full responsibility for it or remain on the lower-level prison-like discomfort of what's 'normal' at that moment. I say it this bluntly because I've done this to myself for too long with certain things. I know how easy it is to deceive yourself and justify mediocrity.

What muddies the waters is that underlying a lack of action might well be the unconscious thought: "I don't really deserve that high level of health/wealth/love/joy". This is even more reason to get serious and, yes, obsessive about making consistent small changes in your life that build self-respect. (See Habit 4, Key 1: Elevate Your Worthiness).

Clint Eastwood said: *"Respect your efforts, respect yourself. Self-respect leads to self-discipline. When you have both firmly under your belt, that's real power."*

Once you start *doing your best* at increasingly more things, you will in time realize that you were wrong to limit your thinking about what you're capable of accomplishing. It's not a fast process; powerful things rarely happen fast. That's why you want to keep adding fuel.

The real question is: are YOU going to step up now so you can mine your own gold?

I urge you to face what's not working and decide to get really proactive about addressing it. You are going to get knocked down as you do. This is life testing your resolve. If it were an easy challenge, you would have figured it out already. But you do want better for yourself, and you are far more capable than you might think. The very fact that others have done it is proof you can too.

Take responsibility for all areas of your life!

Fuel up often!

CHAPTER 6

Ignite Your Regrets

Sometimes it helps to get clear on what you don't want first.

Bronnie Ware was an Australian nurse who spent several years working in palliative care, caring for patients in the last 12 weeks of their lives. In 2012 she wrote *The Top Five Regrets of the Dying*. This is as good a place as any to start on the topic of not living your life filled with unaddressed regrets. Here's what she found:

1. **I wish I'd had the courage to live a life true to myself, not the life others expected of me.**

   We hear some sayings such as 'be true to yourself' so often that it's hard to absorb what it can really mean. One of the most common limiting behaviors I see coaching others is the desire to please others too much. It's very easy to rationalize pleasing others which suggests it's a grey area.

   It doesn't help that as children we learn to please our parents and teachers who want us to do many things a certain way – their way! We become socialized to behave certain ways – someone else's way. I'm not saying this is all bad (as parents we all do our imperfect best), just that we have many learned behaviors, and it can get hard to know what is being true to ourselves and what is conforming or trying to please others.

Then if you throw in worthiness and buying into daft ideas that some people are better than you for whatever reason, again we behave in ways counter to our true selves.

It's probably worth journaling on this:

If I were really being true to myself, what are some things I would do in an ideal month or year? Then afterwards examine your list and say: are there things on this list that I do to please or impress others? How much do I genuinely enjoy them? This is just to check that your memory isn't flawed.

2. I wish I hadn't worked so hard.

We live in a culture that currently values being extremely busy all the time. Is anyone ever praised for how well they spend their non-work time (except the uber wealthy)?

Yes, the material rewards typically come from hard work and inspiration. But that's not what matters most. We all want the same thing in life: to love and be loved.

It's worth pausing and remembering someone you knew who died prematurely. None of us has total control over what happens. Any of us can get a terminal diagnosis or be in a fatal accident. What do you think that person would say about working hard?

Journal: if I was told I had six months to live, how would I spend my time?

3. I wish I'd had the courage to express my feelings.

I understand shying away from stating your feelings. I grew up with a volatile parent where conflict felt rife and moods unpredictable – walking on eggshells. My survival was to hide in my bedroom and read. And as an adult, I've often avoided conflicting conversations: I've not always had the courage to express my feelings.

I remember being 25 and living alone and thinking to myself: "I like this. NO ONE is arguing. And I don't have to deal with anyone's bad mood." A few years later, I graduated to having a dog and didn't get married until I was 44. Avoiding conflict made the first few years difficult with another A type who was also used to doing everything her way. At times, I became a doormat as a result – too nice and unwilling to argue or express what I wanted because I lacked the courage. I was unwittingly living a hard-wired way of being even though it didn't serve me. And only when being that way was clearly damaging my self-respect too deeply did I realize that I had to change.

The exercises in Habits 1 and 2 can help you bring to the surface which behaviors no longer serve you anymore. For current pressing issues, try journaling: What do I REALLY think about (not getting a dog, living with my mother-in-law, my son wanting a motorbike etc)?

Honesty starts with you telling yourself the truth even when it's difficult to digest. This includes our human imperfections. Just don't forget you're still lovable!

4. I wish I had stayed in touch with my friends.

The trend I've 'noticed' in the last 20 years has been men having few or no friends and virtually no one to confide in or talk to. And despite this chasm many men have, almost no one does much about it. They accept it as 'normal now'. Overtures get made but are almost never sustained, as if that's too much of an admission of weakness. It's as if it's not socially acceptable to let a male friend in. And given how much everyone works or busy everyone feels, friendships are made to feel like a luxury.

I almost always had good friends. It used to be a real strength of my life. Becoming self-employed at 35 was the first time I put less effort into having friends and, once I got engaged, it felt like a nice-to-have that I couldn't find the time for.

Only during the Pandemic did that make a change for the good as it became a necessity for me to stay sane and find connection with others. And since the Pandemic, it's declined again.

5. I wish that I had let myself be happier.

So few people seem to go about their day as if they're having any fun at all – again, almost as if there's something wrong with you if you are. Certainly, the volume and depth of problems we have seem to grow as we get older and, yes, the only people with no problems are in the cemetery. There has to be a better way.

Interestingly, many people I've met who have had a lot 'success' tend to be more optimistic and grateful. It's a common theme that the people at the 'top' tend to be nicer – it's rather like the comment I hear frequently that people's top clients and biggest, most complex clients are the nicest to work with and the ones who pay the least often quibble about the fees and are often the most demanding. I have heard this so many times it is well worth reflecting on!

I would venture that many of the people who have had these outcomes have been close enough to people who did not enjoy similar outcomes - and how that could have been them. This is partly why they are - even subconsciously – more grateful and positive. They have an awareness that they were somewhat fortunate. Certain things could have easily gone another way in their lives. I can think of a few people immediately who were wonderful people who made one mistake in business or with a relationship choice and it changed the course of their lives for the worse.

The most useful insight is to be grateful for all you do have and let that feeling grow. Stop seeking happiness 'out there.' Tune into your Unconditioned (original) self vs. your ego and to know you were born happy. You were born as loveable. See the world through your heart and actions from a place of love not your fear. All greatness comes from within.

No Regrets?

"No regrets" is a popular tattoo and common sentiment echoed by a wide variety of people from Bob Dylan, Angelina Jolie and Justice Ruth Bader to Norman Vincent Peale, Tony Robbins, and Edith Piaf and her famous 1960's song: "Je ne regrette rien".

But in his book, *The Power of Regret*, Daniel Pink says **this is not a healthy recipe for a good life.** Regret is in fact "universal," "valuable," and "needn't drag us down; it can lift us up." Repressing or ignoring regrets is unhealthy and foolish. It can often stop us from doing the work we need to mine our gold! Bottling up regrets can also lead to negative health consequences over time.

Here's why acknowledging and exploring your regrets can help you mine your gold (since it is a painful thing to do):

> a) **Better future decisions - use past regrets to improve your future and clarify your values**

Some of what we value most comes from regrets. For example, as I tried to explain Pink's book to my then eight-year-old daughter, I reminded her that one of my life regrets was that I only told my dad that I loved him once in my life – and it was the last time I saw him before he died of cancer. And that this was why I so frequently like to express my love to her and her brother.

b) Improved performance from instilling deeper persistence

Failing to succeed at something can deepen our resolve and cause us to try again even harder, e.g., failing to land a big prospect or coming second in a contest. Regret can help us develop a **"journey mindset"** which helps us SUSTAIN good habits *after* we hit a goal and not unwittingly slack off.

This makes me think of one-hit wonders who perhaps arrived at their success too young, too quickly or too easily. Some failure and frustration might have given them the resolve they needed to keep working on their craft knowing that good things often don't come easily.

Michael Jordan was cut from his high school team as a freshman and the pain of this is something he never forgot and often used as motivation to prove the world wrong. Even when he was inducted into the NBA Hall of Fame, he made reference to the person who made his high school team instead of him.

c) Increased sense of meaning and connectedness

One of my biggest life regrets was not staying in a relationship during my university years with a wonderful young woman called Catharine. I decided to end things because I was going overseas for an exchange year to study in the USA. I wanted to be 'free', and I didn't trust my feelings: I was afraid that if I missed her too much, I would come back home and 'drop out' of the year.

It was a legitimate concern because I'd done that two years prior after arriving in Germany for a job I'd arranged right after high school. That was over a girl called Sue. That had been the lowest point of my life and had been very hard to dig out of emotionally.

So I broke things off saying I needed to listen to my head not my heart. It was about seven months before I wrote to her saying I'd made a mistake. I hadn't met anyone new either. But she didn't reply.

What this really painful regret taught me was the value of loyalty. I was not loyal to her. I've been much more conscious since then about standing by great people.

Regrets from relationship failures can help us make better decisions in the future or to right past wrongs so we don't repeat past painful experiences.

As you read through these questions, write down increasingly more of your own regrets. This is not an easy assignment. I found myself getting temporarily really sad. I realize no one wants to feel that way, but the deeper you dig, the closer you will get to topics that you can use as fuel. <u>That fuel will help you mine your gold.</u> And you will probably need all the fuel you can get. I promise you it's worthwhile – almost a mini test for the actual mission you're on.

REGRET SURVEY

Answer these questions followed by the question: <u>What's next/ How to Leverage for Fuel?</u>

There doesn't always have to be an answer here, but it is designed to make this exercise valuable by becoming more open to how you would like to change and rewrite a different future. It's also okay to start prioritizing and respond with: 'Maybe in five years I will…"

1. Who do you wish you were in better contact with?
2. Which past conflict do you wish you'd resolved?
3. When do you think you were living a life expected of you rather than one where you were being true to yourself?

And when do you fall into that trap currently (ouch)?

Achiever types in particular tend to have the plug in too tight. Since this was the biggest regret Bronnie Ware encountered, we are fooling ourselves if we think we don't do the same thing! We are rarely conscious of how much our surrounding culture and other people influence us. We usually convince ourselves that we are making all our own independent decisions, but in her book, *Influence is Your Superpower,* Yale professor Zoe Chance says: *"Influence doesn't work the way we think because people don't think the way they think they do...most behavior reflects very little "thinking" at all."*

I remember when my twins were toddlers, I felt like I had lost my identity as I just automatically played the role of 'robodad', thoughtlessly doing all the parent and household tasks I was supposed to and never doing anything that I wanted to do.

4. Education: What do you regret not better applying yourself to learn?

5. **What actions do you regret NOT taking in your life?**

Think REALLY HARD about this one and **start a list. This is a really powerful question.**

6. Who do you wish you'd declared your feelings for?

7. What challenges do you regret taking on or not taking on at work?

8. When do you wish you'd listened to your intuition or instinct better?

9. Where do you wish you'd made a bigger impact?

10. During which part of your life do you wish you'd not worked so hard?

11. **What habits do you wish you'd had earlier that would have set you up better for long-term success?**

12. What part of your life journey do you wish you'd enjoyed more at the time?

13. Which morally dubious decisions do you regret making?

14. Was there a college you still regret not getting into or attending?

15. Which concerts/performers do you wish you'd gone to?

16. What did you lack the confidence to do as a teenager?

17. Which job or professional opportunity do you regret not getting?

18. What trips do you wish you had taken?

Next, answer from these five questions for the following life areas. It's okay to respond to some of these and come back to others over time. Do it based on what value you're getting and on how much you can handle at any one time!

1. **LIST** YOUR REGRETS in each area

   Daniel Pink recommends the next two questions:

2. How could the decision I now regret have **turned out worse**?

3. What's one silver lining in this regret? Pink shares his own example, "Going to law school was a mistake, but *at least* I met my wife."

   "How would I complete the sentence? **"At least…"**

   Lastly, answer this:

4. **What experiences do you wish you'd had** in this area?

5. **What's next**/How to leverage for fuel?

Summarized:

> List regrets: I wish…
> Turned out worse?
> "At least…"
> What experiences do you wish you'd had?
> What's next/How to leverage for fuel?

Remember, the ultimate purpose to these questions is to find more fuel for mining your gold:

a)   Your key relationships:

b)   Your business/vocation:

c)   Your finances:

d)   Your physical health:

e)   Mental health:

*Your self-belief:
*How confident you feel:
*How much you respect yourself:
*Your sense of worthiness to achieve your long-term goals:

*How happy you feel:
*Degree to which you feel positively challenged:
*Degree to which you tune into your intuition and trust your gut instinct:
*How constructively you deal with anger and other negative emotions:

f)   Sense of spiritual connection:

g)   Adventures/fun/hobbies:

h)   Contribution and giving back:

i)   Living your purpose:

You may also find use for this phrase:

<u>What's the healthiest mindset to have about it now?</u>

This time around on Earth, I wasn't meant to… be with this person, become a doctor, have children, be a refugee in a war-torn country etc.,

I was meant to take a different path this time around, my purpose is to do my best…

Lastly, from your thinking above, pick your top 10 biggest regrets that you can do something about.

ANSWERING THESE QUESTIONS IN DEPTH is HARD. When I did this most recently, I felt so sad. I hate to admit, but at first I actually felt depressed. It's hard to face your own shortcomings and wonder how you made such a mess of something or reacted in such a 'dysfunctional' way.

This is not an easy assignment but persevere because it can be *very* powerful – can I get a show of hands on who wants to live with regrets?! The deeper you dig, the closer you will get to topics that you can start to use as magnificent fuel. Within a short time, you will feel differently and have tapped into new fuel that will help you surge. You will probably want to right some wrongs from your past and prove that YOU are holding the pen that writes the script of your life, not someone else. **This is all fuel that will help you mine your own gold** (which is the only reason I'm sharing this with you)

For example, when I listed out my regrets, I was surprised to see that most of them were areas I could still improve on now and make a very positive difference in my life. Even if they've hurt my happiness and effectiveness to varying degrees in the past, it doesn't mean they have to be a life sentence. Same with you.

I wrote:

I regret living too close to my comfort zone for so long. Scared to date. Scared to take bigger biz risks. **Playing too small.**

Low on self-belief so growing too slowly in biz.

Regret trying to be too nice to/soft on clients (allowing them outs) and not pushing them enough.

I regret under-charging for my services for too many years (low self-worth).

Regret letting my mother and wife upset me so much – being a puppet to their words and unhappiness and bad days

Wish I hadn't taken life so seriously.

Regret making myself feel so guilty for so long about emigrating when that was what my heart always wanted.

I regret not dealing with feelings of frustration better – that started (I think) with my boyhood choir experiences and that were channeled mostly at my mum. And denying its existence for a long time.

Regret having **doubted my self-worth** for too long.

Regret being down for so long after my 2012 burnout and frustration – marital, parenting, biz quagmire combo.

ACTION! How to start addressing your regrets

At a minimum as you look at your own list, you can be clearer about not making the same mistakes again and living on a thoughtless autopilot.

What would be a breakthrough for you with this past regret?

Here are some examples of how I responded to my painful past regrets.

*To stay out of my comfort zone, I have often had "4%" as a Power Habit. See Chapter 24 to learn about this strategy.

*Self-belief and self-doubt for me were best addressed for me by using my Habit Tracker every day. This provided proof to my brain that I was doing my best to be my best (most of the time!).

*I reminded myself on my Big 5 (Chapter 8) to push clients based on the knowledge that everyone has a vein of gold to be mined and I do no one any favors by letting them off the hook

*I have a reminder on my Big 5 to charge what I'm worth

*I created an identity to work on (see chapter 16) and a daily question (See chapter 20) to address not being easily set off by unhappy people

*I added to my Big 5 not to take life so seriously

*I have a daily question (chapter 20) to remind me about how well I'm dealing with things that frustrate or upset me

You will probably want to **prioritize your list and only work on a small number at a time** as it is not realistic to focus on multiple *anything* and do it really well. As the Chinese proverb says: *He who chases two rabbits catches none.*

You might need to *experiment* with the 'right' number for you. I *love* this concept because it gives you permission to make mistakes, change your mind and not be perfect about it. A-types typically try to do too many at once and usually get frustrated and give up – I've done this far more times than I'd ever care to recall. Experiment and if you are trying to change too much too fast, then re-prioritize, shorten your list, and make a note to revisit your list in a future month. **We have to go to the gym forever**, so whatever you decide, IT'S *OKAY*. Just stay in the race!

Stop living like a caged lion.

In Tim Grover's book *Relentless*, he reminds us that we've been taught a lot of limitations since childhood and stopped doing many things naturally. Rather like the king of the jungle that naturally chases a zebra until it's put in the zoo and is handed food, you can't be great if you stuff up all your crazy urges, ideas, and desires.

Lastly, I want you to know: it's okay to feel whatever you feel from processing through these difficult questions to remember that the value in feeling the pain is so you do not live the rest of your life blindly anymore but do your best to steer your thoughts and actions into more proactive directions. That is all you can control now. And you don't have to be a reactive puppet now you've shone a bright light onto events from the past that you wish you had handled/experienced differently. And this process may take a little time for you.

Done right, this thinking can give you power and help you build new skills and habits that fuel a much brighter future. Most of us have many years left to make all kinds of magic happen. All of us can do something impactful today. Accept your humanity and imperfection and live the life you've always wanted to.

Mine your gold often by addressing past regrets!

Fuel up often!

CHAPTER 7

Define True Success and True Failure

Felix Dennis lived with his grandparents for many years as a child in the 1950's. His father had left him and his mother behind for Australia when he was two. They were extremely poor and had a bucket in a shed for a toilet and at times had to use squares of newspaper for toilet paper. Even though he says he had a happy childhood (and he didn't know anything different at the time anyway), it instilled in him the fuel he needed to mine his own gold: a hatred for having nothing and a fire to become rich. He went on to become one of Britain's wealthiest self-made entrepreneurs with an estimated fortune of $650m and a next-door neighbor to Mick Jagger on the island of Mustique.

Yet in his book *How to Get Rich*, he shares this:

"Happiness? Do not make me laugh. The rich are not happy. I have yet to meet a single really rich happy man or woman – and I have met many rich people. The demands from others to share their wealth become so tiresome – and so insistent, they nearly always decide they must insulate themselves. Insulation breeds paranoia and arrogance. And loneliness. And rage that you have only so many years left to enjoy rolling in the sand you have piled up."

THEN he adds this about the previous remarks: "In my heart of hearts, I know it (is) *the* most important bit you will read in this book" – even though his book is about how to get rich.

He also says that if you want to be rich, you have to "cut loose" from loved ones to focus on making money: *"I have heard of very few men or women who made a ton of money who did not leave, or divorce, their wives or husbands or lovers sooner or later. Or who were not estranged from family members, often their children. It comes with the territory."* He said it happens because the person making the money valued the time it took to succeed more than spending it with their loved ones.

I tell this story because you bought this book to mine your own gold. Because you know it's there. And you will need a deep tank of fuel to get you there because this supreme task is unlikely going to be easy (sorry). It will require you to show up on the days you don't feel it. You're capable of this and you want as much fuel as possible.

But as you source your fuel, you want to be clear about what success really is for you, you want it to align with what you really want, with what you truly value, with how you want to make a difference, and with what will make your life rewarding and meaningful.

Felix Dennis made a lot of money and deserves praise and admiration for all he accomplished, for his courage, brilliant resourcefulness, and how much he learned and taught others from running so many successful companies that provided thousands of jobs. His initiative and resolve are *inspiring* – as with many entrepreneurs. But would you have really wanted what he had? It's easy to knee-jerk think '$650m? Yes!', but there was a side to his life you may not have wanted:

He was a cocaine addict in his 40's. Slept with over 100 prostitutes. Smoked his way to a painful death by throat cancer at 67. Never married or had children.

His book is practical and insightful but *at no point* states that getting rich will bring joy to your life. He never promises that because he didn't experience it. It leaves you torn – **how do you balance wanting to get up to something big and not alienating your closest**

family and friends? What is true success? This is a question Robert Holden started asking over twenty years ago.

Lost on the Road to Success

One Saturday afternoon when he was 16, he was late to meet some friends outside a record shop. Rushing down the high street of his hometown in England, something caught his eye: It was a homeless man lying face down on the sidewalk.

"We all pretended not to see him," explains Holden in his book *Authentic Success, "But something made me stop."* The man was wearing a ragged coat, he reeked of alcohol and had a pair of smashed glasses next to him. *"His face was a mass of cuts and bruises. He was barely conscious. He smiled at me. 'Hello Dad.' I said."*

His father, Alex Holden, had been a well-respected executive with various multi-national corporations and had raised his family on three different continents. He owned a lovely country home and had a family who loved him. He was successful by virtually anyone's standards.

The doctors diagnosed alcoholism, but the more time Holden spent with him and his vagrant friends, he came to a very different conclusion: *"my dad was not ill; he was lost.* **Somewhere along the road to success he had got lost**...*of what is real...he had also lost sight of himself. And then the meaningless and valuelessness set in. Slowly killing him."*

Holden's life as a teen was literally gut-wrenching: *"The pain I felt was beyond words. I woke up every day for ten years with a sharp, stabbing ache in my belly. I was having a mid-life crisis in a teenager's body."* Perhaps not surprisingly, Holden was deeply motivated to understand what happened to his father and, in time, to help others avoid making the same mistakes. Here are some of the things that ate away at his father that affect us all, some suggestions on what you can do to address them and then tie this into what true success is for you:

1. **We are always busy** (which is often a major block to success in work, relationships, and life).

   *"The major challenges we face today require not more effort,
   but more wisdom."*

   Many people are running and trying too hard or simply
   burning out and becoming ever less efficient. Faster in life
   and business does not always mean better. Constantly feeling short of time has so many negative consequences: *"True
   success should not have to cost you your joy, your health,
   or your relationships. On the contrary, true success is about
   enjoying these things."*

   We have confused speed and adrenaline with purpose. You
   can't do *everything* faster.

   Yet we want everything by yesterday. Permanent busyness
   is not only a badge of pride, it is almost socially unacceptable to be anything other than this! While we all aspire to
   have a thriving business, being busy all the time ceases to
   be productive. We all need to recharge but our culture does
   not support it.

   When writing his book, Holden tells the story of a taxi driver
   in central London who told him: "Most people think this
   taxi is an ambulance. They act like everything is a life-or-
   death emergency. I should fix a siren on my roof." He went
   on to explain that he drove for ten hours a day and never
   clocked up more than 80 miles each day. "Everyone is in a
   hurry and the fastest we go is eight miles an hour. It's bloody
   madness."

   Busyness at its worst can become an addiction. It conve-
   niently helps us avoid facing something about our life we
   don't want to face – a relationship, yourself, your purpose,

shame, guilt, or even success. And workaholism is one of its socially acceptable forms.

What really cut through my own noise was his point that **endless busyness wasn't just socially acceptable, but it was a way to hide a broken heart.** It slowly helped me acknowledge that working all the time was a convenient way for me to avoid thinking about feeling lonely and confront my lack of being in a relationship and pursuing personal happiness.

Solutions:

*Get more aware about the pace you live your own life and start questioning when moving fast serves you and when it absolutely doesn't.

*Put space in your calendar – let life in: 'When the student is relaxed, the breakthrough appears.' Don't try too hard all the time.

*Answer this: If I were less busy and had no fear, what ache in my heart would I do something about?

2. **We are flying through life as almost complete strangers to ourselves**

    We are so busy that we have little idea what being true to ourselves even means because we don't make time to reflect.

    Solution:

    *Raise your self-awareness. Journal. Holden cites the benefits: *"The better you know yourself – what you value, what inspires you, what you are made of – the more effectively you will live, work and relate to others."* It's too easy otherwise to get sucked into chasing marketers' version of success – a world where you never have enough and there is always something missing.

*Increase your awareness of your self-talk and catch what you say that holds you back.

3. **Our behavior as consumers adds no meaning or happiness to life**

You can never get enough of what you don't really need in the first place. **Happiness is not an 'it' you can buy**. It is inside you waiting to be unwrapped.

Solutions: It's quite easy to get addicted to buying things but the dopamine hit you get is embarrassingly fleeting

*Pay more attention to how inter-connected everything is. Want to argue with Leonardo da Vinci? In the 15th century, he noted: "Everything comes from everything, and everything is made out of everything, and everything returns to everything."

*To build inner happiness, connect beyond the immediate stressors of your life and to the world beyond time and space through meditation or prayer.

4. **Many of our communities are broken**

Holden's father was perhaps the first generation of executives and managers to be stationed in multiple countries. Many people in these roles travel away from home for multiple nights per week disconnecting them from loved ones. Our long work weeks also make us too tired to socialize so instead we watch so-called reality TV and, over time, lose connections with friends and neighbors.

Solution: If you are away from home a lot for work, keep reading this chapter and see how well it aligns with your definition of true success and purpose.

5. **Our culture of individualism leaves many feeling lonely**

Loneliness is spreading. The UK and Japanese governments now have a Minister for Loneliness. This is exacerbated by a highly competitive business environment which often discourages collaboration.

Solution: Interact! It becomes a matter of life and death (See Habit 3, Weed 2: Mostly Avoidable Weeds).

6. **A life of shallow conversations**

Our long hours and constant distraction from technology leave us too tired to have conversations of any substance most of the time. This too leads to feeling empty and alone on the inside because we're rarely connecting on any meaningful level with others. We mostly exchange quick texts.

Solution: Schedule the time to talk to people, and for date nights with your partner and your children. Put the screens away.

7. **The pace of change leaves most people feeling ever less in control of their own lives**

This topic doesn't get enough airtime. All of us resist change in certain ways and learning to adapt challenges most of us at times. The default is often to find something simple to blame that you don't like – a war, a government, global warming, or a group of people – when this is almost always multifactorial.

Solution: The best way to handle this is through continuous learning so you're more aware of what's changing (so well done for reading this!): Then it's easier to regularly improve your own skills and knowledge so you can pivot and adapt. We also need to have more faith in ourselves and in our higher power that gives us strength too.

8. **'Up' isn't the only way to success**

There are many inspiring reasons to grow but it is not *always* the wisest step. It can add stress you don't want. It can take you away from what you value most. It can become pur- poseless. You can risk missing out on life along the way.

Solution: As you've read from Felix Dennis, going up the food chain or making more money usually requires more time. When is it worth the sacrifice of time? Work on your definition of true success (keep reading!)

9. **We have forgotten love from our definition of true success**

Love has been separated from work yet **love inspires success**.

Solution: Let love drive your decisions.

10. **We suffer from "Destination Addiction"**

Robert Holden coined this phrase to describe how we are always in a big hurry to get somewhere and as a result we never enjoy the present moment we are living in. Nor do we ever get 'there'. There is always another destination. There is no purpose. The achievements will supposedly give us time for joy, relationships, and health in the future, but we get permanently impatient and addicted to always needing to get somewhere else. We never get 'there'. Life passes us by.

Solution:

*If you're going to chase 'more' in life, chase more happiness, more meaning, and more love: *"We do not become happy* *because we are successful; we become successful because we are happy"* – because we are pursuing what inspires us.

*Believe in grace – where the world conspires to help you in unpredictable ways. Find a way to believe that everything will work out in the end. Holden adds: *"Success is easier when we trust in our inner wisdom and accept God's helping hand."* Many spiritual texts subscribe to the ancient proverb: 'When the student is ready, the teacher appears.' On a deeper level, it means the teacher is *waiting* to be noticed and is here already. We just weren't ready. Holden concludes: **"True success is something we feel when we allow the grace of God to inspire our endeavors."**

Find Your Road to Success - DEFINE TRUE SUCCESS AND TRUE FAILURE

We have no definition of success besides the ridiculous one our culture feeds us – and you want your own definition to make sure you don't get lost.

True Success starts with being aligned to what you value

Here's an embarrassing story. When I was 28, I was training to be a schoolteacher and running a before and after school program in LaCrosse, Wisconsin. One afternoon, Brandon, one of the children, asked me what I most valued in the world? Without thinking, I said: "My Wisconsin Badger season tickets." He looked taken aback and said: "What about your family?" I could feel inside that I'd said the wrong thing, something shallow.

I don't remember how I backtracked, but my first answer was the true one at the time. I had so many unresolved challenges from my past that more than anything else I had wanted to emigrate and try to forge my own path. The topic of family made me uncomfortable and confused, and I wasn't quite willing to take responsibility for it at that time. I blush out of embarrassment even now writing this.

There are many things we can value: a nice house, a prestigious job title, a rare or luxury car, speaking to large audiences, fine jewelry, a hobby, closing a big sale, or owning a prized collection.

And then there are other value items: people. People often define our purpose. I have often put health before people, not in a selfish sense, but in that I'm no good to anyone if I don't take care of myself. Living to your full potential can be something you value. Meaningful work. Serving others.

Take a moment to identify what you value most at least as a starting point to get more clarity:

> Your key relationships:
> Children:
> Family members:
> Friends:
> Your business/vocation:
> Your finances:
> Spiritual life:
> Your physical health:
> Your mental health:
>> i) Your self-belief:
>> ii) Your confidence:
>> iii) Your self-respect:
>> iv) Your sense of worthiness:
>> v) Your happiness:
>> vi) How positively challenged you are:
>> vii) How you want to feel
>> viii) What you say to yourself
> Adventures/fun/hobbies:
> Community involvement:
> Living Your Purpose:
> Following Your Heart:
> Listening to Your Soul:

It's not a black and white topic because sometimes we have to prioritize differently. We almost all have to make a living so can't *always* put our loved ones first. The real value of the task is for it to help you make better decisions that align. Too often in today's world, for example, we say we value family first, but we often put work first.

Success does not equal MORE

We are sold the message that success equals *having*. But there is almost no scientific evidence among advanced industrial societies between income level and subjective wellbeing beyond a surprisingly low household income. We fail to focus on living a life of purpose that serves others.

And why – when we think about success – does it *always mean needing MORE*? It never considers that what you have now might be enough or as close to great as it's wise to expect.

In Chapter 4 you looked closely in the mirror for where you are today. This can provide quite a lot of fuel especially if you're not feeling good right now. And there are other important layers to building your motivation.

a) A great question to ask yourself first focuses on *being*: **'What type of person do I want to be?'** When people write their own obituaries, they rarely mention their possessions. They write about relationships, quality of life and having made a difference. As Gandhi said: "Be the change you want to see." (More on this in chapter 16)

b) According to Holden, "***the key to feeling truly successful***" is to know the answer to this question**: What do I really want?**

What do you really want?

This is usually a challenging question because we have been so (unwittingly) influenced by the culture we grew up in. Most cultures throughout history and today perpetuate the myth that happiness only comes from striving for 'more': more possessions, more money, more power, more everything: The More Monster.

Not only is this a guarantee to never feeling fulfilled, it leads to another cultural myth: that **there is never enough**.

How do you feel when you keep telling yourself there is not enough of something (usually money)? You *always* feel negatively. It NEVER makes you feel good about yourself. And, as I learned from studying human behavior with BJ Fogg, founder of Stanford University's Behavior Design Lab, since **we change best when we feel good not when we feel bad,** this immediately has us taking steps backwards every time the thought crosses our minds. There's usually only so much of that discouragement most people can take. I know you don't see yourself as 'most people', but either you're setting yourself up to make your gold mining efforts much harder than they need to be or, quite possibly, to give up at some point.

How often do you inflate the importance of money? Sometimes I feel like I have a balanced handling of it and other times it consumes far more of my thinking than is healthy. And I know that more of it probably won't make me happier. It can buy more fun experiences around the world, but to make that money generally takes time away from my loved ones. Which isn't particularly good for them or me.

Twenty years ago, I spent some time in Moscow and, as I walked about the streets day after day, was struck by how unhappy people looked. When I got back to the US, I was shocked to notice that people here didn't look any happier - especially when they were driving! Now I live in one of the top 20 wealthiest neighborhoods in the wealthiest country in the world. And I cannot honestly say that the people I meet are any happier here than anyone else I've met. They all talk about their problems with the same levels of worry and stress. Even if many of their problems are 'first world' challenges; mentally people respond the same.

It's a warped message that our culture sends us. According to Daniel Pink's research in his book, *Drive,* 75% of people are *not* motivated by money but are motivated intrinsically – that they find their meaning in life on the inside and not by money and possessions. Surely this then leaves many of us questioning our own intrinsic drive as somehow flawed given that popular culture suggests that the way to go is the high-net-worth lifestyle – that 'real' success only comes when you've hit certain financial levels; that finding your work or your relationships rewarding in and of itself isn't enough.

Couldn't Gandhi, Mother Teresa, Nelson Mandela, or Amelia Earhart have written a fabulous personal development book about true success? Van Gogh, Beethoven and Emily Dickinson all died relatively poor or penniless – yet isn't our world so much better for their contributions and didn't they also teach us much about true success? Van Gogh lived long periods of his life existing on bread and coffee. What about all the men and women who contributed to fighting the Axis Powers in World War Two? If there is an afterlife, I couldn't look any of them in the eye and tell them they weren't successful.

Why does it seem like almost everyone in the world aspires to be rich and, worse, feels something of a failure when they're not? What makes me feel frequently torn is having all this 'knowledge' and living with my own desire to grow financially too - as if I'm missing the most important point about life. One weekend my (then) eight-year-old daughter performed some impromptu songs. One of them was about a 'dad' who didn't have time to play his daughter and how sad she was! Ouch. But the waters can be muddy as what drives me *mostly* is a desire to provide more educational and life opportunities for my wife and children.

As before, it's easiest to start by breaking down into areas of your life and asking yourself:

What do I really want?

> Your key relationships:
> Children:
> Family members:
> Friends:
> Your business/vocation:
> Your finances:
> Your physical health:
> Your mental health:
>> i) Your self-belief:
>> ii) Your confidence:
>> iii) Your self-respect:
>> iv) Your sense of worthiness:
>> v) Your happiness:
>> vi) How positively challenged you've been:
>> vii) How do you want to feel?
>> viii) What do you want to say to yourself?
>
> Spiritual life:
> Adventures/fun/hobbies:
> Community involvement:
> Living Your Purpose:
> Following Your Heart:
> Listening to Your Soul:

What is your definition of true success?

Only you can answer this. One of my favorite definitions of success is: "to spend your time doing what you love". Here are some other thoughts – the first four are paraphrases from Robert Holden:

True success is to keep saying 'yes' to what truly moves your soul.

True success is about finding something you believe in so much that you will risk giving your heart for it – something you love.

True success is something we feel (love) when we allow the grace of God to inspire our endeavors.

True success is serving and inspiring others

True success is choosing GRATITUDE over frustration

"Success is peace of mind which is a direct result of self-satisfaction in knowing you made the effort to become the best you are capable of becoming." - John Wooden

"Life is either a daring adventure or nothing." - Helen Keller

"This is the true joy in life, the being used for a purpose recognized by yourself as a mighty one: the being thoroughly worn out before you are thrown on the scrap heap; the being a force of nature instead of a feverish, selfish, little clod of ailments complaining that the world will not devote itself to making you happy." - George Bernard Shaw

1. What did you learn from your parents about true success?

2. **If you were presenting to a group on five major lessons you've learned about true success in life, what would they be?**

How well have you learned each lesson?

It's likely a combination of things you did right (and got positive reinforcement from) and the things you messed up on – and had to learn the hard way. Maybe one of the five is a lesson you learned from a parent's mistake or something they modeled really well.

These should help you get closer to a useful definition of success for you.

WRITE DOWN YOUR DEFINITION/S.

Next, there is a useful flip side to this:

Also Create a Definition of True Failure

You want one that allows you to CONTINUE pursuing what you love in life

"I've failed over and over and over again in life. And that is why I succeed." - Michael Jordan

None of us wants to fail. No team wants to lose. None of us wants to get ill, injured or have an accident. We want our children to achieve exclusively great things. Yet each of us knows that this is not reality: we have all fallen short with relationships, work assignments or jobs, and meeting all our health and financial goals; we've all been thrown off course and interrupted unexpectedly (most days!) by life events. We've all made mistakes. It's an innate part of living a human life. Challenging things happen to our children.

Failure is nothing to fear even if it's not enjoyable. It usually provides us our most valuable lessons in life. Typically, when we are ready to reflect on something that didn't go as well as wanted it to, we can identify mistakes we made. Our problem lies in how we think about it. Gareth Timmins learned this from his time training as a Royal Marine Commando: ***"Failure is a misused ...label...it does not highlight the different avenues (such as perseverance) a person can take to learn, get better, and make a successful attempt."***

As discussed in the Divine Dozen Part 1: **Forgive yourself for your mistakes and let them go.** I realize this is much easier said than done.

What you need is a way to look at 'failure' such that you rebound from setbacks and accept them as part of life.

Here's my most recent definition of failure. Feel free to use it as a starting point for yourself:

True Failure is having the epitaph: "Too scared to go all in on your dreams."

True failure is giving up on what you love in life and giving up on yourself
True failure is no longer learning, creating, and growing
True failure is when you stop dreaming and loving everyone
True failure is *ceasing to serve and inspire others*
True failure is not being grateful for what you have

When you can define (your version of):
"True failure for me is having the epitaph: "too scared to go all in on his dreams" and
"True success for me is to keep saying 'yes' to what truly moves my soul,"

then how you handle setbacks gets easier and how you make decisions and spend your (one life) time gets centered on your world (not your parents, or Hollywood's or marketer's), it is purpose-driven and a whole lot clearer.

Just remember to keep what you come up with top of mind so it stays with you.

Define true success and failure and keep mining your gold.

Fuel up often!

CHAPTER 8

Discover More Purpose

A perfect day is any day I am vertical…and any day God disturbs me to move outside the normal noise of my life and serve a greater purpose - Bonnie McElveen-Hunter

The purpose of life is a life of purpose - Robert Byrne

Nine months before the end of World War Two, Simon Wiesenthal was a death camp inmate taking a break next to an SS corporal who asked him what he would tell people in the USA "if an eagle took you to America."

Fearing a trap but deciding to be honest, Wiesenthal haltingly said: "I believe I would tell the people the truth, Herr Rottenfuehrer."

The SS man did not shoot him but simply said: "You would tell the truth to the people in America. That's right. And do you know what would happen, Wiesenthal? They wouldn't believe you."

This was the defining moment for Wiesenthal and his purpose became clear: should he survive the rest of the war, he would commit himself to tell the world the truth about the Holocaust – one in which he lost 89 relatives including his mother. He devoted the rest of his life to tracking down Nazi war criminals and, after the war, he helped to bring over 1100 Nazis to justice including Adolf Eichmann and Josef Mengele. It's a stunning story.

Ever had a "moment of truth" conversation? Ever been told you couldn't do something, and you vowed you would prove that person wrong?

I don't know about you, but I've often felt a bit daunted by the topic of 'finding your purpose in life'. I've tried so many times to do the exercises in books and at workshops. It can be harder to find your purpose if you haven't had a Wiesenthal experience or have a cause that prompts a huge sense of injustice (and forgive me because I know there are plenty of them).

This is one reason why the first chapter of this book is about love. It can make life far simpler to acknowledge what matters most and let love be your purpose and guide for life.

Some people of faith tend to find it easier to feel purpose. This is one reason why it was an early chapter in this book too! Mother Teresa described herself simply as "God's pencil." That was all she needed! My Sikh friends Harpreet and Sukhi (both financial advisors) are very clear that their faith drives them to make an ever more positive mark on the world. They are inspiring to spend time with. Harpreet recently started a Men's Wellness Circle focused on mental health. Oprah Winfrey gives herself to God every morning.

When love and/or God are your guides, you are going to focus on serving others. Stephen Covey said it best: "**The key to life is not accumulation; it's contribution."**

Sometimes I wonder if you struggle more with finding a purpose when your self-worth is wobbly; in other words, if your inner dialogue is: "I'm not sure how much I deserve a mighty sense of purpose because I'll never be Martin Luther King or Mother Teresa." As a result, you don't persevere to work on answers (for solutions to this, see Habit 4, Key 1: Elevate Your Worthiness). Then again, if you're focused on your cause/purpose, then you aren't thinking about your own insecurities because you've got more important things to do!

Many people are driven to make a difference in an area that has personally affected them – that becomes their cause. They lost a child to a drunk driver. Or they are like Jenna Benn Shersher, an amazing woman I interviewed for my podcast who survived a near-death cancer experience and started an inspiring charity called Twist Out Cancer that provides psychosocial support for people with cancer through creative arts programs.

Finding a deeper purpose is a longer journey for most people that requires more digging and re-visiting. **Keep mining.** I think people with quite a bit of past trauma can find *drive* more easily because they have a lot of internal energy pushing them to make a mark on the world. Some charge ahead to make a positive difference in the world after having experienced such negativity in their past. Some just charge ahead to 'achieve'. But I'm not sure if most of those people are any clearer about their *purpose*.

Many of us are unwittingly 'chosen' by our vocation although we tend not to see this as our purpose: The person who becomes a police officer because she was bullied as a child or couldn't protect a family member from harm; the nurse who, as a child, couldn't make everyone feel better when a loved one died and it left its mark; the financial advisor who grew up with parents who spent more than they earned, got downsized, divorced, and who experienced a difficult childhood so is driven to help others avoid making the same mistakes his parents made.

And, yes, me – powerless to help an unhappy parent chase her dream so subconsciously drawn to a vocation where I can help people achieve this. But it's taken me decades to be able to clearly understand this.

Some people are driven to serve their partner or their children – and perhaps that is your driver, especially if you felt that your parents were rarely there for you, or you've been at a point in life where you feared you could not support your family. This can be a very powerful motivator – to be a role model to your children. It's worth digging deeper to find out what drives you to be your best. And not be beaten down by life that you lose the spark that you were born with. We all have that vein of gold in our core. And you know it too.

What are the great benefits to defining your purpose?

"What is the use of living, if it be not to strive for noble causes and to make this muddled world a better place for those who will live in it after we are gone?" - Churchill

1. Neurobiologically, purpose alters the brain by shifting the attention off us and it attracts outside assistance. It boosts motivation, productivity, resilience, and focus.

2. Clarity: It helps you focus on what matters most

3. It helps you feel more grounded and centred

4. Your purpose is long-term mission driven

5. It's easier to listen to the voice who wants you to be better

6. It gives your life more meaning. John Assaraf reminds us that our purpose can go deep: "When we have a strong sense of what that purpose is, we tend not only to be far happier, but also far more effective at what we're doing."

7. **Your purpose gives you FUEL to persist towards mining your own gold – think SERVING OTHERS and think: Mother Teresa, Gandhi, Nelson Mandela, a Suffragette like Elizabeth Cady Stanton**

I realize most of us aren't fighting for a mighty cause. But what is your driving purpose? Have I covered it already in the previous examples? I do not want you to overthink this either.

You know you've found your purpose when you can feel it. It helps you most days to think less about what to do and more about getting the work done. The financial advisor schedules the meetings with prospects and clients so s/he can help people. The writer writes. The parent takes care of his/her child.

There's no 'right way' for how you express it.

Write out your Big 5:

Of all the ways to help identify/express your purpose I've seen over the past thirty years, my favorite is based on an idea I got from Robin Sharma's book, *The Everyday Hero Manifesto*. He calls it the Big 5. When he was on a safari once, he was told he'd get to see the 'Big 5' animals of the continent. It prompted him to wonder what the Big 5 things were for his life.

a) **List out the different *roles* in your life** (parent, partner, vocation etc.).

b) You might list out the different *areas* of your life (health, relationships, professional, financial, spiritual etc.).

c) You can also think about causes you are passionate about and how you would like to make a difference there.

d) Ask yourself: What type of parent/partner/leader to my clients do I want to be? How do I want to make a consistent difference with…?

e) Revisit your past life regrets, then reverse them, and inject them into your Big 5, e.g., as a teenager, I had so much anger towards my mother that I fell into the unconscious habit of blaming her for much of my unhappiness or things I didn't like about my life *instead of taking ownership for everything in my life.* Unfortunately, because I hadn't resolved all of this negative hard-wired reactivity even by the time I got married (ouch), I unwittingly did the same thing with my wife for the first few years. As a result, I still find it important to have on my Big 5: "Be a human being who fiercely works to TAKE FULL RESPONSIBILITY FOR EVERYTHING IN HIS LIFE (no blaming!)"

While it makes me a bit uncomfortable sharing mine with you and putting myself out there in public, if it helps you get started then it's worth it because the benefits to having such a clear sense of direction are so helpful – especially on the harder days.

Mission Statement – to Do My Best to…

1. Be a human being who fiercely works to TAKE FULL RESPONSIBILITY FOR EVERYTHING IN HIS LIFE (no blaming!) and evolve **4% DAILY** towards his potential (personal mastery - no more being timid and playing small!). **Feels calm, strong, and FULFILLED with a *journey* mindset** (who deals with anger and is <u>*non-reactive*</u> to the words of the unhappy)

2. Love on and **PUSH** as many people as possible so they **feel worthy, confident, and bold** to face their fears, experience breakthroughs, and fast track to fulfil their potential

3. Shower love on and raise confident, intrinsically motivated, and kind kids

4. Be a responsible, principle-centered provider and protector for my family who knows there is enough, and I am enough (my own resources are DEEP)

5. Be a **content creator** and role model who does *outstanding* work DAILY, charges what he's worth, and doesn't take life so seriously

   As with most exercises, just start. Even if it's five minutes in the car. Keep revisiting the idea of purpose: what drives you most? As Mary Shelley said: "Nothing contributes so much to tranquilize the mind as a steady purpose - a point on which the soul may fix its intellectual eye."

Then keep what you come up with highly visible – it will make your days richer, and you will feel more aligned about what matters most to you.

"He who has a why to live for can bear almost any how."
Nietzsche

Discover more purpose! Serve others!

Fuel up often!

CHAPTER 9

Unearth and Max Out Your Zone of Excellence

You've probably heard about the concept of your zone of excellence - **it's what you do best and love to do**. It goes by other names too – zone of genius and unique ability – but I prefer zone of excellence because this feels achievable, and I don't want you to think you've got to differentiate yourself completely from seven billion people. That isn't particularly helpful or necessary for 99.9% of you reading this unless you are determined to be the next Elon Musk. What matters is that feeling of flow you get where you don't notice the passage of time because you are so immersed in what you're doing.

Don't be lulled into thinking it's a nice-to-have that you might not be quite worthy to identify and pursue. It's where your vein of gold lies. The reasons to be clearer about yours can be the difference between having an *okay* life (really?) and loving it (much, much more of the time)!

Benefits:

*You will enjoy your days, weeks, and life much more. (Do you really need another reason?!)

*Because you enjoy spending time on it, it makes you feel good and that gives you even more positive momentum and feelings of flow state. There is a lot more love going on.

*Because it's something you're good at, it builds your confidence – not least because you're *not* spending your time on things you're not as good at and enjoy less.

*The odds are high you will enjoy breakthroughs in your life because of who you become along the way.

I would read those again and let them sit for a while – hopefully for obvious reasons.

How do you figure out your zone of excellence?

1. List out separately what you spend your time on now:

    a) The things you are really good at and love to do

    b) The things you are good at but don't *love* doing (this is often quite a long list)

    c) The things you are not good at and don't enjoy.

2. Ask ten people who know you well what they think you do best.

    These insights might help you attain more clarity. Don't be surprised if several don't reply (either because they are too 'busy' or because you've asked a question that can require a lot of thought), but those who do will provide some useful insights.

3. Zone of Excellence Questions:

    a) What do I most love to do?

    (I love it so much I can do it for long stretches of time without getting tired or bored)

    b) What work do I do that doesn't seem like work?

(I can do it all day long without ever feeling tired or bored.)

c) In my work, what produces the highest ratio of abun-
    dance and satisfaction to amount of time spent?

(Even if I do only ten seconds or a few minutes of it, an idea
or a deeper connection may spring forth that leads to huge
value)

d) What is my zone of excellence?

(There's a special skill I'm gifted with. This unique ability, fully
realized and put to work, can provide enormous benefits to
me and any organization I serve)

e) Articulate your zone of excellence further by answering
    these questions from Gay Hendricks' outstanding book
    The Big Leap:

    i) I'm at my best when I'm…

    ii) When I'm at my best, the exact thing I'm doing
       is…

    iii) When I'm doing that, the thing I love most about
        it is…

If at first you are not feeling as clear as you'd like, see this process
as one that may well take time. **You may need to revisit the topic a
few times**. It's not one we've often been encouraged to do.

Too often our areas for improvement get far more focus. One problem with that is it sets you up to waste your life working on weaknesses that will never be strengths or things you even enjoy. I can't
think of anything more tortuous than having to spend time trying to
improve my woodworking, car maintenance, coding, or bookkeep-
ing skills. And don't forget that there really are people who enjoy

these things, who love doing the things you don't, and they are good at them too.

Vern is a one of the most accomplished investment consultants I've ever met in my twenty years coaching people in that industry. His zone of excellence lies in his ability to synthesize a lot of complicated financial data and communicate in an extremely *personable* way that anyone can understand and feel smart about. He will go so far as to put himself in the shoes of the other person and give them examples from *their* world to make sure they fully understand. This is really rare.

Heather is a child psychologist who has been helping our son, Callum, adjust to and thrive since his diagnosis of ADHD and being on the autism spectrum. Her zone of excellence is her ability to communicate with him on a level that both teaches him and makes him feel *loved* and accepted. Callum would see her every day if he could because he feels understood and empowered – something he seldom feels elsewhere. And she can communicate with me and Erica equally effectively in ways that are practical, caring, and empathic. I would consider going to her for counseling if she offered such services!

My dentist Bill has run a flourishing practice in high-rent downtown Chicago for decades. I can't know that he's the *best* practitioner on the planet but where he is stunning is how he treats his patients (my wife and mother-in-law go too). It's far more than white glove bed-side manner. His zone of excellence is his insatiable curiosity and deep concern. He enquires about your family, your hobbies, and all your health habits from A-Z beyond dental: everything we put in our mouths and everything exercise-related. He fully lives the notion that much of our health starts with our mouth and our dental hygiene and, as importantly, you don't just feel his genuine interest and con-cern, it wraps you tight like a blanket! It's remarkable especially for an industry not noted for personal dynamos!

In the past I don't think I always took this topic seriously enough. As a result, I've done too much work I wasn't passionate about. I've taken on big projects I wasn't excited about – that were in my 'good' zone. Interestingly, I think this is where our level of worthiness kicks in: we don't bother digging into this topic because we wonder deep down if we even deserve to do all the things we love. (For more on this, see Habit 4, Key 1)

In the past, I didn't focus enough on the flow in my days and how to generate more of it which is where I get the best results and have the most fun. Funnily enough, the flow 'flows over' into other areas more when there is more of it and those areas go better too.

I urge you not to make the mistakes I did by figuring yours out now. Give it time and make your goal to incrementally increase how much time you spend on it. Then watch your life change!

Get in your zone of excellence!

Fuel up often!

CHAPTER 10

Follow the Ghost of Christmas Yet to Come

"Answer me one question. Are these the shadows of the things that Will be, or are they shadows of things that May be?

Men's shadows will foreshadow certain ends, to which, if persevered in, they must lead,' said Scrooge. 'But if the courses be departed from, the ends will change."

As Scrooge looks at his own grave in Charles Dickens' *A Christmas Carol*, he pleads with the Ghost of Christmas Yet to Come: *"Assure me that I yet may change these shadows you have shown me, by an altered life! I will honor Christmas in my heart and try to keep it all the year. I will live in the Past, the Present and the Future…I will not shut out the lessons that they teach."*

It's an excruciating final straw for Ebenezer Scrooge when the third ghost shows him his miserable future – a desperate and lonely death. The pain is too much to bear as he sees three scavengers trying to sell his few final possessions in the seediest part of London and gradually learns that not one person is mourning his death.

None of us wants to get towards our later years and admit we were fools. Fools because we didn't take care of our health, didn't save enough, didn't face our fears, and do what we really wanted to with our lives. Granted, as flawed human beings we all make plenty of mistakes, but what would you see if a ghost took you 20 years into the future and all your current habits and ways of being are still the same?

Think I'm exaggerating about the unlikelihood of change? In Joe Dispenza's most recent book, *Breaking the Habit of Being Yourself*, he writes: *"Psychologists tell us that by the time we're in our mid-30's, our identity or personality will be completely formed. This means that for those of us over 35, we have memorized a select set of behaviors, attitudes, beliefs, emotional reactions, habits, skills, associative memories, conditioned responses, and perceptions that are now subconsciously programmed within us. Those programs are running us…* **About 95% of who we are by midlife is a series of subconscious programs that have become automatic.***"*

That leaves a paltry 5% of new actions from your conscious mind. One thing to do with it once or twice a year is to **look at your FUTURE present situation. What are the consequences of not making any changes?** These are your regrets of the future.

First, write down the date TWENTY YEARS FROM TODAY: e.g., June 1, 2044.

<u>*YOUR AGE:*</u>
Ages of other key people in your life:
Partner:
Children:
Parents:
Siblings:

ASSUME YOU'VE NOT ADDRESSED ANY KEY AREAS IN YOUR LIFE DIFFERENTLY SO THEY HAVE STAYED ON A PREDICTABLE TRAJECTORY. YOUR HABITS HAVE STAYED THE SAME.

In other words, if an area is on a downward trajectory, it will continue downward if you let it. WHAT IS INEVITABLE OR HIGHLY LIKELY IF YOU TAKE NO ACTION? (And what's really painful is the *odds* are the vast majority of us won't take any lasting action).

Answer these four questions for each area:

1. What is STILL the **reality** in this area?
2. How do you *really* feel about it?
3. **What (if anything) needs to change so 20 years from now doesn't happen?**
4. **WHEN does this need to happen?**

   A) Your key relationships: 20 years from now

   B) Your business/vocation: 20 years from now

   C) Your finances: 20 years from now

   D) Your physical health: 20 years from now

   E) Your mental health: Comment on the following or score them on a scale of 1-10:

      i) Your self-belief:
      ii) How confident you feel:
      iii) How much you respect yourself:
      iv) Your sense of worthiness to achieve your long-term goals:
      v) How happy you feel:
      vi) Degree to which you feel positively challenged:
      vii) Degree to which you tune into your intuition and trust your gut instinct:
      viii) How constructively you deal with anger and negative emotions:

   F) Sense of spiritual connection:

   G) Adventures/fun/hobbies:

H) Giving back and contribution

I) Living your purpose

Based on your answers for today if little changes, 20 years from now:

How focused are you on what you do best and love to do (your zone of excellence)?

Where are you making an impact?

Which are your better habits that set you up for long-term success?

Most importantly, how much are you enjoying your journey?

I acknowledge that this can be a painful process and you may feel sadness and concern about what is likely ahead if you do not course correct. Scrooge "had been sobbing violently" during his night with the three spirits. It's okay to feel the feelings.

And I implore you to then take that worry, pain and frustration and wake up as Scrooge did on Christmas morning and realize your game is *far* from over. You can do many wondrous things in the future to mine your gold regardless of your age.

As he opens his eyes that morning in bed, Dickens writes: *"Best and happiest of all, the time before him was his own, to make amends in!"*

"'I don't know what to do!' cried Scrooge, laughing and crying in the same breath. 'I am light as a feather; I am as happy as an angel. I am as merry as schoolboy. I am as giddy as a drunken man. A merry Christmas to everybody! A happy New Year to all the world!'"

Scrooge starts donating his fortune to charity, he becomes a generous boss to Bob Cratchit and second father to Bob's son, Tiny Tim. *"He became as good a friend, as a good a master, and as good a man, as the good old city knew, or any other good old city, town or borough, in the good old world."* Why? Because he saw his terrible mistakes and excruciating regrets, he saw what he didn't like about his past and present and he saw what was in store for him if he did not change his ways of being, thinking and behaving.

Dicken's story resonates every year with so many people 200 years after it was written in 1823 because it reminds us not to value the chase for more over our loved ones and over people and relationships. It probably also hits a nerve with most of us because we are not always living aligned with our values or doing our best to fulfil our potential.

And, once you've been honest about where you are probably going, you have a lot more fuel to help you mine your own gold. What are you waiting for?!

Walk with the Ghost of Christmas Yet to Come!

Fuel up often!

HABIT 3:
PULL THE WEEDS FAST

CHAPTER 11

Understand Your (Brain as a) Garden

Now your fuel tank is full of love, drive, and desire, it's natural to want to start charging towards what you really want in life.

But first you need to understand your mind better so you can use it to serve you better. How do you do that? Understand why it may not appear to serve you as easily as you want it to and understand all the weeds still in place that need to be pulled – despite all the additional fuel and clarity you now have. These weeds will slow down your mission significantly unless you pull them.

Hurdle 1: Your brain is biologically hardwired in ways that make your gold mining tougher

Unfortunately, your brain is not all set up for helping you. It has some biologically hardwired qualities that explain why most people can set a goal easily enough but then fail to reach it. These exist through no fault of your own!

a) **Hardwired for survival:** Our brains have not evolved as fast as humankind and our society has and are still hardwired for survival mode. Not many generations ago (and for ALL the generations before them going back 10,000's of years), your ancestors were only worried about whether they had enough food, clothing, and shelter to survive. The vast majority of people on this planet today are still anxious about these things most days of the week and whether they have enough money.

Your brain has not had enough time to evolve, and it can resist your attempts to change and pursue new goals because this can feel too risky, i.e., a threat to your survival. Our brains are rather like an old house that we try to add a brand-new renovation to.

In addition, the brain tries to keep you in your comfort zone – even if that 'comfort' isn't where you really want to live your life. For your ancestors, it helped them survive. Plus, we fear losing what we have more than trying to gain something new.

Lastly what all this means is your brain does not do a good job of telling the difference between a rational and irrational fear. Most of the things we worry about and that cause us stress are nothing like as threatening as what stressed our predecessors such as large, hungry predators or severe weather, *but the brain still reacts as fearfully.*

This is a lot! Typically, we want to change when something is going badly in life – a job, relationship, a health or financial situation. Most of these can be really difficult changes to make: Your brain is somewhat irrationally hardwired to see change as potentially life-threatening sometimes.

These are weeds of fear that need pulling!

b) **Efficiency:** Years ago, I remember being taken aback when reading a book written by Harry Hoopis, a legend in the life insurance profession who ran a very successful agency. One of his early chapters was about how he thought most people are lazy and will often not do the hard work they need to do, be resourceful, or follow the proven process. I had expected him to be far more optimistic and positive about people given that his agency had achieved such impressive results.

However, what I didn't know at the time was this: our brains have many jobs to do to maintain a healthy body. We take them all for granted that our brain is helping our heartbeat, oxygen flow, and vital organs tick along nicely. The brain craves efficiency which means that if a task does not seem essential, it may often talk us out of bothering to do something new or different. **It feels like too much extra work** and **your brain's priority is energy conservation**, so new efforts to make change will often be resisted.

We are fighting against our own brain's natural default! That's what Hoopis was referencing.

These are weeds of doubt that need pulling!

c) **Hardwired for the negative:** Steven Kotler cites research in his book, *The Art of Impossible* that our brains think nine negative thoughts for every one positive. This immediately turns your desire to change into an uphill battle because most of your thoughts are fear-based, efficiency-based, and hell-bent on keeping you in your 'normal' operating zone.

In other words, your brain is not exactly installed with the latest operating software in how to be highly efficient and effective! All of us has our work cut out for us if we want to make lasting positive change.

These are weeds of negativity that need pulling!

Hurdle 2: Pull the weeds that are blocks to mining your gold

"Feelings left unfelt form a subconscious Field of Hurt that degrades your genius, cheats your promise and blocks your greatness." - Robin Sharma

Be more aware of your suppressed emotions (even if it is unpleasant) and work on letting them go because there is no other way to become enlightened – rather like doing the hard yards of exercise. You must pull these weeds. Psychologist Carl Jung wrote that this shadow side "forms an unconscious snag, thwarting our most well-meant intentions."

Sigmund Freud said the same thing: "Unexpressed emotions will never die. They are buried alive and will come forth later in uglier ways."

All too often you start chasing a goal or new year's resolution and end up talking yourself out of your big dreams.

Or you only crawl your way to a little bit more success because you're weighted down by past baggage.

Or you achieve some (even significant) professional success but mess up other areas of your life.

Or you achieve some (even significant) professional success but don't enjoy most of this journey and look back on those years feeling like a bit of a fool.

In his excellent book *The Everyday Hero Manifesto,* Robin Sharma levels with us all by stating that suppressed negative emotions and experiences get buried in our subconscious and are *"the main reason you are procrastinating on producing your magnum opus, resisting the installation of virtuoso-grade habits, sabotaging healthy relationships...or increasing addictions that range from too much time on social media to too much time shopping or drinking or complaining and basically missing out on the opportunities right in front of you to realize your giant promise, lead a phenomenal life and serve many people in the process."*

Michael Singer does a beautiful job of explaining the damage done by holding onto emotional baggage. He compares our thinking when we are born to a river where all the water flows freely. Then, as we start to accrue strong positive and negative experiences, they tend to stay in our 'river' of thoughts and act as rocks that mess up and influence the flow of our thinking and how we experience life. Revisit chapter 2 for ideas on how to release these blocks through meditation.

We become puppets to these past experiences and have immediate positive or negative associations to certain things. This skews our present and even what's 'real' because of our emotional, reactive bias. We simply see certain things from the same perspective and make it always mean the same thing.

Singer believes that in order to enjoy all that life – the present – has to offer, you want to let go of these past experiences, so they do not get in the way and hold power over your thoughts, feelings, and responses. Think about it, do you really want the dog to be taking you for a walk? Jerking towards one dog smell after another? Metaphorically that's how we behave with past jilted lovers, family members we've divided with, broken business relationships – even fears we are afraid to face.

If you don't address these blocks, you do what most people do unwittingly which is to self-medicate – you try to bury them away with external distractions such as alcohol and other drugs, shopping, work, pornography or extra-marital affairs, gambling, or computer games. But the anesthetic always wears off, your addiction grows, and you are never closer to feeling happiness or joy. On the contrary, you become numb to the pain in the world.

Happiness comes from within, from being true to the real you - not from who you project yourself to be to the outside world.

Addictive states such as anxiety, guilt, shame, self-importance, fear, depression, or hatred form our personality and cause us (unwittingly) to seek out experiences that reinforce them. This identity is attached to the environment. In his book, *Changing the Habit of Being Yourself*, Joe Dispenza found that: "The personality (ego) does everything it can to hide how it really feels or to make that emptiness go away" through acquiring material possessions, working too much, television, or by needing thrilling experiences.

Suppressed emotions and past traumas are (big) weeds to pull!

Hurdle 3: Understand that your subconscious mind is the *gardener* and how to rewire it so you can mine your gold more easily

In his 1937 classic *Think and Grow Rich*, Napoleon Hill revealed his TWENTY-year research project of over 500 self-made millionaires. Hill had been sponsored by Andrew Carnegie to work on the book, who at the time was the richest man in the world. In it, Hill explained that if you wanted to grow rich – indeed, if you wanted to achieve 'riches' in any area of life - you had to work on influencing your subconscious mind.

A) Understand Your (Brain as a) Garden

Hill described the subconscious mind as a 'fertile garden' where you could plant and grow 'desirable crops' or have 'weeds in abundance' – and that you might need 'everlasting persistence' to get the results you wanted. 85 years ago, this was very abstract thinking because Hill had little science to lean on, 'only' an extremely impressive array of case studies.

The science arrived in this century with the advent of neuroscientific technology that can read neural pathways and scan brains. The book that best explained the connection to me between the physical world and the world of our thoughts - and what to do about it - was John Assaraf and Murray Smith's *The Answer* in 2009: *"Everything is energy – it's all made of molecules, which are made of atoms…which are made of nothing but vibrating packets of energy."*

They outlined that before matter becomes something physical, it comes from the quantum field. That's also where ideas start. And that the simple act of observation could influence the behavior of particles (focus!). Beneath this level of energy is a **"sea of pure consciousness, from which matter emerges in clustered localities."** The universe is *made* of consciousness – matter and energy are simply two of the forms it takes.

Their conclusion 72 years after Hill: *"THOUGHT creates the physical world."*

"Thought is the most powerful force in the universe…***The truth is more like this: You'll see it when you believe it…***your beliefs don't simply *reflect* your reality, they *create* your reality – and that applies to the reality of massive success in business." Interesting how consistent this is with Michael Guillen's lifetime research in science and religion.

It's why you live in a land of what author Robert Holden calls *"make-believe. Your beliefs literally move the world around you"* - you believe it; you see it. You *believe* it, you *make* your gold mining happen. For more on this, see Habit 4, Key 2: Elevate Your Beliefs.

Most people still struggle to buy into this line of thinking. Yet this was exactly what Napoleon Hill popularized in *Think and Grow Rich*.

Assaraf and Murray went on to explain that the events and circumstances of your life or your business do not ORIGINATE in the seen world. The unseen world is vastly more powerful; it is the world of *cause*. Matter, energy, and consciousness are not separate but are merely different frequencies along the same continuum. Cause and effect apply to your thoughts too. "Events in your business are a reflection of your thoughts."

They then share about **three related laws:**

i) **The Law of Attraction** is about FOCUSING energy on a specific frequency to resonate with every other form of energy in a similar pattern – together with cause and effect. In the same way an acorn becomes an oak tree if planted in fertile soil, you attract the nutrients, water, and sunlight you need for your business and life by reconditioning your subconscious mind.

For your business and personal life, you start with the part nobody else sees: the vision. Make this strong and **crystal clear**.

ii) **The Law of Gestation** means you need to allow time to let your seeds be watered and grow. Don't keep digging them up. Don't force it with your impatience. If you consider the reality that it took your current thinking, feelings, and actions years to get you what's hardwired now, you've got to accept that your brain needs time and patience before you reap the rewards of your new thoughts, feelings, and actions.

iii) **The Law of Action** – you can't just sit around and visualize all day. The power of the focus is to create cognitive dissonance in your brain. This means that as it starts to believe in your new beliefs, it's saying: "What are you DOING about this to make it happen?" In other words, an 'error' message will come up if there is not a match – if there is not congruence – between what you're thinking and what you're doing.

Your conscious brain has to come up with the goals and create the vision, but astonishingly it only does about 3-5% of the actual work to get you there.

What you MUST understand is that if you want to mine your vein of gold, your subconscious brain is the gardener that you need to influence and help you do the work.

THAT is why you want to use the strategies that influence it so that what you want gets hardwired in your subconscious and converted into action by the gardener. Your physical and mental habits all lie in the subconscious.

In terms of changing beliefs, your beliefs are not all true. They are simply neural patterns in your brain that are so ingrained they've become automatic.

Your beliefs are self-fulfilling prophecies.

You want to change your *limiting* beliefs because that leads to limiting emotions and actions. However, wanting to do this is not going to help much unless you work on influencing your subconscious mind because "**beliefs and habits are thousands of times stronger than desires**". You might want new, exciting outcome A, but if deep down you still believe B (something to the contrary) it won't happen.

Most neuroscientists agree that only about three to five percent of what's happening in your brain occurs at the conscious level of awareness. The other 95% of your behaviors are buried in your subconscious and are automatic. This means that we are unconscious 95% of the day to what we do and operating on autopilot – that's why setting a goal in the conscious mind is not enough.

b) Two positive brain qualities to leverage

There are two encouraging things to know about your brain so you can change your beliefs:

    i)   **Leverage neuroplasticity:** you make new neural connections and new brain cells all the time. "The number of potential connections your brain can make over your lifetime is about one followed by six MILLION zeroes," Assaraf and Smith share: "**Not only *can* your brain change dramatically, but it *is designed specifically* for you to be able to do exactly that.**"

ii) **Leverage your reticular activating system (RAS)** so it focuses on what you want. Your brain processes 400 billion bits of information every second so you need the clarity of focus. How do you make this happen? Imprint on your subconscious what you really want.

A simple example of how your RAS operates is when you buy a new car. Before you owned it, you probably hadn't really noticed this particular car and its color, but once you own one, you notice them seemingly everywhere! Or when you or your partner becomes pregnant, you start seeing pregnant women wherever you go.

Hurdle 4: Really tune into your brain's autopilot!

As I mentioned in the previous chapter, by our mid-30's most of our thoughts, feelings and actions are on automatic pilot and will get us the same outcomes we're used to getting. 95% of what we do is dictated by our subconscious mind. Much more alarming: our bodies have become *addicted* to the emotions it's used to having. **Unconsciously we become addicted to our problems that feed our deeply engrained survival-oriented emotions.** This explains a lot about why we don't change. We become bottom-feeders to our pain.

Sooner or later, there are emotions that are going to get in the way that can include:

Guilt, self-doubt, shame, fear, anger, and unworthiness.

Each of us has a norm for how we are used to feeling. This feeling varies from person to person. One person might be used to generally feeling quite good most days; another person might be used to feeling quite miserable or anxious – that is their norm. It's as if we have an unwitting thermostat set for how we expect to feel in the same way we set a thermostat to maintain a certain temperature in our house.

It's crucial to understand that this has nothing to do with happiness. Your normal thermostat could be set to 'mildly unhappy' – you could be used to feeling subpar most of the time. Only by working on your subconscious can you change that wiring, that way of being and feeling. Otherwise, your thermostat will keep trying to reset you back to fairly miserable all the time!

This thermostat for our feelings is trying to keep us 'safe' in our comfort zone. When we deviate too far off course from this – either too low or too high, this autopilot kicks in. Maxwell Maltz wrote about this in the 1950's and called it our psycho-cybernetic mechanism.

Maltz was a plastic surgeon who couldn't understand why his patients would often feel no better about themselves after their corrective surgeries, so he decided to explore the subject.

Each of us also has this 'thermostat' with money. If you are in sales and used to earning $120,000/year (to keep the numbers simple) and find yourself way below your $10,000/month average, you will pull out all the stops to get back on course to what you're used to. Unfortunately, it works the other way around too. If you're having a great year and are way ahead of your usual earnings, *unwittingly* you'll find yourself uncomfortable with this new high and often find ways to drop balls and not pursue opportunities and slip back to your typical norm.

The problem is that you interpret your brain's alerts as a danger signal because you are not familiar with your psycho-cybernetic mechanism. Being outside your familiar territory and when you make a change in your life does not mean you are in danger (usually!), it simply means you are changing direction.

What if you want to make a change to the path you're on (as I'm sure you do otherwise you wouldn't be reading this)? The harder part is that just cognitively *understanding* this in your conscious brain is not enough. What you need on your side is the immense power of your subconscious because it is the tail that wags the dog. It is the gardener most of the time! The only way to make lasting change is to address this is in the subconscious brain.

Assaraf and Smith implore us to notice that **the most important thing to do is to interpret your change "as a sign that a breakthrough is in the offing rather than seeing it as a threat."** This can be challenging as **the discomfort can last a while** and you may not feel 'right'. I've fallen into this trap where the discomfort is so new and the change or result you want isn't happening yet that it's hard to adjust. It's tempting to revert to all your old ways of thinking and habits.

"Anytime you learn something new, whether it's riding a bicycle, making more money than you have ever made before, entering a brand-new relationship...there's going to be a point of resistance, a point of fear where you will feel discomfort. <u>Here's what that means: You're growing</u>."

One powerful solution to this challenge is to remember Habit 1: Let love drive. Lean on the universal intelligence of the quantum field and believe that God/your universal spirit has got your back. Believe that there are guardian angels who are looking out for you. They have got you through challenges in the past just fine (remember?) and now it's time to understand that they are doing their work now. Their solutions might not come in the next ten minutes, and they might come from an unexpected source, but this has happened before.

Robin Sharma argues that "dark nights of the soul are - in truth - faithwalk experiences. In other words, they show up at the perfect time to help you trust in a force larger than yourself." We return to letting God drive. Life is being put together in a better way and taking you to a better place.

Now you understand more about your subconscious brain as the gardener, how do you influence it so your actions change too?

Pull the Weeds Fast!

CHAPTER 12

Weed Your Garden

1. Don't run away from the truth that you are capable of mining your gold

As I walked up to the microphone in the aisle of the large auditorium in Seattle, I waited for my turn to ask the venerable speaker a question. I was feeling very self-conscious because, even though I'd spoken to audiences of a similar size, this 77-year-old man was one of my heroes and he was the expert while I was just another attendee sitting at one end of row 12. His books had been a revelation to me, and he was one of my top role models.

I was particularly nervous because I couldn't quite think through exactly how I wanted to phrase my question to Stephen Covey. For fifteen years - ever since I'd first read his book *The Seven Habits of Highly Effective People* - I could not for the life of me understand a key point in his book. In it he stated that we all had the ability to choose our attitudes and choose our own way even when all our freedoms had been taken away from us.

Covey cited this fundamental truth that Austrian psychologist Victor Frankl had learned surviving the concentration camps of Nazi Germany and described in his own book *Man's Search for Meaning*. That afternoon I again heard Covey reference Victor Frankl's epiphany. I just couldn't take it anymore that I didn't understand this key point he was making yet again when it mattered so much. Even though I feared I might be the only person in the huge audience not to understand what he was talking about and that I was about to make a fool of myself for being so dense, I had to try and get some clarity.

When it was my turn at the microphone, I just started talking: "Can you help me understand what I'm missing about Victor Frankl's comment? I can't relate to his point. I've never experienced anything like a concentration camp or even fighting in a war. It feels too far removed from anything in my own world. How am I supposed to understand what he was trying to say?" I highly doubt I was that eloquent or succinct, but I will never forget how Covey responded:

He bored his eyes into me from quite a distance on the stage to where I was standing halfway up the auditorium and I felt completely rooted to the spot. With a moving intensity as if I were the only person in the room, he said: "My friend, what Frankl was trying to say was this: **You can choose your beliefs. You can do anything you set your mind to**." He paused to let me digest this a little.

"That was what Frankl learned. He discovered that your brain has the freedom – has the capacity - to make that choice and no one can take it away from you. It was an epiphany for him that he learned from being in the worst possible human circumstances. But you don't need to go through what he experienced to learn what he had to learn. *Your job is to apply his hard-earned lesson:* And first, you just need to believe it."

Then he refreshed his intense stare and repeated to me: "YOU can do anything you set your mind to," and continued his stare *as if to say*, "and don't you dare doubt it."

That was the closest thing I've ever had to a religious experience and, while I felt like I'd just been handed the Holy Grail, I didn't think I was quite worthy to do anything with it. Yet. But I still remember lying in bed that night knowing he had shared something monumentally powerful. **I think I was too scared to carry the torch.**

Have you ever had this happen? Someone tells you: "You 'just' need to believe in yourself to succeed!" Or you hear a motivational speaker say it on a video or at a conference. It was really moving to hear Covey tell me I could do anything I set my mind to, but the sad truth is that inspiration – even knowledge - like this doesn't last. It became a fond distant memory.

I wanted to believe him. For a few fleeting moments my instinct told me he was right – **I think we all have moments when we sense that we DO have a vein of gold inside us that we could achieve the remarkable** - but to believe it was really true for *me* felt like too much of a stretch at the time. Easy for the bestselling author of an iconic book on stage getting paid $50,000 to believe it. But *me* do *anything* I set my mind to? Exhale. Really? So, I did what Churchill once observed: *"Men occasionally stumble over the truth, but most of them pick themselves up and hurry off as if nothing had happened."*

I couldn't get myself to believe it, so the next day I got on a plane to England for a speaking engagement, got busy with my life, and forgot about all it.

Looking back, on the rare occasions I thought about it, I told myself it was too far-fetched, and I didn't know how to build my self-belief. The weird part about this is I *had* worked diligently on influencing my subconscious mind for months prior to this; I can't understand why I 'forgot' this when it had led to so many remarkable outcomes *that year*.

Covey probably believed that if you followed his seven habits and were so clear about your life purpose and had your clear end point in mind, you could do anything you set your mind to. I agree - if you are clear about your powerful purpose, but if you feel rather foggy about this as I did for much of my life, then the 'set goal – follow the plan

- achieve success' concept is not simple at all. We are inconsistent, fearful, and have brains hardwired to talk ourselves out of anything that looks like change, risk or playing bigger than our fragile ego will allow.

2. Accept that knowing isn't doing.

It doesn't work to just tell someone: "You have to believe it" or even "you just have to believe in yourself." Beliefs are developed through repetition generally from personal experiences. Often, we think that when it comes to changing, all we need to do is learn something new that shows us how to get there. But more often the sticking point is not knowledge, skill, or motivation, what needs to be addressed is inside us.

If it were simply about knowledge and even sometimes, achieving, John Assaraf asks in his follow-up book to *The Answer* called *Innercise*, then how come:

95 percent or more of dieters regain all the weight they lost?

80 percent of new businesses fail within five years?

40 percent of the marriages of young couples end within five years?

Over 70 percent of lottery winners lose their money within three years?

A 2009 *Sports Illustrated* report estimated that 78% of National Football League (NFL) players file for bankruptcy or are experiencing financial stress only two years after retiring and 60% of National Basketball Association (NBA) players suffer the same fate after five years of retirement.

Before you can plant new flowers - new beliefs, new goals, and new dreams - into your garden of a brain *so that you can most effectively mine your gold*, you probably need to pull more weeds. Where do you start?

3. Become aware of your weeds

Joe Dispenza recommends answering this question: **What negative energy am I holding onto from past experiences that reinforces my past identity and emotionally attaches me to current experiences?**

In theory, if you apply the principles of living in the present discussed in Chapter 2, you're not thinking about the past and are beyond old negative energy. But I don't know anyone who is always fully present and who hasn't unwittingly hung onto some past negative emotions. Being present to me is like holding a compass. It points you to a true north.

What you want to do is focus on being present for one strategy AND for another strategy have a GPS too to redirect you. You do this by confronting your negative emotions, the negative ways you see yourself, and then reduce their influence and replace them with positive, present, and productive ones. Your feelings can be powerful and, because most of them have been stored in your subconscious, you need to diminish their impact so you can move them out of your own way.

What negative memories and feelings come to mind? I found my answers to this kicked in after I had started dreaming big and thinking about some new, exciting things I wanted to do. It took a little while, but then the fears started to creep in.

You may need to start out by thinking about a big goal you have too before you experience something similar. When the doubt starts to show up questioning whether you really can achieve this goal, pay close attention to your self-talk and what negative thoughts and emotions your ego communicates to you.

Shine a spotlight on your weeds and how you currently handle them

When I did this with my new and exciting goals and vision, I was surprised at how unaware I seemed to be of these weeds. And I was surprised and dismayed by how old these thoughts were – they dated back to disappointing outcomes I'd had many years ago. It was as if my brain had already come up with a case prepared to explain to me why my latest goal would end in disappointment. Can you relate? My mind had already piled up the evidence to talk me out of it.

I had some initial excitement for my new goals and visions. I cut out pictures and put them on my vision board. I started to visualize them twice/day. But my mind would wander and throw a wrench in the works, and I'd have to course correct to keep up the excited emotions.

Then I started thinking about putting my dreams into action. That was when the fear really arrived. And painfully quickly, old memories came up of previous ventures I had thought were great ideas. The emotions that came up were disappointment and low self-worth, of not feeling as good as others, of not seeing huge wins but very small ones that weren't worth the effort. And I remembered trying too hard to make them work while not really expecting them to work. I wasn't one of those types of people who had the big successes. They happened to a more confident species, to people who had had more 'success' than me – who seemed to have better ideas and more resources. Urgh. The old unhelpful mental loop of thoughts. Ever been there?

Yet again it's a rather distressing experience to start noticing the low-level thoughts and emotions you have - especially when you start to get up to something bigger. It's very possible that you have unwittingly hardwired your subconscious to bring up negative emotions related to a long-past experience that starts to demoralize you and talk you out of making these positive changes.

Remember from Habit 1: Your ego is the one with all the self-doubt and anxiety, not your true self. It is your learned self that needs to be faced and rejected. It tries to hide behind the image you project in public. Most people try to ignore these negative feelings of guilt or insecurity throughout their lives. Worse, you start to say to yourself: 'this is who I am.'

4. Own it! Only you can pull your weeds

If you want to breakthrough and mine your gold, you want to address these vulnerabilities and weed them out of your garden. Own it! It's *your* garden, not someone else's. And let love drive. That's who you really are.

Yes, we have all been emotionally scarred by past events. You are not alone! One problem is that you relive them over and over and they engrain themselves in you and how you then respond in the future to similar circumstances or people. They end up becoming personality traits. You may not notice them for a long time because you are out there busy living life. But eventually, these limitations catch up to you as you are unable to stave off these painful emotions.

You self-medicate with your favorite distraction which changes your emotions without addressing the problem. Depending on some-thing external that makes you feel good only works for a brief time. And doing more of the addiction doesn't work because an addiction is never a solution.

"Behind every addiction, there is some memorized emotion that is driving behavior," explains Joe Dispenza: ***"We've got it backward. We have to become happy BEFORE our abundance shows up… true happiness has nothing to do with pleasure, because the reli-ance on feeling good from such intensely stimulating things only moves us further from real joy."***

Nothing in your external environment is going to 'fix' the way you feel and help you mine your gold. This is an inside job for you and you alone. Take charge. How?

5. Confront your weeds because they are choking your progress

Face the negative ways you see yourself, then cut back their influence. Release them. PULL THE WEEDS FAST and replace them with positive and productive elements to help you access your vein of gold such as inspiring beliefs, gratitude, positive acknowledgments, supportive people, and activities that raise your confidence (see Habit 4 for all of these).

As I shared earlier, Napoleon Hill described the subconscious mind in his book *Think and Grow Rich* as like a 'fertile garden' where you could plant and grow 'desirable crops' or have 'weeds in abundance' – and that you might need 'everlasting persistence' to make this happen (weeds grow back which means 'make it a habit' and 'you have to go to the gym forever' - not that it necessarily takes a lifetime to achieve).

You can't just start planting new flowers (mining your gold) in a garden with no room for anything, where new growth will be crowded out. First, you have to pull the weeds. It's rather like trying to add something new to your already full schedule, something has to give. You can't simply keep piling on more meetings and events without removing other activities.

HOW TO WEED YOUR GARDEN:

   a) **OBSERVE: The first stage of weeding is to observe (meditate and journal on) the thoughts, and feelings that do not make you feel good (the weeds!)**

Name them. Pay really close attention to this otherwise you will stay at the same emotional level as before and not understand what's happening inside. The negative emotions stuck in your body need to be liberated too. This cultivation is a regular process – just as you would frequently tend a garden. This is done purposefully. The goal is to create a new reality.

Dispenza explains that: *"Meditation opens the door between the conscious and subconscious minds. We meditate to enter the operating system of the subconscious, where all those unwanted habits and behaviors reside, and change them to more productive modes to support us in our lives."*

This can start to release positive energy as you reduce emotional dependency on feeling a certain old, negative way. You have to look at your 'mess' of weeds and acknowledge that *it's not serving you anymore and has never helped you mine your gold.*

As you weed your garden, you make room to elevate positive emotions. You no longer live in a state of lack and can more easily take constructive actions to help you be, do and have more of what you really want in your life.

The most effective way to observe a negative emotion is to choose ONE of the following survival emotions to neutralize.

It is a familiar feeling for you and something you would like to change. Here are some examples from Dispenza's book:

Insecurity, hatred, judgement, victimization, worry, guilt, depression, shame, anxiety, regret, suffering, frustration, fear, greed, sadness, disgust, envy, anger, resentment, unworthiness and lack.

Hardwired feelings condition us to think, feel, and act in certain ways every day so it's crucial to get clarity here.

Next, OBSERVE THESE THOUGHTS, FEELINGS, and BELIEFS centered around the ONE negative emotion – it's okay and, indeed, wise to spend time on this. I'd recommend writing down examples of these thoughts as they come up. This is the 'part' your brain plays when you feel angry/anxious etc. These are the lines it has been hardwired to say to you! Clearly these lines have not served you and they have led to correspondingly negative feelings. They are not the 'truth'. You will be alarmed at how often you've had that thought in the past. Don't just 'glance' at the ugliness and pain and run away.

"ALMOST EVERYTHING YOU HAVE DONE IN YOUR LIFE HAS BEEN TO RUN FROM THIS FEELING. YOU USED EVERYTHING OUTSIDE OF YOU TO TRY TO MAKE IT GO AWAY...this feeling influences everything you do." – Joe Dispenza

    i)   **Write out your limiting thoughts** – your mental weeds.

What are some common thoughts you have repeatedly that express your primary survival emotion?

e.g. I'll never…
I can't..
I must…
There's not enough…
I hate…

    ii)   **Write out your limiting actions** – Actions (weeds) that you often do after you have your limiting thoughts. These self-perpetuate your negative emotion.

When I feel frustrated, I...

Get easily irritated with my children
Worry about my finances even more
Get sucked into social media
Watch TV or porn
Have a drink
Crave ice cream
Work even harder

List out how you distract yourself and self-medicate to avoid or dull your painful emotion.

b) Start to unlearn these mental weeds – thoughts, feelings, and beliefs – and admit your faults and failures to a higher power.

Identify what you don't like and what doesn't feel good and speak it aloud to God. I realize this is quite a leap of faith, but it is easier than sharing it with a loved one as there's no fear of being judged or rejected. Put the past to rest. This is the hardest part.

Remember, it takes a huge amount of energy to pretend to be someone else and bottle up the survival emotion. Release that negative energy so you don't keep attracting in what you've always gotten. Don't forget that your negative emotions primarily hurt you and make you feel badly.

As Robin Sharma says in *The Everyday Hero Manifesto*: "Dislodge the frozen pain…Trust this process…this exercise will leave you more intimate with your gifts, more friendly with your strengths, more connected with your courage, more awake to your aliveness, more trusting of your instincts and much closer to your loving nature."

State aloud your primary survival emotion, e.g.: "I have been an angry person for as long as I can remember."

c) Surrender your weeds to a greater power and let it resolve your limitations.

To paraphrase the well-known observation from Einstein, your same level of consciousness cannot solve a problem it created, so you need to let it go to something greater than you. All potentials exist in the quantum field; why not let God resolve it? Trust in an outcome you haven't thought of yet. Even this concept can help you be less tense about forcing an issue and stop trying too hard.

The best thing you can do is to say a prayer of surrender to your higher power. Give yourself up to the loving presence that created you – at least to a loving universal spirit. Then GIVE THANKS.

It's going to be a process of observing the negative, releasing it, and redirecting your thoughts. And it will probably take time.

6. **Replace your weeds with flowers: See Habits 4 and 5 on how to plant your garden.**

   Habit 3 focuses on removing the weeds fast.

PULL THE WEEDS FAST!

Pull the Weeds Fast!

Weed 1: Fear of Success

"The mother of all fears that's so close to us that, even when we verbalize it, we don't believe it: fear that we will succeed. That we can access the powers we secretly know we possess…This is the most terrifying prospect a human being can face because it ejects him at one go, he imagines, from all the tribal inclusions his psyche is wired for and has been for 50 million years. We fear discovering that we are more than we think we are, more than our parents, teachers and children think we are…That we actually have the guts, the perseverance, the capacity. We fear we truly can steer our ship, plant our flag, reach our promised land."

Steven Pressfield, *The War of Art*

Compared to the fear of failure, fear of success does not get much airtime and is less understood – and it could well be the most obstinate weed stopping you from mining your gold.

The 4 Fear of Success Dragons

Dragon 1: You fear ostracizing yourself from your 'tribe'

I met Nadia networking at a high-end jewelry event in London. I was helping out a client's wife by making introductions to people in my UK network so she could expand her brand in Europe. When I struck up a conversation with Nadia, I was struck by how much fun she was having. When I later interviewed her for my podcast to learn her story, she told me that she had started out in the working world as an air hostess. Her family, devout Muslims, had no issue with this, but when she started building her own business as a celebrity make-up artist, there was instant tension.

"I always had a passion for art…what excited me about make-up was the transformation – that it could help women look amazing. They could be the best version of themselves." Her parents discouraged her, so at first after leaving school, she acquiesced and went to college to train as an accountant. "They didn't see being an artist as a talent. It was not very respectable, not a high-profession job – they were influenced by the community… Sitting behind a computer, IT WAS NOT ME!"

In the end, Nadia dropped out of college and got a job for British Airways figuring that at least she could work with people more and travel. Then one day when working in business class, one of her passengers was Charlotte Tilbury, the world-famous make-up artist who has her own skincare brand, was honored by the Queen with an MBE, and has worked with many of the world's top models inc. Kate Moss and Kim Kardashian. Tilbury was impressed with Nadia's knowledge of make-up and offered her a chance to train with her.

Nadia's family did not want her to do it, but she really felt she was making a difference for the first time in her life. "I have come across a lot of obstacles from family. (They'd say:) "People will talk about you. You are not part of this family. Don't put your name out there." I had to stand up for myself and say: 'This is what I love.' I'm not doing anything wrong. If you support me, fine and if not, fine, but I'm going to go ahead and do what I love and what I have a vision for." Fortunately, her parents came around over time and are now happy for what she's achieved.

You too may feel a pull from your family or your community that playing full-out to mine your gold may alienate you from what's socially or culturally acceptable in your family or social circle. It may threaten other people's status quo too much. Steven Pressfield describes this fear as "terrifying." It's also possible that you hadn't been able to name the fear or its source before.

Do you feel safe emotionally (and supported) to shine – at home, at work and in your community? Surely in your one life you want the real you to live out loud.

As a parent, I know it's not easy to keep your own opinions and biases to yourself and let your children march entirely to the beat of their different drums. Nadia adds: "That's the hardest part. You have to be strong when you feel down and don't have family support. You have to ignore what people think. **Luckily, there are other great people who will support you such as clients and colleagues."**

Make a point to really seek these supportive people out (see Habit 4, Key 10: Elevate Your Support Team) **and spend much more time with them and ever less time with those who give you mixed messages and undermine your morale.**

She got to work with Middle Eastern VIP clients during the launch of a Charlotte Tilbury event in Kuwait and oversee the Arabic Fashion Show in Dorchester, England in 2016. Nadia went on to coordinate events with 20 of the top Middle Eastern fashion designers and be responsible for numerous press events and shop launches in the UK and internationally and take care of high-profile clients from the Saudi Royal Family and do work done at the personal request of a family member of the Bangladeshi elite.

How has she handled going from being a trainee accountant to having 90K+ Instagram followers? "I'm very genuine, honest, and simple. I love what I do. I care about and love people. If I interact with somebody, I always give my best advice. I see their beauty."

The key to her finding peace with the conflict between doing what you most want in life and fear of becoming estranged from your family or community is this: **"I LOVE this. I enjoy it and I see myself at other levels. I see no limits. I've become someone who took risks, is a hard worker, is strong, determined, and clear about what I want."**

Nadia deserves huge accolades for her courage and overcoming the fear that holds so many people back. In his inspiring book *The War of Art*, Steven Pressfield writes about how hard it is to overcome the fear that we will succeed and risk being alienated from our tribe: *"We fear that we actually possess the talent that our still, small voice tells us…What will become of us? We will lose our friends and family who will no longer recognize us…But here's the trick: we wind up in space but not alone. Instead, we are tapped into an unquenchable, undepletable, inexhaustible source of wisdom, consciousness, and companionship. Yes, we lose friends, but we find friends too in places we never thought to look and they're better friends, truer friends, and we're better and truer to them."*

Pause for a moment to do a gut check about your willingness to shine in your community. Don't subconsciously or consciously hold back because you're afraid your greater success will make someone you care about feel badly or that they won't talk to you anymore. Avoid being around anyone where you find yourself playing smaller. As you increasingly mine your gold, what you discover on the other side of your fear is exhilarating. You may well feel separate from your old world until you pay attention to all the new connectedness that exists. Remember Marianne Williamson's words too: you will inspire other people to shine too.

Let your love drive and listen to your heart and soul.

Do you fear outshining loved ones (and thereby ostracizing yourself from your tribe)?

You don't want to make your father, mother, or partner (or some other prominent person in your family or life) **feel badly by outshining your accomplishments**. This is not something you usually do consciously. You might have grown up it - in the culture of your family because perhaps one of your parents was quite the 'superstar' in the bubble of a world you grew up in.

You might chance into a different culture and gradually play smaller. When I first met my wife, I became aware that she was the hero of her family. Not only was she the first to get a college degree but she had also become a doctor. She had done better than me financially from her many years as a physician. Her schedule took precedence at times because babies and surgeries generally can't wait but some of my work could! Cumulatively this new 'culture' that I lived in started to affect me and I started talking less about my own accolades and playing them down. I didn't want her to feel that I was stealing her hard-earned spotlight.

Is there room in your life for the real you to fully express yourself? *How can you lean into that – even with small steps?* This is how to pull the weed even if you're not feeling any support – and to know your world is not going to end.

Dragon 2: Your ego tells you that you are not worthy of big successes, so you think and play small

To address not feeling like you deserve it or not, see Habit 4, Key 1: Elevate Your Worthiness and apply the 5 Mindsets of Worthiness. You tend to think and play small because you don't feel you 'belong' on the 'main stage' the big players. I can fully empathize with this fear.

Sometimes we mistakenly tell ourselves it's Imposter Syndrome - this is where you feel somewhat fraudulent about the work you're doing or that you're not 'there' yet. This is very common when are new to a career and realize in your new vocation that you don't know that much yet...but it can stick especially in sales roles where every January you start at zero production again. If you are new, tell yourself that you're building a custom private jet and that this high-end vehicle is your developing future business (or vocation) with limited seats only for the best people and opportunities.

Granted, some people can feel like imposters because they do receive acclaim early in their careers when perhaps they got a bit lucky by being in the right place at the right time and had not developed their skills well. A few people can make their peace with that and keep growing, while many others unwittingly self-sabotage. Think of how many one-hit wonders there are in the world of music.

There is always a way to look at something in a new light and see the reasons to step up. Perhaps it is time for a breath of fresh air in your profession.

You achieve your success to the extent that you think you deserve it: What do you tell yourself you must do in order to deserve success (and is that mindset limiting you)?

See Habit 4, Key 1: Elevate Your Worthiness.

In my life experience, when you can focus on the worthiness mindsets, understanding that people believe whatever they want, then you can focus on feeling worthy, pushing through past obstacles, and getting to work on what will help you go where you want to in life. It will also help you to set some bigger goals and ask: Are my goals worthy of me?

As Marianne Williamson wrote: "Your playing small does not serve the world. There is nothing enlightened about shrinking so that other people won't feel insecure around you. We are all meant to shine, as children do."

Pull your fear of success weed!

Dragon 3: You fear shining in the spotlight

By the time Payal Kadakia was nine, she'd become quite good at Indian folk dance and couldn't wait to perform in front of her elementary school in Randolph, New Jersey. As she prepared for the talent show, she put on her sari and combed out her long dark hair. But once she began to dance, a few children started laughing. Then more laughed. That was when the booing started. "It was at that moment that Payal decided she would never again blend her two lives – her Indian life and American life – together. Or so she thought," writes Lowey Bundy Sichol in *Idea Makers: 15 Fearless Female Entrepreneurs*.

Another way fear of success shows itself stems from an emotionally negative experience in your past when you put yourself in the spotlight and felt either humiliated or taken advantage of. Then you *unwittingly* vowed never to do that again. Could that be what's held you back from pursuing your passion?

While Kadakia did continue to take private dance classes on weekends with other girls from Indian families, it was *ten years* before she plucked up the courage to organize a traditional Indian dance group in college (because she couldn't find one anywhere in Boston) and perform in front of a general audience at an MIT cultural show.

Facing her fear of shining proved life changing and led to a fascinating journey. After graduating college, she moved to New York and started an Indian dance troupe there. It fueled her love of dance in general. The turning point came at a friend's birthday party in San Francisco, when she met dozens of entrepreneurs who were either starting a company, launching a new app, or had created a platform around their passion.

THE 5 HABITS TO MINE YOUR GOLD

In 2011 it led to her realizing that she had her own need to fill which was to create an app that helped people find and book health-related classes. Through various iterations, it became ClassPass which just nine years later was valued at $1 billion.

If you've been burned trying to do something you loved or fulfill a dream, breathe in Payal's words and reframe your own past to get back up and go bigger again: "I felt like I was put on this earth to do this...I'm a dancer and a businesswoman. I am short but I am powerful...I kept dancing because it gave me clarity, helped me guide my decisions, helped me connect to the product."

Marianne Williamson notes the ripple effect of you shining: "And as we let our own light shine, we unconsciously give other people permission to do the same. As we are liberated from our own fear, our presence automatically liberates others."

Who are you not to play big? **How does hiding yourself serve the world?** If you've felt punished for trying to shine in the past, that was the past. Live in the present (return to Chapter 2!)

Dragon 4: You fear that mining your gold requires too much hard work or sacrifice

"(True) success requires you to sacrifice what is not important for what is." – Robert Holden

The idea of mining your gold can feel too daunting for many people, that it requires too much sacrifice and hard work. When you read about high achievers, it is easy to notice how hard they almost always work. I think of people like author John Grisham, who wrote his first novel by getting up at 4am every morning and working from his laundry room while keeping his 'day' job as a lawyer. That takes enormous self-discipline and purpose.

I remember a telling story of a rising star in the Irish golf world. He had done well in one particular tournament, had enjoyed celebrating with dinner and drinks afterwards and then noticed some lights on outside on the golf course that night as he was leaving the clubhouse. He wondered over to see what was going on and realized it was one of his rivals still out on the course practicing by the headlights of his car. He went over, shook his hand, and exchanged a few words. Then as he headed back to his own car, he noticed his hands were wet. Once in his car, he saw that it was blood. His rival had been practicing so hard, his palms were bloody. "That was the day I realized I did not have what it took to be the best," he said to himself.

"My mother taught me that anything in life you want, the price has to be paid in advance," Solomon Hicks once told me. Sol has been the remarkable and inspirational top producer at Prudential Financial *globally* for 12 out of 15 years – in his 60's and 70's!

Clearly one of the challenges to us mining our gold is the truth of these stories.

Why might you be afraid of mining your gold?

Steven Pressfield acknowledges that we can all sense our vein of gold; we all know it is there. Marianne Williamson wrote that: "Our deepest fear is that we are powerful beyond measure." I'm guessing that's why you are reading this book. They think that what holds most people back from mining their gold is point 1 above: their loved ones or 'community' will reject them.

What this says to me is that we all have a problem in our own minds that first needs to be addressed.

And it depends what you want, doesn't it? If you want to be the best in the world or the richest in the world, there is a big price to pay for that. If you're going to be a top footballer or rock star, you're not going to be home that much and when you go out, most people will stare at you and want a picture with you. Privacy will be what you crave most and pay a premium for. If you want to run a $1bn company, you will have to make that your priority in life. There's a reason billionaires don't write books and run workshops on how to raise a happy family! Their partners and children don't see them much.

Remember what Felix Dennis said about the rich people he knew in his life, how he'd never met a happy one, and the sacrifices they had made to get rich? And that they couldn't even enjoy their wealth that much because other people were always hounding them for a piece of it? It is understandable to be apprehensive about mining your gold if it requires you to work 80-hour weeks and the rewards are unclear.

We all want to read a book that explains how we can have it all, but our inner wisdom is not stupid, and it can sense that if we want to mine huge amounts of gold, something has to give.

I wouldn't be writing this book if I felt the task to mine your gold and love your life was not very achievable, but it would be disingenuous of me not to acknowledge why many people might hesitate to dive in if the sacrifices feel too large.

It's why I wrote chapter 7.

*Make your definition of true success and true failure your compass and then go about mining your gold.

*Understand fear of success so it does not cause you to play small any longer.

*Play as big as you want so long as it aligns with what true success is for you!

Do you procrastinate?

Two rarely acknowledged fears that lie behind procrastination are:

    a)   "What happens if I succeed?"

It's legitimate in that you are sensing your vein of gold! The prospect seems so daunting that it psyches you out of starting. What if it works? You say to yourself: "How could I handle all that success and attention?" The potential change can look scary. Change can feel a threat sometimes even when it looks so much better; it's still a big change.

b)   "This is mountain of a task!"

It looks like too much work and intimidating to know where to start. You just have to start and put one foot in front of the other.

This procrastination can last a lifetime; over the years you just change your excuses and reasons for not doing anything to make your ego feel better.

Revisit Habits 1 and 2 since you're low on purpose, love, and fuel. Having an ever more compelling 'why' will make the biggest difference to getting into action plus a great support team. It is an inside job, so you do need to step up and own your challenge.

CHOOSE YOUR HARD

"You simply cannot achieve anything worthwhile in life without sacrifices to your time, health, comforts, and social relationships. Acknowledge that is often only temporary in relation to the rest of your life. In that sense, it is not a difficult trade-off."

Gareth Timmins' dream was to become a Royal Marines Commando and earn the coveted Green Beret. In his account of the unbelievably gruelling 32-week training, *Becoming The 0.1%*, he explains that 99.9% are told to not even apply.

The book is a gut-wrenching account of the almost impossibly challenging physical and mental ordeal that recruits have to endure usually on next-to-no sleep and little food. If you have a hard project or big goal ahead of you, this is the best book I could ever recommend to remind you that almost nothing really worthwhile comes easily and to help you stay on the path.

Let's have the reality check first. We should not fool ourselves: getting great outcomes in any area of life almost always requires a lot of work. I learned a powerful concept from financial advisor Eszylfie Taylor that I referenced in the introduction when I was on a top producer panel with him at the Beirut Life Insurance Seminars in 2022:

Being successful is hard. Being a failure is hard.

Being rich is hard. Being poor is hard.

Being married is hard. Being divorced is hard.

Being fit is hard. Being unfit is hard.

CHOOSE YOUR HARD.

Mining your gold is hard. Being too scared to mine your gold is hard – choose your hard.

Understanding that there is no short cut or free ticket is important. When you look at a high achiever's routines, these are simply not what average people are willing to do - consistently (for more on this simple but challenging element, see Habit 5). BUT it is enormously empowering to know that you can choose your hard too. Yes, it is hard to be, do and have many of the things you want in life, *but the alternative is hard too*. Frankly, **it is harder to live with disappointment and underachievement** because you know that you could have tried harder. You could have done the work, but you made the many small daily decisions not to.

Pull the mental weed that mining your gold is "too hard."

Knowing there is a hard to choose can be reassuring and make it easier to get out of bed early to exercise (or write your book – what

I'm doing right now on the day of this writing!). **"I'm choosing my hard."** It can make it easier to make extra prospecting phone calls or go to additional events to promote your business. "I'm choosing my hard." It can make it easier to go out to meet a new date when you'd rather curl up at home and watch a movie. "I'm choosing my hard." It can make it easier to ignore the desserts. Gradually these daily decisions can help you to build your self-discipline muscle.

Whenever we hear the words "hard work," we tend to recoil and secretly say to ourselves: "Man, I wish there was an easier way." It can sound too daunting, but:

i) Don't let it psych you out of trying your best

ii) Consider the alternate 'hard' choice.

Then it goes back to fuel and how much you want something.

Weed the Fear that You Must Sacrifice Something Important.

Reframe what you tell yourself: YOUR sacrifice is for something MORE IMPORTANT.

You can still unwittingly make everything harder than it needs to be because you believe that *all* progress comes either through pain or that there's an unpleasant price you must pay. This price feels so high that you end up being too scared to pursue what you want because you fear a hefty penalty, e.g., thinking you can only be more 'successful' if you work many more hours and thus not be available to spend any time with your family.

Robert Holden points out that: "We routinely sacrifice our relationships, our families, our values, and our health for success…People are often afraid of the next level of success because they fear that more success demands even more sacrifice."

The empowering belief is to be clear what true success is for *you* so that you aim for that on your gold mining journey (See chapter 7). This probably will involve choosing your hard, but it doesn't mean you have to sacrifice what matters most to you.

The choices can still be hard *at times*. I'm writing this section on a five-day business trip to the UK and I'm choosing to work on this rather than meet my cousins or several other business contacts who could potentially generate new business opportunities for me. I'm also choosing to work on this rather than go to a museum, read, or sightsee. Something has to give but writing this book is part of my purpose in life.

Weed the Fear that Success Can *Only* Come Through Painful Hard Work.

This is one of the most common blocks I've seen. While few would argue you don't need to work hard, I've seen many clients over the years who were **trying too hard**. Frankly, I have tried too hard too often myself. And it leads to heartache and projects miserable energy out to the rest of the world which definitely doesn't help!

Robert Holden argues that this is limiting because this mindset "does not believe in natural talent, inspiration, synchronicity, flow and effortless accomplishment." It certainly doesn't allow room for God to drive. Life is telling you to take a break, do something relaxing, and stop taking yourself so seriously.

Pull the Weeds Fast!

SUMMARY

12 Solutions to Slaying the 4 Fear of Success Dragons

> Dragon 1: You fear ostracizing yourself from your 'tribe' - including a fear of outshining loved ones

1. **Choose**

   LOVE (of all you could contribute to the world)

   Over

   Fear (of succeeding)

2. **Remember you were born loveable** (chapter 1). Stop holding back because you're afraid your greater success will make someone you care about feel badly or that they won't talk to you anymore.

3. **Find new friends, colleagues, and supporters** (Habit 4, Key 10). Avoid being around anyone where you find yourself playing smaller. Put yourself in places where you feel safe/emotionally supported to shine.

4. **Make your purpose greater than you fear** (chapter 8). Let love and your passion drive. Feel the fear and do it anyway (Susan Jeffers wrote that book: thanks Susan!)

Dragon 2: Your ego tells you that you are not worthy of big successes, so you think and play small

5. **Tell yourself: "If not me, then who?" "I've worked really hard to get here."** How does hiding yourself make a contribution to the world? (Habit 4, Key 1)

6. **Dream BIG dreams and set BIGGER GOALS** (Habit 4, Key 12) **and ask: Are my goals worthy of me?** Make room for natural talent, inspiration, synchronicity, and flow.

Dragon 3: You fear shining in the spotlight

7. **Do the work to resolve past trauma** (chapter 12)

8. **8. Live in the present** (chapter 2) **and keep your eyes on the prize: Be clear about your vision of what you want** (Habit 4, Key 2)

Dragon 4: You fear that mining your gold requires too much hard work or sacrifice

9. **Reframe what you tell yourself: Only sacrifice for something MORE IMPORTANT.** How can you make more room in your life for the real you to fully express yourself? *How can you lean into that – even with small steps?*

10. **Choose your hard: Mining your gold is hard. Being too scared to mine your gold is hard. Overcome procrastination by showing up every day. Do your best to DO THE WORK whether you feel support from your tribe or not.**

11. **Elevate your beliefs: there is something exhilarating on the other side of your fear** (Habit 4, Key 2)

12. **Play as big as you want so long as it aligns with your compass of true success!**

Weed 2: Mostly Avoidable Weeds

Tom is a top producer in financial services. His teenage son has a drug problem and quite debilitating anxiety. Tom has had numerous extra-marital affairs throughout his marriage. Mike is a very successful partner at an accounting firm. His teenage son was in trouble with the police and dropped out of school. Mike was a workaholic who was rarely home. He went onto have a stroke followed by a divorce. David is a high-flying international investment consultant for a private equity firm. In his mid-40's his obesity is causing him heart tremors, frequent shortness of breath, and seriously high blood pressure issues.

All three of these people are (or were) friends of mine (one I lost touch with). And you've experienced or heard very similar stories of people who were so good professionally that they overlooked a key area of their life. I recently watched a documentary on Netflix about one of the world's most accomplished tennis coaches who went through *eight* marriages. One of his wives told him: "I never see you."

As a flawed human being myself, I am not writing this to judge others. I've had plenty of my own challenges and Tom, Mike and David are or were really good friends of mine. What I want to do is recommend you get clear about the mostly avoidable weeds in life.

While pursuing "success" can *sometimes* feel somewhat intangible:

Sense of purpose   Great health
Loving and fulfilling relationships and social connection
Positive challenges – feeling like you make a difference
Meaningful work – preferably pursuing your passion

Acts of kindness   Great health

By contrast, knowing what NOT to do can often seem more straightforward. Warren Buffett sums this up well when it comes to the business world:

THE 5 HABITS TO MINE YOUR GOLD

"Charlie (Munger) and I have NOT learned how to solve difficult business problems. What we have learned is to avoid them."

The same can be said for our personal lives. Big weeds to avoid is a long list (courtesy of getAbstract co-founder Rolf Dobelli from his book, *The Art of the Good Life*) but it's worth having on hand. Even if you're fortunate not to be affected yourself with any of these, you won't have to look far to know someone who is.

WEEDS TO AVOID:

- Alcoholism
- Drug addiction
- Chronic stress
- Noise
- Lengthy commute
- A job you loathe
- Unemployment
- Dysfunctional marriage
- Stupidly high expectations
- Poverty, debt, and financial dependence
- Loneliness
- Spending too much time with negative people
- Overreliance on external validation
- Constant comparisons with others
- Thinking like a victim
- Self-loathing
- Chronic sleep deprivation
- Depression, anxiety, rage and envy

- YOU CAN'T LEARN TO LIVE WITH ANY OF THESE WEEDS IF YOU WANT A GOOD LIFE and want to mine your gold.

You may think Dobelli missed some key ones: Disease, Disabilities and Divorce. But countless studies have shown however that the negative impacts of these three things diminish over time – more quickly than we imagine.

I know this may seem like an unusual topic for a book about mining your gold. It's certainly not uplifting. But the more I re-read this list, the more I realize how important it is to keep it top of mind so that you don't tolerate or ignore something that could become a significant weed that you need to pull – even ones that on the surface don't seem so jugular like tolerating too many mediocre nights' sleep or being jealous of someone.

They are all toxic to you making progress and are worth addressing as quickly as possible if one of them rings true for you, a loved one or a client.

Here is my best solution to avoiding these weeds:

Keep a journal. This is the best way to raise your self-awareness and to reflect on how you're feeling. It's also a useful way to make sure that your busyness is taking you in the right direction and aligns with your values. If you don't do this or feel that at this point in your life that you don't have time, at least **Do a Monthly Review** (see chapter 14, Key 3: Elevate Your Awareness). This will help a lot.

As Samuel Johnson said: "The fountain of content must spring up in the mind, and he who hath so little knowledge of human nature as to seek happiness by changing anything but his own disposition, will waste his life in fruitless efforts and multiply the grief he proposes to remove."

PULL THE WEEDS FAST!

Weed 3: Feeling Beaten After a Setback or 'Lifequake'

Bruce Feiler, a bestselling author, PBS presenter, husband, and father of two young children, was 43 when he was diagnosed with an aggressive bone cancer in his left leg. He spent a grueling year going through sixteen rounds of chemo and a seventeen-hour surgery to remove his femur, then spent two years on crutches: "Every step, every bite, every hug I've taken since has been haunted by the long tail of fear and fragility."

If that wasn't enough, he nearly went bankrupt: "I woke up three nights a week in a pale sweat, staring at the ceiling, wondering." To make matters even worse, at the very same time, his father made several suicide attempts as he struggled with the mobility and moods often associated with having Parkinson's disease.

Trying to hold down some writing work to support his family, Feiler became awed by some research about children who thrived. Emory University psychologists had found that the children who handled life better were those who knew their family histories as narratives that *oscillated* – meaning these histories revealed ups *and* downs, triumphs *and* tribulations rather than children who were told either a family hard luck story, a simple rags-to-riches story, or just got a highlight reel of different relatives' best life outcomes but never heard about their flaws and crises.

Feiler decided to explore how other adults thrived after major life challenges like his and spent three years interviewing 225 people from every U.S. state and of all walks of life aged from 25-85. What he learned and reported in his book *Life Is in the Transitions: Mastering Change at Any Age*, is that: **"We've been led to believe that our lives will always ascend, for example, and are shocked to discover they oscillate instead."** No wonder we feel so much anxiety and overwhelm.

When disruptive and unexpected events happen, rather than responding with a 'well it's normal for one of these things to happen every 12-18 months' (what Feiler's research found), **our typical response is: 'This shouldn't be happening.** This is not the life I expected.' Living a typical life includes dealing with various hardships that often do not happen in any predictable order. Not only that, these types of transitions are happening more often.

The biggest problem we have is that we don't know how to handle these challenges. When we have a chain of disruptive events or one hits us at a vulnerable time, they can last an average of *five* years and happen, on average, 3-5 times in our lives (half our adult years!). Feiler calls them 'lifequakes' and defines them as: "A vital period of adjustment, creativity, and rebirth – that helps one find meaning after a major life disruption."

Have a Setback Plan

Several years ago, Christopher, one of my clients at the time, attended a breakfast workshop I was giving on how to develop profitable centers of influence (referred to as 'introducers' in the UK and some other countries). Almost on a whim I had added a final slide recommending having a Setback Plan. "It can be a frustrating, uncertain process building business relationships and wondering who and when someone will come through for you," I said. "Pretty much every week you need to detach emotionally from your efforts and do your best to remember you are planting a garden. The rewards can be remarkable, *and* these things usually take time."

Afterwards Christopher came up to me and I asked him what he thought was most helpful. "That last slide," he confided. "A plan like that would really help me." I remember being really surprised to hear this. I'd been coaching him for several months and I had no idea he was so troubled by people's silence and the rather slow process of developing great relationships. He'd never mentioned it before - never suggested that it was something that bugged him.

In the end, he couldn't wait. 18 months later Christopher left his business development position. Tragically, a year after that he took his own life. I'm sure there were many reasons for his suicide but in his eyes cumulative 'failure' was certainly a big part of it. He had also grown up in the shadow of a father who had become a multi-million-aire in business and figurehead in the community. As a result, I think he'd always felt a need to achieve his own big results to feel 'enough' (see Weed 4 to avoid: Envy and Comparison).

We all need a Setback Plan for when we have 'lifequakes', feel beaten or badly deflated.

There are many varying degrees of setbacks and **potential lifequakes** for you or a loved one. They can include death of a parent/sibling/child; major health change or turmoil with work; succumbing to an addiction, relocating or your child having troubles. And it can be a combination of seemingly smaller challenging events. These sound rare - and sometimes they are - but as Bruce Feiler found, at other times in our lives events like this come one after another.

You want to have some kind of plan for this rather than flailing in the dark every time and letting your great habits derail. I know it's almost a cliché but, as you've heard many times before, it's not what happens to you in life but how you handle it that counts.

Here is a process to take and make your own. Experiment next time you have a setback to bounce back from and keep the bits that work for you:

1. **Stop and Forgive:**

   a) **Forgive yourself** and others for the setback. Breathe. Remind yourself: "This happens to EVERYONE. *Everyone*. Rome wasn't built in a day".

   b) **Vent your frustrations**. Do this like letting air out of a tire. You don't want to repress negative feelings and store them in your body, but you also don't want to keep venting endlessly either and fueling wild negative fire.

We all experience setbacks, but you don't want to keep watering these weeds.

c) **Find ways to feel even slightly better** that DON'T sabotage your goals much (psychologically it's okay to rebel a *little* – sometimes us A types do have the plug in too tight).

d) **Avoid more crises** (Weed 2) to make sure your slippery slope starts to even out a bit.

e) **Allow time to recover**. Mourn if necessary. There is no set timeline on grief. Revisit point 10 about the forgiveness process in Chapter 1.

2. **Accept your present**

a) **Accept what is.** This might be the hardest part. Try not to resist or deny 'reality'. The longer you do, the longer it will take you to progress again. Try to dwell on the people who have exceptional responses to hard times – the ones who transform their lives from circumstances where the social convention is often to be lost.

Bruce Feiler recommends that you **turn inward and assume responsibility for making it better** (revisit Chapter 5). Those he met had success doing the following:

*Imagine situations worse than yours to help you accept what is ("at least I'm not…"). *See the positive: one interviewee in his book who had imposter syndrome at getting a better-than-expected CEO position said: "It drove me to work harder and learn more than anyone else."

*Get to work – dive right in to avoid letting self-doubt build up.

*Show yourself some empathy: some negative emotions can lead to feeling unworthy of love, success etc. The solution to shame is empathy.

c) **Let go of some old ways** of thinking and old ways of doing things. Shed some of that skin.

d) **Research your options**. If you've been diagnosed with a serious illness or new health condition, learn more about it and how to be proactive about it now.

e) **Seek out support.** Rather like Key 10 in Habit 4, you need a support team and people to lean on and empathize with you.

f) **Remind yourself:** High achievers know that it's not what happens to you; it's how you handle it. Look in the mirror and ask: How am I handling it? Do I need to go back to #1 on the list?

g) **Return to Habit 1** in this book: **Return to love; live in the present not the past or future; let God (love) drive.**

h) **Refuel**. Revisit Habit 2 in this book for suggestions when you're ready.

i) **Gratitude practice:** Do your best to be grateful for what you do have. At least ask yourself: what could I be grateful for?

j) **Reverse the Fear Spiral**

> *"Nothing in life is as important as you think it is while you are thinking about it."*
>
> - Daniel Kahneman

All of us have worried too much and experienced fear spirals more times than we'd care to mention. We've all had setbacks. What you and I need are strategies to catch worries and fears and redirect them back towards an empowered track that gets you taking positive action. You want a better plan next time to pull this weed fast.

Cognitively it can be helpful to remind yourself what Psychologist Daniel Kahneman has found that when we think about something a lot, we unintentionally inflate it out of proportion and lose much of our perspective – hence, a "focusing illusion."

What can you do to halt the spiral and shift your thoughts from worry to something empowering?

Review the chapter titles of what you've read so far. Every single chapter offers a way to redirect your thinking towards something positive. You may only need *one* that works at a time.

3. **Experiment with 'Be and Do the Change Consistently' (Habit 5)**

   a) **Consider the timeline to recover.** Accept this as best as you can.

   b) When you feel somewhat ready, think on paper. **Write your responses to: "What can I do about this now?" Think about what you *can* control and do that's positive in your life.**

   c) **Get help:** Very, very proactively seek out sources of any and all inspiration (because you probably won't feel like it and they will do you a world of good): books, songs, people, films, comedies. It's a curious thing, but when we're feeling low, we tend to avoid people.

      Yet what can often help us the most is actively reaching out to other people. We especially need reminders that **_everyone_** up to something big has to endure tough times (and the bigger the quest often it seems like the tougher the times). I try to remember the words of world champion athlete Amanda Allen: *"When I thought I couldn't go on, I just did the next most important thing. I just kept turning up."*

What is your next most important thing that you just need to 'turn up' for?

You might well need to find someone like a coach to gently push you outside your comfort zone. And, as I also discuss in Habit 4, Key 10 you might need someone to cajole you and get in your face to help you get a reality check to take action. Usually, these people show up uninvited. Also look out for role models that you may or may not know personally. Sometimes these can be people we look up to who inspire us enough to get in action.

d) Experiment with new things: Transitions can be like hitting refresh or restart. Bruce Feiler found that when times get really tough, some people get very creative. As they shift from the natural journey though isolation or disconnection, they create new attitudes, aptitudes, skills, talents, and means of expression. Some people reconnect to their childhood and become consumed with a desire to create and transform. They rekindle former passions, childhood fantasies, and long-dormant dreams. One interviewee told him: "God's given me a second chance."

Most importantly, understand that these changes are something you have to CHOOSE to do. Most of them won't just happen to you.

e) **Elevate your control!** Read the many suggestions in Habit 4 of this book to help you elevate your life to help you get back on track.

4. **Create new meaning**

a) When you are ready, **write down some lessons learned** from this setback so far to build your foundation for the future, e.g., "This too shall pass." "I've been here before and what doesn't kill you makes you stronger." "My body heals and at its own pace." "If others have pulled through this and gone onto shine, I can too". "Less time for 'a' means more time for 'b'."

b) **Be and do the change** (Habit 5 in this book). EASE back into your empowering past habits and add new ones that reflect the type of person you now want to be. If you need to lower your targets to get back in the game, do it now. Just get back on the field – whatever that looks like and even if it scares you greatly. *Just turn up.*

Ask yourself: **Which activity will build my self-respect/ morale quickest?** If you have a peer group, do not compare yourself to any of them. Compare yourself ONLY to your *recent* past self, your own expectations, and goals. Listen to your inner hero who wants great things from you, not your inner critic!

c) **Don't get complacent** or smug about *starting* back on track. That's your ego getting in the way. Don't fool yourself that your recovery is easy or assured. Prove it to yourself by staying on track week-in and week-out and use the setback as mojo.

d) **Become part of the solution rather than part of the problem**

One summer in 1996, about a year after graduating from Yale, Anne Wojcicki was visiting her sister, Susan, in California. Susan had rented out her garage to two men who had just left Stanford to start a new company.

After getting to know them better, Anne started to open up about how bad she thought the healthcare system was in the US and how its primary focus was on making money rather than offering care for all and doing what was right for the consumer.

Many of us have a negative viewpoint about something. Just the other day, a wealth manager client of mine was telling me that his father had raised him to believe that all wealthy people had made their money in a "nefarious way." My mother used to say the same thing.

Anne's family had been scarred by an experience that her mother, Esther, had had as a young child. Esther's 18-month-old brother had found a bottle of aspirin in a medicine cabinet and swallowed the entire bottle. Because the family was poor, they had no money or medical insurance and so were turned away by the first two hospitals they went to. "By the time they found a hospital that would take Esther's brother, the little boy was in critical condition. The next morning, Esther's brother was dead," explains Lowey Bundy Sichol in *Idea Makers: 15 Fearless Female Entrepreneurs.*

As Anne continued to yet again malign the health care industry, one of the men, Larry Page – who was busy building Google – said: "Anne, you can either be part of the solution or part of the problem. Right now, you're part of the problem."

This wake-up call led to her blending the genetics revolution with social networking and crowdsourcing. She founded a company called 23andMe named after the 23 pairs of chromosomes in a normal human cell. The purpose of the business was to provide consumers affordable information about their genetic information and diseases they were at risk for that could help them make more empowered health decisions.

"She also wanted to work together with scientists and pharmaceutical companies," adds Sichol, "and help them create drugs that work better." By 2021, rather than still complain about how awful the health care industry was, Anne had empowered over 12 million people. Her problem became her cause. This is how some people respond to a lifequake.

e) Find meaning in your new story and <u>make your purpose greater than your fear</u>

Your search for meaning comes from **reframing your story and retelling it so it's one that empowers you and then empowers others.** Bruce Feiler says this is a scary and necessary step. Essentially, your story says: THIS PAIN HAPPENED AND I CONVERTED IT INTO POSITIVE FUEL, A CAUSE, and NEW RELATIONSHIPS. You create a new story that ties the transitions together and creates or cements meaning. *You start to see the possibilities.*

The most important thing is to make meaning from what has happened to you. Piece your story together so it empowers you. **Tell your story and, even though you may not believe it 100% at first, your feelings will follow;** you become the narrative. You bring the meaning to it. And you can change your story any time – even when an 'ending' seems like a failure!

Through his three-year journey, Feiler learned that stories empower, connect, and inspire us. He says that we don't tell our stories much and that this contributes to us being a generation of malcontents. "Learning to bring meaning from our life stories may be the most indispensable but least understood skill of our time." It goes deeper than happiness. The quest for meaning is part of what makes us human.

Any setback or frustration, argues Pema Chodron, "shows us, with terrifying clarity, exactly where we're stuck." If we view this only as pain and discomfort, we miss opportunities. **Transitions aren't going away. Face them:**

"Don't shield your eyes when the scary part starts; that's when the heroes are made," urges Feiler: **"The woods are full of people just like us."** The moral of the setback story is to push through and know you're not alone. Get through the woods and then once you're out of them, plunge back in again to face down another wolf and dream another dream.

Knowing how to handle life's inevitable slings and arrows of outrageous fortune means you can bounce back harder and mine more of your gold. You can handle it!

PULL THE WEEDS!

Weed 4: Avoid Envy and Self- Comparison

"I know people with hundreds of millions of dollars who feel like failures because their friends are billionaires. There are famous Hollywood celebrities who are depressed because someone else is <u>more</u> famous."- Arthur C Brooks

How often do you unwittingly compare yourself to someone else? Once you start catching this, you might well be alarmed. From Greek philosophers to holy scriptures and fairy tales, we have been warned about the damage done by the malignant weed of ENVY.

According to Rolf Dobelli, **"Envy has a bigger impact on your life situation than physical affliction or financial ruin, and the ability to manage it is fundamental to the good life."**

This comment *really* struck me. I never considered that it could be such a tumor until I thought back on my upbringing. I recalled the searingly negative emotion directed by my mother towards people who had more money than us. This stuck with me subconsciously. I'm ashamed to say that it then reminded me of some people's success that I've resented and, yes, envied over the years. Most days as a competitive A type, I used to have to catch myself when I saw people "like me" with nicer cars, nicer clothes or, in the gym, with Planet of the Apes frames!

And that's how it works: *"Above all,* **we envy those who are similar to us in terms of age, career, environment, and lifestyle***…you're not comparing yourself with the Pope…Alexander the Great or a super-successful Stone Age human from your part of the world."*

Yet how do you feel when you think these thoughts? You *never* feel good, do you? And this matters to the high achiever because you change best when you feel good, not when you feel bad.

This is challenging because it is (unfortunately) human nature to compare; it's actually even an animal instinct (based on research with primates). So, what can you do?

How can you reduce feeling envious and messing up your thoughts and days… and lives?

What's the best way to feel less envy and pull the weeds fast?

The primary solution is to STOP COMPARING YOURSELF TO OTHERS!!!

In the early years of being self-employed, my inspiration and role models were Stephen Covey, Brian Tracy, and Jack Canfield. I wanted their everything: their reputation, their influence, their travel schedule, their bestsellers, their fame, their happy families that they wrote about, their apparent confidence, their expertise, their luxury lifestyles, and the really positive difference they made.

In the early years this was a guiding light. But at some point – without me realizing – it undermined me as I unconsciously started to compare myself to them. For a while I could reassure myself that they were quite a lot older than me, so I had time.

But at some point, I started subconsciously feeling "less than" and badly about myself because I wasn't anywhere near where they were. While my book sold 10,000's of copies, I may have been travelling half the globe, I got married and had two great kids, I hadn't written the timeless classic, I hadn't produced many volumes of self-help guides, and I wasn't being offered $10,000's for keynotes.

I didn't notice my many successes and that I had my own story to live. I had my own life to live. I had a different path to walk on that couldn't be exactly the same as theirs or anyone else's. And I had to break from the comparisons because they no longer helped.

What I've learned is that somewhere in the mix of wanting to grow, the art is to find a balance between:

a) What inspires you to grow and fulfil your potential with feeling sufficiency
b) How to do it in a way that comes from love and makes you fulfilled most of the time
c) What aligns with your purpose, values, and conscience
d) What you're best at doing

How often do you unwittingly compare yourself to others?

It surprises me how often clients of mine compare themselves to others they work with or know well from their company or industry. This could sound benign enough, but it rarely is. It almost always make them feel worse about themselves. Last year I worked with the managing partner of a law firm who had made herself unhappy for many years because she too frequently compared herself to the other owners of her firm and how they brought more revenue in than she did.

It's a hardwired way of living. Think back to when you were a child. How old do you remember being when you realized that there were other kids your age who could run faster than you? Draw better than you? Figure out math questions quicker?

I was the second fastest child on the playground but could never outrun Peter Gandy. I was probably five or six. I will never forget a picture that Martin Loughbridge drew in my class when we were eight. He had drawn a person and had angled the feet in the way that we actually stand rather than sticking them out at right angles the way I still drew people. And on the shiny shoes, he had even drawn a little shape to show that their polish reflected in the sun. I was amazed and announced to myself that I did not have that talent and would 'never be good at art'.

Regardless of the context, comparing yourself to anyone else is almost always unhelpful and usually quite a toxic thing to do. Presumably it is not easy to focus instead on comparing yourself to your past self, yet this is by far what makes the most sense for you to grow.

Solution: Compare yourself to who you were in the recent past.

Ten years ago, I used to travel for business on average ten days/month, but that was before I had children.

16 years ago, my wife ran marathons and half-marathons. Now she has a husband (me), two school-age children and a department to run at work – plus her extremely demanding primary work.

In a Clubhouse room I once hosted on Tiny Habits and Confidence, a gym owner told me that he had master athletes who were constantly unhappy because they kept comparing themselves to their past self and their glory days when they were stronger, fitter, and faster. Compare yourself to a recent past self!

It may not be realistic or worthwhile to reach a past goal or achievement from 20 years ago. Things may well have changed for you since then. Your commitments and priorities may have shifted.

1. **Compare** yourself to this time last year, how would rate yourself on a scale of 1-10 with your:
   a) Your key relationships:
   b) Your business/vocation:
   c) Your finances:
   d) Your physical health:
   e) Your mental health:

   *Your self-belief:
   *How confident you feel:
   *How much you respect yourself:
   *Your sense of worthiness to achieve your long-term goals:
   *How happy you feel:
   *Degree to which you feel positively challenged:
   *Degree to which you tune into your intuition and trust your

gut instinct:

*How constructively you deal with anger and other negative emotions:

f) Sense of spiritual connection:
g) Adventures/fun/hobbies:
h) Contribution and giving back:
i) Living your purpose:

Now this is too long of a list to *focus* on, but it gives you the big picture. **Then you can choose two areas (no more) to focus on improving most and measuring most closely.**

2. **Compare Yourself to Your Recent Self: Create Daily Questions**

Marshall Goldsmith developed these working with Fortune 100 C-suite leaders. They all begin with the wording:

"On a scale of 1-10 today, did I do my best to…"

You can decide what your priorities are and measure yourself against your recent self. Examples include:

a) Set clear goals?
b) Be engaged at work?

c) Meet my prospecting targets?

For more on this, see chapter 20.

3. **Compare Yourself to Your Recent Self: Use a Habit Tracker**

Decide which habits are important for you right now and track them daily, weekly, and monthly. Again, focusing on your own activity compared to your previous activity **keeps**

your thoughts on what you can control and off what others are doing.

For more on this, see chapter 19.

4. **Compare Yourself to Your Recent Self: Do a Monthly GPS**

Once per month, I recommend scoring yourself in key areas on a scale of 1-10 (health, key relationships, professional and financial to name a few).

Then I urge you to ask yourself **what to stop/do less/keep/do more/start/accept** moving forward. It's a great way to make small adjustments and to preserve a LOT - even if this feels less exciting. (Successful people already have a lot of good habits but are often tempted by the concept that change always equals progress).

For more on this, see Habit 4, Key 3: Elevate Your Awareness.

5. **Compare Yourself to Your Recent Self: Every Evening Identify Five Things You Did Right**

This is one of my favorites. For years I had this awful evening habit of perseverating about the one or two things that hadn't gone well that day – the 'no' I got or the person who said they'd get back to me and hadn't. By that point in the day, I was already tired and emotionally depleted. It was a terrible way to end a day when I had done many things right and to the best of my ability – but I wasn't noticing the 80% of things.

I'd go to bed feeling badly about myself. And when our brains start on a negative spiral, it's easy for the inner critic to show up and say something unencouraging like, "I bet so-and-so is doing better than you!"

The solution is to write down (or at least mentally list), five things you did right that day. Get your brain to focus on positive actions you took. These are all free of envy and address things within your control that deserve applause.

End the day on a high note.

Be consistent with this and you'll be amazed at how much more content you will feel.

6. **Understand the fallacies of envy (this knowledge is power if you use it)**

   a) **When you envy someone else, you are assuming (unwittingly) that s/he is happier than you** and that everything in that person's life is better than yours.

   Yet how many times have you later found out something about another person only to be relieved you're not in their shoes?

   One summer I remember standing behind this immaculately dressed man at my local coffee shop, and I started imagining his huge lake-view home with a blissfully happy stay-at-home wife tending to her organic garden, polished exuberant children probably at first class summer camps, dogs with endlessly wagging tails, and various luxury cars outside.

   Then when I went to sit down, I looked out the window and saw him sitting with a large young man in thick glasses making loud squealing noises rocking back and forth in his seat to calm himself. As I watched, I realized it was his son, who was severely cognitively delayed. A flood of emotions came over me from embarrassment, shame, and upset at myself for feeling envy and then a deep appreciation for all the experiences I've been able to have with my own son.

You know what really got to me the most? It was the realization that he could never have a thoughtful conversation with his son – never be able to reflect on life with him. Now I see him outside the coffee shop every morning (which feels like an unexpected reminder).

"If we all threw our problems in a pile and saw everyone else's, we'd grab ours back." - Regina Brett

And this isn't the entire point either, **it's also crucial to be happy for other people's successes and wish them well.** You and I have no idea what someone went through to accomplish their wins. Being jealous of others gets you nowhere. The recipes for what it takes are public information; the other truth is most people are not willing to do what it takes – to do the hard, hard work, take the risks, and pay the price. It's easier to have sour grapes.

b) **The things you envy are far less important than you think they are.**

Many of my neighbors have swimming pools and my kids sometimes say, "That's not fair; they're so lucky." On bad days I used to feel envy too and a bit of a failure as if I am being a negligent father and denying my kids what some of their peers have.

On the vast majority of days (thankfully), I remind myself the rather ridiculous notion that there is no extensive scientific double-blinded research proving that the presence of a pool determines whether my children grow up to be happy, kind and confident contributors to society!

c) Rolf Dobelli has a *'last resort'* suggestion to remove envy which is to identify the worst aspect of a person's life that you envy and imagine them struggling with those problems.

7. **Avoid social media**

   How do you think most people feel after scrolling through Facebook or Instagram? How do you feel most of the time noticing people's seemingly perfect family, holiday, or evening out? Researchers at Humboldt University found many users felt: *"frustrated and tired."* Dobelli adds: *"The internet has turned jealousy into a modern-day epidemic."*

   We change best when we feel good, not when we wish we had someone else's life. And the last time I went to a cool, picture-worthy professional sporting event, my son ate too much junk food and threw up all over the urinals.

8. **Let it be: Accept that there's always someone somewhere doing better than you**

   While this isn't something we like to think about, it is pointless to deny.

   It could bring us plenty of peace not to obsess with having to be the 'best' in the entire world out of seven billion.

   Then we can just get on with being our best selves.

   As you become more self-aware to your thoughts, you can notice the weeds of envy and comparison quicker.

   PULL THE WEEDS FAST!

Weed 5: People Pleasing

When Zoe Chance started to achieve a certain level of success as a researcher in behavioral economics and as a Yale professor, she received an increasing number of invitations to speak around the world. "I was thrilled…but these opportunities left me overwhelmed and stressed," she explains in her book *Influence is Your Superpower*. Her coach told her that her enthusiasm was burning her out, so Chance decided she had to start saying no more.

She called the upcoming month NOvember and vowed to say no to everything from speaking invitations, to coffees, nice people, and requests from senior colleagues: "as the month progressed, I started to feel less stressed and more in control of my decisions, my time, and my life," – so much so, that she started to track her nos.

Her MBA students are assigned a 24-hour "No" challenge on the first day of class. Through her work, she has found that many people – especially nice ones – find it impolite to say no to requests and invitations. She argues that we have been socially conditioned to be giving of our time and the end result is we feel stretched in too many directions and resentful: "you have to start with no to expand both your comfort zone and your power." The challenge is intended for you to be kinder to yourself and make more space in your days. "Practice saying no even to people close to you, even to things you want to do, even to things that are small."

Saying no 90% of the Time

Warren Buffett is credited with saying: *"The difference between successful people and very successful people is that very successful people say no to almost everything."* He and his business partner Charlie Munger have a five second rule: when asked for something, to give it five seconds thought, and then, 90% of the time, say no.

People pleasing is a giant weed!

For most of my clients the idea of saying no is emotionally laden because as they grow their business, they amass more and more clients that they don't want to say no to when they hear from them. This is a challenge in some industries such as being a financial advisor because you are expected to review plans with clients 1-4 times/year depending on the complexity – and then there are market crises that panic everyone. There is a finite number of people you can work with at some point. Yes, some of my clients will hire extra staff and some will sell parts of their book of business, but they almost always have too much on their plate and too many people to please.

It can be difficult to say no to people. And what businessperson isn't clear that customer service is enormously important? This means that promptly responding to client needs is important (often feels urgent), it can often come first and then get in the way of strategy, your plans, and your growth. This isn't as selfish as it sounds because all healthy businesses are either growing or declining. It's a difficult dilemma.

I've found that people pleasing can really limit your growth. It's like the dopamine hit you get from receiving a text or a 'like' on social media. It feels good in the moment to address a quick client need or reply to a message, but it takes you away from what you were working on that was often more important. You've already determined your priorities *before someone calls or emails interrupting you with their 'agenda'.*

Yet again the topic of worthiness raises its ugly head. If your self-worth is shaky, you are going to put others first every time. This can happen at work and at home and you end up putting yourself last. You have to fight for your time.

People pleasing can also confuse us into giving all of our business clients/customers exactly the same amount of time. This is quite a common mistake. If you give your lowest-paying clients the same amount of time as your highest-paying because you have confused the idea of equal treatment of human beings with how to run your business, you can easily get sucked into spending a lot of time on people who do little to help you feed your family. It is also a danger because the lower-paying clients are often the neediest, most demanding, and most sensitive to money-issues. Yes of course you treat everyone with respect. But in business, you cannot give everyone the same amount of time.

People pleasing can halt your gold mining. It is a call for better planning that aligns with what (and who) you value most. If you need to allow flexibility for client needs, then schedule that too and be clear about what is truly an 'emergency' where it is justified to drop everything else.

Lastly – and I hate to suggest any gender stereotype here – but in my life experience as a coach I do hear female clients of mine who are mothers fret about being conflicted with time between work and their children. Many carry a lot of guilt about this.

In 2009, before I had children of my own, I was paired up at a workshop with a female executive who was deeply distressed about this: "I feel like I'm doing a terrible job with my daughter. When I'm at work I feel guilty about not being at home and when I'm at home, I feel like I should be getting more work done. And I'm worried about how my daughter is doing in school. She's behind in reading, writing and math. I think I should get her tested."

Based on the tone of what I heard, I assumed her daughter must be about 16 or so. But not knowing how to empathize about it at the time, I opted to make conversation and asked her: "How old is your daughter?" She replied: "She'll be six next month." Conversely for most men, I think it's still not socially acceptable to admit this conflict even though it is of course very real.

I hear it from my wife too: the frequent feeling that she is doing everything in an average way because she has such a conflicted relationship with time – her primary work, her role as department vice-chair, her parenting, even her role as a daughter and wife. It's a painful place to be and I can feel it when she talks about it. One solution is saying no more.

Beware your ego

Many years ago, I had a client called Hugh who was highly respected in the UK financial planning community and was frequently being asked to speak at events all over the country. He didn't get paid for any of this nor did it lead to any new business opportunities, but it took a lot of willpower on his part to admit the real problem. "It's my ego. Knowing where I started in life, it feels really good to be asked to present to all these people." He loved the recognition and acknowledgement for his achievements.

The problem was that it put no food on the table and took him away from his family. It's one thing to want to serve others and give back. This absolutely has a powerful place and can be part of your purpose; just make sure that it's not a blended combination of not being able to say no, people pleasing, and your ego loving being in the limelight.

Ideas of how to actually say 'no' to people – verbal ways to pull weeds that can interfere with your big plans:

Stephen Covey tells the time his wife was invited to serve as chairperson for a local committee in his book *The Seven Habits of Highly Effective People*. She didn't really want to do it but felt pressured and finally agreed. Then she called one of her closest friends to ask if she would like to be on the committee. Her friend replied: "Sandra, that sounds like a wonderful project, a really worthy undertaking. I appreciate your inviting me to be a part of it. For a number of reasons, I won't be participating myself, but I want you to know how much I appreciate your invitation." After she'd hung up, Sandra turned to her huband and said, "I wish I'd said that!"

On another occasion, long before he wrote the book, Covey wanted one of his managers to work on an urgent project that had come up because of his own lack of foresight. This manager showed him all the other projects he already had and said: "to do the jobs that you want done right could take several days. Which of these projects would you like to delay or cancel to satisfy your request?" Covey didn't want to be responsible for cancelling anything, so he gave the work to someone else who, while less skilled, "was (also) a crisis manager"!

Covey also wrote about 'No Deal' in his Think Win/Win chapter. If a win-win agreement can't be found, he recommends that you say no – to agree not to make a deal because down the road the party who conceded would grow resentful. "*No Deal* basically means that if we can't find a solution that would benefit us both, we agree to disagree agreeably."

Zoe Chance suggests these ways to say no effectively:

To a social event: "Thanks for asking, and I would absolutely love to do something like that with you another time."

To a salesperson: "Thanks but I'm not interested."

To a romantic overture: "My intuition says no – it's a gut feeling and I always listen to those."

To a task you don't want at work: "Thanks for the compliment, but that would my absolute nightmare. My soul would shrivel. Is there any alternative?"

Talk about what you are focusing on or, in business, specializing increasingly more on.

The easiest example I can give is writing this book. I have to say no to numerous worthy personal and professional activities otherwise I'm just not going to find the time. As the saying goes, the enemy of great is good. For me that might include saying no to a later evening activity with a family member so I can go to bed early (and get up early to write). It means often skipping church with the family so I can write on Sunday mornings. It means negotiating about ride shares to get the kids to school so I can free up a whole day to write. Professionally it means I don't pursue as many business opportunities as I might so I don't end up with full days and no time to write. It has meant doing a lot less exercise than in the past.

It's okay to tell people you are focusing your time on:

*One of your children because s/he was recently bullied at school

*Taking care of an ailing parent

*An important project at work with an imminent deadline

*Rehabbing after an injury or surgery

*A committee fundraiser

*A side hustle business that you're excited about

*Coaching your kid's (pick your sport or extracurricular activity!) team

Something has to give, right?

In business, I recommend sharing to clients that you're shifting your area of specialization based on your acquired expertise. "I'm focusing increasingly now on working with (state your niche) e.g., business owners who are selling their companies" so that the other person can't really object. Or you could say you're now working only on "more complex planning cases such as 'a' or 'b'." If your general practitioner said, "Sorry, I'm no longer doing GP work, I'm specializing now in orthopedics," you couldn't tell them: "You shouldn't have done that!

The idea of saying no sounds straightforward enough when you *read* about it. Give yourself more time to think and respond more slowly to most requests that come your way from now on. Tune into *your* values. Ask God for guidance. Avoid saying yes out of guilt, obligation, ego, or habit – anything to help you gradually open up more time for what matters most. If you want new results, it requires new actions that require your time and *focus* that you have strategized for in advance. Time is all you have; it's not guaranteed to be here next year. Slow down and you will NO what to do.

PULL THE WEEDS FAST!

Weed 6: Emotional Attachment to Your Efforts

I think the biggest challenge when you're trying to make changes is that you can put in quite a lot of work and sometimes not see any noticeable new outcomes. You are emotionally invested in what you are doing but hoping for more positive signs sooner than may be realistic. In chapter 11 I wrote about this as the Law of Gestation: sometimes it takes time for the flowers to show.

The weed to pull is the frustration you have with your results taking longer than you want. You don't want to get discouraged.

One of the challenges of being self-employed is trying to detach from your prospecting efforts and not obsess about when the business or payment will come.

You must have been down this negative spiral. You've got a big opportunity. To you it means everything – *"Then why the hell aren't they calling me back? They seemed very interested and a 'yes' sounded to me like a formality. They seemed sincere and enthusiastic. They made all the right noises. Why aren't they calling me back? All they have to do is (fill in the blank) confirm my text, sign the contract, pick a start date (etc.). It will only take them a few minutes. What's the matter with them?"* And on and on the neurotic voice in our head goes.

I wish I had had lessons on how to deal with this 20 years ago. I'm sure my hair would be less grey, and I'd have enjoyed more days, weeks, and years. All the stress and perseverating.

So, what can you do? Work on detaching emotionally. Yes, this is definitely easier said than done.

1. **Give everything because it feels so good to do so – and detach.**

Take the leap of faith that good things will happen when it's the right season

A few days before Liverpool won the English Premiership for the first time in 30 years, their manager, Jurgen Klopp, was interviewed in *The Guardian* about why he believed he had achieved so much success in such a competitive business. He said in his German English: *"I give everything, but I don't expect I get something for it."*

This is the problem many of us have:

We DO expect something, and it drives us nuts because we don't get it NOW.

And it's really hard to run your business just for the pure joy of it. (Although it was Richard Branson who coined the phrase: Work hard, have fun and the money will come). This is a great time to remember Habit 1: Make love your purpose.

Think about thought leader Adam Grant's compelling findings in his book *Give and Take*: Givers in sales make *50% more money* than everyone else because they give without holding out their hand and saying: "Come on! Where's my piece of the pie? Huh?" The other 90% of people are "matchers" – people who only do good deeds to those they expect something directly back from.

As Bob Burg writes about in the inspiring tale of *The Go-Giver*, you can't make this a 'technique' to grow your business: *"The point is to give them more. You give, give, give. Why? Because you love to. **It's not a strategy, it's a way of life.** And when you do, then very, very profitable things begin to happen."*

I'm reminded of one of Oprah Winfrey's three principles to success: Newton's 3rd Law: For every action, there is an equal and opposite reaction. Her definition: the more good you put out into the world, the more it comes back to you. What brings Oprah the most joy is giving without expectation of return. Giving because of how it makes her feel. (It's in her book *What I Know For Sure*). Oprah is a *billionaire*. Klopp was paid $12m the year his team came top. Obviously, there are other ingredients to their success, but do you still think this joy and giving stuff is fluff?!

A few days before me writing this, I met with Harpreet Atwal, a friend and UK financial advisor who was in Chicago for a Million Dollar RoundTable committee meeting. He has started a fascinating mental health group for men that meets up for dinner every six weeks. It's taken up quite a lot of his time. In other words, he has done a lot of giving. When he described it to me, he said more than once: **"If you're serving humanity, everything is going to be okay."** Give everything and detach.

Then later he connected a different dot, leaned in, and slightly abashed, confided: "Matt, business has been up 25% this year!" To me, the look on his face was: "Only God works in ways like this." To Bob Burg's point earlier, Harpreet isn't doing this as a prospecting technique. Please be very clear about that. He is doing it purely from his heart. Business talk is not allowed at his events. He has a greater purpose: love. He's giving everything and receiving in many ways.

That's how you mine your gold.

2.   Have a little perspective and detach

I know this is a rational argument on an emotional topic, but you know **people have lives and other priorities that are theirs not yours** – whether you agree with their priorities or not. You've had many experiences in the past where you finally heard back from someone, and they said what they said – even if it wasn't compelling – and you forgave them because you realized that you are not at the center of anyone else's world but your own.

Everyone is winging it through life. No one taught us how to parent brilliantly. No one can give you the exact recipe for running your business along with all the dynamics to what's in your personal life and help you find peace, happiness and – yes – hopefully some joy in your life.

Focus on what you can control doing – your best. Try not to listen to the neurotic voice in your head because *you are not your thoughts anyway.* Or your emotions for that matter. I concur with those who say we are spiritual beings – souls - having a human experience. Even if you're not a person of faith, put your spirit into your profession and then DETACH from the outcomes as best as humanly possible. Maybe it will not win you the League Title or get you ALL the stuff, but it will bring you far greater rewards and much more joy which, deep down when we're honest with ourselves, is what we all want more of anyway.

3. **Give everything then detach: move on and give every-thing to something else**

I am the last person to claim this is easy. I grew up in a scarcity household where there was never enough. The pie on offer in life was usually shrinking in size and the bigger dog always got his piece first (and it was never us).

However, our brains have plasticity. Through repetition, you can shift how you think and respond. It may take you many months – after all, it took you years to forge your current reactions. You must be patient and persistent. The rewards come.

After you've done everything, you can to make sure your big prospect knows what the next step is, fight your mind to focus on something else and give everything to that. When your unhelpful neurotic self -talk reminds you that you've still not heard from Big Prospect, remind it back that the season will come, and you are going to focus your thoughts on something else. It really helps if you have other prospects to get in touch with (even if they're not as big).

Marketing guru Seth Godin recommends focusing on being *market-driven* (versus marketing-driven) – in other words, to focus on how you can serve and love on your clients and others who make ideal prospects for you. Get in a value-adding mindset because that too is where the rewards lie – again, probably not today but for sure your season will come.

Almost every week as a coach I talk to a client who is anxious about a big opportunity that isn't moving along according to plan. The prospect has not been in touch when they said they would and this silence leads to a lot of handwringing, frustration and worry. If you've been in a business development role for more than a few weeks, you will have had this experience.

The scary part is that whenever we start getting edgy about this opportunity, the universe decides to have some fun with us and knows – every time – just how easy it will be to wind us up further and drive us even more crazy. So rarely do these opportunities ever progress at the pace that we want them to and all too often it is our own anxiety and impatience that messes up the whole deal and we lose the chance to do business with that person or company.

I truly empathize. I have had the exact same mental challenges and fully understand the excitement and power of the big, juicy business opportunity and the impact it could have on your bottom line, your finances, and your family – where you've already started spending the money you anticipate making.

What we really need to learn here is how to emotionally DETACH from these opportunities and do all we humanly can to think about something else – anything else frankly. The easiest thing to focus on are other opportunities. While these aren't usually as exciting, they offer some distraction. If you don't have other big opportunities to think about, then get busy doing more prospecting, so you can create more opportunities.

Let's not forget the rest of your life.

What else is happening in your world that you can get distracted by and focus on more?

What fun event is coming up soon?

What are you looking forward to doing this evening or this weekend?

What can you plan for that would be a good distraction?

This is the perfect time to dive deep into your network to seek other opportunities, dive deeper into important personal relationships, dive deep into a great book or bigger project.

In the same way that high achievers bounce back from a business 'failure' so much quicker than medium and low achievers, you want to shift your mental focus to other things. Put in your calendar when you're going to follow up next and then 'hide it in the safe' so it's out of sight.

I've found that it's almost best to forget about the big opportunities so you can be relaxed when you do follow up. On some level it's almost a game - as if you're acting like this opportunity is no different than all your others and checking in on it is no different than you would *casually* check in with a loved one or colleague on the way to a coffee shop by asking, "I'm going to Starbucks. Do you want anything?"

Don't misunderstand me. I'm not suggesting you act like you don't care. I'm not suggesting you don't express your deep desire to help that person or express your confidence that you can make a really positive difference. But you act without too much emotional attachment. People can sense fear and desperation. They can sense when working together is no longer about their wellbeing but yours. They can sense when you're focused only on your agenda and your timeline versus theirs. You will blow this deal!

I've learned that detaching takes practice and a lot of reminders and self-awareness. **A practical step is to rate yourself daily: "On a**

scale of 1-10, did I do my best to detach emotionally from the outcomes today?"

By scoring yourself on this for a few *months*, gradually you will relax more realizing that it's the only way to succeed. Slowly you will ease up on your mental perseveration. You cannot obsess most of the time and expect great outcomes.

Avoid emotional attachment to your hard work.

PULL THE WEEDS FAST!

Weed 7: Your Ego and Inner Critic

Not long ago I was preparing for a big presentation, and I was introduced by the managing partner to Melanie, an insurance professional based in Dallas. She told a story about a referral she got to a law firm in Houston that was so good that it prompted her to plan a special trip there. Her goal was to spend a few days there and try to set up as many prospecting meetings as she could. She called around her network asking for introductions to people they knew in Houston.

When she got there, she had some meetings planned but could not get an appointment with the best opportunity she had – to the lawyer she was referred to. While the average salesperson will follow up once or twice and give up, Melanie *kept calling*. She said: "I got to know the receptionist who answered the phone. I asked her about her kids. I brought treats. I kept calling. Finally, towards the end of the week, the receptionist called me saying, "My boss had a cancellation. Can you be here in 45 minutes?"

"I was pretty new at my company, and I did not really know what I was talking about. Luckily it was a quality referral otherwise they would never have met me. While the attorney I met with has not become a client yet; he has referred me to several of his colleagues who have."

I asked her: How did you get past feeling like a pest when you kept calling? Her reply was priceless: **"I listened to the louder voice that said: "Keep pushing. They don't know they need this, and you do."**

There are two voices in your head. An ugly weed to address is to adjust the volume on your egoic self-talk. You want to:

    a) Expose your inner critic (your ego – which spends its entire time planting weeds)

b) Tune in more proactively to your inner hero – your heart, soul, gut instinct, and your joy that pulls the weeds and moves you towards mining your gold.

1. **Face Your Inner Critic - Why you aren't achieving the level of success you want?**

The story you tell yourself (often unwittingly) day in and day out about why you are not where you want to be becomes a self-fulfilling prophecy. Scary thought, isn't it? As much as you probably don't want to answer the question, I'd urge you to:

a) List out your responses in detail: I'm not where I want to be in my life because...

You've got to be totally honest with yourself. Were there experiences you had as a child that have limited who you think you can become and what you see yourself capable of doing? It's no new revelation that our parents were flawed human beings who did their best with the skills they had. But you don't want to give anyone the power now to determine who you are going to become. As Solomon Hicks says: "No one can write your story unless you give them the pen."

We've all had hardship, problems, and setbacks. Some people have been through real trauma. And this is all relative. Just because your past may not sound as challenging now as someone else's, it doesn't mean it hasn't cramped your true style. Conclude your response to the question with: "I'll never achieve the success I want because…"

You want to look at the story you've been telling yourself and feel *disgust*: see it dripping with *excuses* and the lack of ownership since you turned 18. Next, read the story aloud. Better, pretend that God or someone you respect enormously just walked into the room and tell them your story. Please, experience this versus just reading this.

If you don't change your story that's rife with weeds, your outcomes will likely be the same for the rest of your life.

b) Journal on this: How do I feel about letting this old story dictate the rest of my life and prevent me from mining my gold? Dig into the emotion of your excuse story.

c) **List out your limiting beliefs:** One of the most telling exercises I know of is this:

> i) **List five things you've always wanted to do but haven't**
>
> ii) **Then write three reasons beside each item**

Avoid putting 'time' and 'money' as reasons you've not done them because these diminish you. Err towards writing 'yet to manage my time effectively enough' or 'lack of resourcefulness.' Take responsibility for all your results. The reason to be clear on these things is to call them out in your new story…

2. **Clarify Your Inner Hero**

a) **Write your new story:** The easiest place to get clear about your own inner hero is by reversing what you wrote about yourself in your old story. If you lacked confidence, then you write about becoming increasingly confident. If you've been too much of a people pleaser, then you're someone who sets increasingly healthy boundaries and for whom 'no' is a complete sentence. Here's how mine opens:

"I am a resourceful, confident, young 55-year-old big thinker and role model who is ready to pursue his TRUEST passion in life and focus on the cool and positive things that can happen because of it."

I'd recommend including these phrases that I got from Dean Graziosi's *Millionaire Success Habits*: "I'm empowered because my childhood circumstances taught me…"

I added: "My childhood GIFTED me..." - and then list your greatest strengths.

"When I combine ...(strengths), my life is limitless."

This is powerful because **you want to see yourself as advantaged because of everything that happened to you.** It's the challenges we had in our past that typically hold us back and act as anchors. But what if that pain was meant to teach you something that only you can use to help others? How can use it as fuel?

I admit the first time I read this concept in a Fiona Harrold book, it seemed too far-fetched, but what's the alternative? Stay stuck? Mired in pain or self-pity? Many of these pain points were probably beyond your control. Now you can you be part of the solution rather than the problem. **One of the rarely spoken secrets to many people's big achievements was that they were driven by trauma. Use it.** (Just remember not let it use you always and forever from a place of pain because you'll never be happy)

> b) **Read your new story aloud at least twice/day and preferably first thing in the morning and last thing at night.** Edit it until you love it.
>
> c) **When you do mine your gold, how will that make you feel?** List out these feelings. Then **add them to your story now**. "Today I intend to feel..."

Why? Because why would not want to feel them now? And it will speed up your trajectory. The truth is you will be more motivated if you feel a certain way. Remember BJ Fogg's research in *Tiny Habits*? *"I change best when I feel good, not when I feel bad."*

Noah St John makes an interesting point in *The Secret Code of Success* when he asks: would you rather earn $1,000,000/year working for someone who treats you like scum and that you hate, or would you rather make $100,000/year doing work you love that fulfils your passions?

What we most want is to feel a certain way. And once the sticker shock wears off, you don't want soul destroying. Nor does it mean you won't make $1m doing what you love.

We think having a luxury lifestyle will guarantee feeling great, but it's not true. Affluent neighborhoods are full of lonely, miserable people. Some of them I see waiting for the early train to go to their golden-handcuff jobs. Some of them I overhear in my local coffee shop. Some gave up their pursuits to marry a very wealthy person. I've lived in one of those neighborhoods for nine years, so this is something I didn't read in a book (!) and I know someone who coaches spouses like this for a living.

d) **Compare the two stories:** Graziosi concludes: *"See how radically different the outcome of yor life will be by not only changing one story or one belief but by changing all the stories that do not serve your higher purpose or your true "why"."*

e) **Rewrite your life trajectory and become the person you want to be:** Give yourself time to see results. I really, really hope you do these exercises and turn up the volume on your heart and soul. Rewrite your life trajectory and become the person you want to be by exposing the weeds, replacing them with flowers and mining your gold.

PULL THE WEEDS FAST!

Weed 8: Going Downhill in the Second Half of Your Life

One evening, Harvard business professor Arthur C Brooks was on a flight to Washington, DC when he couldn't help but be absorbed by a quiet but emotional exchange between an elderly couple sitting in the row behind him. "It's not TRUE that no one needs you anymore," replied the wife to her despondent husband, "Oh, stop saying it would be better if you were dead."

He pictured an old man filled with regret because all his hard work had only led to unmet dreams and a lifetime of frustration and disappointment. Brooks continues: "As the lights switched on after touchdown, I finally got a look at the desolate man. I was shocked: I recognized him – he was well-known; famous, even. Then in his mid-eighties, he has been universally beloved as a hero for his courage, patriotism, and accomplishments of many decades ago." How was it possible he wished he was dead?

This led to Brooks looking himself in the mirror and looking at his own future. What he saw unsettled him – enough to write a book about it. He realized he was on the same path as the man on the plane – and as what he describes is true for most 'strivers' – people who have worked hard in the first half of their life and enjoyed their share (or bountiful) success. He explains this path in his book *Strength to Strength* as an unsustainable one that denies inevitable human decline and leads to desperate unhappiness and rage as you age and feel increasingly irrelevant.

First it helps to understand that, in his work, he found two types of intelligence. Fluid intelligence serves you well in your younger years and is based on reasoning, thinking flexibly, and solving novel problems. But this intelligence wanes in nature like athletic ability (only a bit later in life) and the only way to feel fulfilled into your 40's and beyond (it varies on your field), is to focus on using your crystallized intelligence which leverages your stock of acquired knowledge.

If you want to continue to mine your gold in the second half of your life – yes, perhaps in a different way – here are some suggestions.

1. Admit your success addiction

There is never enough success. It is easy to get hooked on always wanting more as you read about in chapter 7 on defining true success. You are not your job. It is not your identity. Release your attachment to success. Pull this weed fast! And keep pulling it.

2. Need less

True wealth is not simply having a lot; it is having enough. It is accepting yourself, it is focusing on what you can control, on what actually matters in life. If you can embrace this, you'll be richer than any billionaire, movie star, or pro athlete. - Ryan Holiday

Avoid the More Monster. Avoid chasing the pretty-looking weeds of money, power, pleasure, and fame because this addictive behavior brings only fleeting satisfaction. The more you have, the more you need, and it's never enough. It is always leaving you wanting more. The solution is to gradually reduce what's essential so you're pulling fewer weeds. As Seneca observed: "There is no enjoying the possession of anything valuable unless one has someone to share it with."

Be more purpose driven and focused on intrinsic (internal) goals. Seek interesting work that's enjoyable *and meaningful.* **"The work you do has to be the reward,"** advises Brooks. No more destinations or you will look for the next one and the next one. Perform your work from a place of love or through God as I discussed in Habit 1. You never know what impact your work will have - think of Van Gogh who never achieved fame in his lifetime. Focus on serving others.

3. Reflect on your death

When Eugene O'Kelly was 53, he was in the prime of his life as CEO of the Big Four accounting firm KPMG (U.S). Then he was told by doctors that he had a virulent form of cancer and most likely only three months to live. How he handled that time is an inspiring and sobering account in his book *Chasing Daylight*, and always worth the reality check that anything can happen to you or me any time.

Facing the fear of your death has great rewards that can help you appreciate the present far more. Live your eulogy virtues now – how do you want people to talk about you at your funeral? I admit this exercise is going to mean more if you are in the second half of your life. I remember doing this exercise after reading Stephen Covey's *The 7 Habits of Highly Effective People* when I was 28 and 39. It was helpful but I'm not sure it really sank in. It felt like I was jumping through the hoops that Covey suggested in order to get a revelation I wasn't ready for. Thinking more about it now I'm 55 and knowing my dad died at 58, it means much more.

The weed to pull is that this is too scary or depressing. Brooks believes that: "Resisting your decline will bring you misery and distract you from life's opportunities. We should not avoid the truth. We should stare right at it." Based on your parents and grandparents' lives, how many birthdays do you have left? For me, its somewhere between 3-40.

4. Build more roots and better relationships

Make relationships your source of meaning rather than your work. According to the longest study ever completed on lifestyles, habits, relationships, work, and happiness about what makes a good life - first started in 1938 at Harvard Medical School - **relationship satisfaction is the most important key to health and longevity**.

The long-time study director, George Valliant, described the most important element: "**Happiness is love.** Full stop. There are two pillars of happiness…One is love. The other is finding a way of coping with life that does not push love away." What did you learn about relationships in Habit 2 after reflecting on your present reality and on your past regrets?

Brooks argues you need *real friends* that bring you pleasure and, even better, where you share a love for something outside you both – not just *deal friends* who are merely useful. The weed to pull is the thinking that it takes too much time. Yes, you've got to want it. Relationships (your love for others) also take the sting out of professional decline. Love people.

5. **Make your weaknesses part of your authenticity and consider them gifts from God**

Brooks tells the remarkable story of Saul of Tarsus whom he describes as the most successful entrepreneur in history. Saul converted to Christianity in the first century and helped to compile a significant amount of the teachings of Christ and then spread that word across Asia Minor and Europe.

According to Brooks, his entrepreneurial genius was in publicly admitting his weaknesses and failings and using them as a source of strength:

"That is why, for Christ's sake, I delight in weaknesses, in insults, in hardships, in persecutions, in difficulties. For when I am weak, then I am strong." In a similar fashion to clarifying your inner hero, **he saw himself as advantaged *because* of *everything* that had happened to him.**

His sadness has attracted literally billions to the Christian faith. Better known as Paul the Apostle, he chose to see his weaknesses and struggles as life working FOR him rather

Definition of a proven process:

A success recipe, a health or sales system or a way to build a business that hundreds or thousands of others have replicated well.

It could include a **workout regimen or diet method** but I'm conscious some of these have pitfalls. *Exact* results vary but by and large it is a recipe - as with cooking - that you can trust will get you very good outcomes. It is not a brilliantly marketed anecdote on social media that worked for one person out of multiple thousands.

There is an infinite list to what might prevent you from doing what has been proven to work for others. While you have been shown *how* to do something…

1. **Cynicism. Maybe you don't believe it is a proven process**. You might be right! Do your homework; revisit my definition above. If it's worked for hundreds of others with enough similar traits/skills to you, you can jump in with both feet. Having a degree of cynicism is wise, but it is typically rooted in low self-confidence and pessimism, neither of which will help you mine your gold.

2. **You may not have the ability** - are there skills you need to help you succeed?

3. **You may not have the motivation** - how much do you want it? (See Habits 1 and 2)

4. **You may well think you know better**. 99% of the time, this is human self-deception at its best. Even my nine-year-old's stagger me with thinking they "know" most things in life (I thought this would happen when they were 14!) None of us can live longer enough to possibly think we will come up with best way to do more than a few things - out of seven billion people!

5. **You may not know how much you embrace *and resist* proven processes**. According to the Birkman Method, a behavioral and occupational assessment that helps people achieve higher performance through positive psychology, all of us vary in our approach to following through on structure and routine. It ranges on a scale of 1-100! Some people just want an outline to follow; some want a definite plan in place. Some of us want a lot of flexibility and others want a detailed, organized, and sequential process. The challenge with this comes in areas where you really may not know how to do something effectively or have a breakthrough - **hence what you _need_ (vs. *want*) is the benefit of using someone else's process.**

The weed in your garden is your resistance to *fully* using this process!

I'd recommend taking this assessment, so you are more aware of your own natural responses to being given a process to follow. I discovered I fall in the middle which means I like knowing there's a process, but I like some flexibility with getting there. This is a problem! If I only *partially* follow a process, its most likely I will end up with partial results and not even understand why! What the assessment suggests is I need to enforce more self-discipline on myself to follow a recipe and to resist my natural inclination to want to reinvent part of the wheel. It's okay for me to find this a struggle; at least I'm more self-aware about my own tendencies now.

I want to take this one step further to help your self-awareness. If you grew up with a micro-managing parent, you probably don't gravitate towards processes because you had your fill of structure growing up. Conversely, if you grew up in a household that was chaotic and unpredictable, you may well really embrace highly structured solutions. The key to this knowledge is to understand better where you might resist being told what to do and need to suck that up better, so you follow the recipe better.

6. **You may be unwilling to do what's outside your comfort zone.** Maybe the recipe subconsciously induces fear of failure (like me with multi-level marketing), so it is easier not to do everything that is recommended because you have unwittingly set up an 'out' you can live with when you don't get the desired results. Revisit why you want better results and face the uncomfortable in small steps**. Follow the habits in this book more closely** remembering that your brain is not hardwired well to support you making change. **I find an almost complete unwillingness to do anything even slightly outside the comfort zone is what stops some people.** They still take courses to learn new topics and might even read this book, but they don't actually take new uncomfortable actions that generate new results!

7. **You just don't do well with being told what to do** - that following someone else's system feels too restrictive for you. It is an affront to your 'independence.' You may have grown up with an overly controlling parent. Can you increase your trust in others while still applying your own common sense?

8. **You feel like you're giving up too much control** by taking the leap of faith. The solution lies in making small shifts. The solution is eased by focusing harder on all the things you can control in your life - and can you be open to letting a higher power drive the rest of the way? Even though Napoleon Hill steered clear of religion in his 1938 classic *Think and Grow Rich*, he had a chapter on the need for faith in order to achieve big results.

9. **You know successful people who don't the use the process *anymore*.** You may already know that others who used to follow the proven system successfully then went on to *change* how they did things and move away from the process – in other words, they did not continue to use the recipe forever. This can make you think that you can make up your own way right from the start. And sure, if you look hard enough, you might eventually find one or two very rare

exceptions of people who didn't follow that process at first who went on to do well. Typically, these are people who tried to do it their own way and hit a profound low in life, felt like total failures, and the pain from this drove them to make significant change in their life. You're making it too hard.

10. **You've picked the wrong time in your life to be attempting to follow the process.** Maybe you just have too much going on that is more important or draining.

11. **There's a strong chance you don't think you 'deserve' to get the same outstanding results as others. Your lack of belief that it will work for you may stem from a lack of worthiness.** (See Habit 4, Key 1: Elevate Your Worthiness)

Your weed to pull fast is whatever your biggest block is to implementing a proven process!

Clearly this is not a simple subject. Most of us are aware that the biggest risk takers and (sometimes) biggest rule breakers have created new businesses and systems that worked better. We forget that this is a *minute* percentage of people so the odds of us doing this soon are remote – and **do you have the time, desire, and money right now to reinvent this wheel?** Someone else has already figured it out.

Having an independence streak and not being a sheep is a healthy trait, but there are times when following a proven recipe just plain works and resisting it is at best stubborn and at worst foolish and a form of dysfunctional independence.

It is highly likely time to LET GO on this one and follow the plan.

I realize this defies logic and shows that how we act is *not* based on logic. Sure, the term 'proven process' is over-used now in marketing. Some proven processes are virtually unsustainable – one health regimen I did in my 30's comes to mind where you had to eat six meals six days/week and exercise with specific equipment six times/

week – but if you want positive change, you can't live life sitting in the stands or being the ship anchored in harbor.

Find your resistance, keep nudging yourself out of your prison-cell comfort zone, polish the necessary skills, show some faith in other members of the human race, and then have faith that you can get ever better outcomes yourself towards mining your gold. **Devote your energy to your zone of excellence** (from chapter 9) and, assuming this lies elsewhere**, follow someone else's proven process.**

PULL THE WEEDS FAST!

Weed 10: Wanting to Quit

In chapter 3, I shared what happened to John McCain's fighter plane when he was shot down during the Vietnam War and how he was a prisoner of war for five years – *two years* of them in solitary confinement.

I think you would agree that this is a life experience none of us can understand without having been through it – the sheer mental turmoil of it – but you can definitely understand wanting to quit. We've all been there. Most of the time, it is an ugly weed.

What can you learn about not quitting from someone who (likely) had it *much* worse than you - and went on to run for president of his country?

McCain's experiences were brutal. His right leg, left shoulder, and right arm were badly broken when his plane was shot down and not repaired properly so he was almost always in constant pain (for five *years*). He was tortured, often beaten and experienced frequent stomach problems; his life was saved by two fellow prisoners who nursed him back to survival. When he left the camp in 1973, he was a badly limping 100-pound skeleton.

How did he dig so deep and not quit? **And what can you replicate when you are next in a tough situation?**

Mark Salter, details this in *The Luckiest Man: Life with John McCain*.

a) **Adopt the McCain mind-set: "You weren't beaten until you quit."** After beatings by prison guards, biographer Mark Salter described how McCain would bounce back right away by banging on anything in reach and yelling out epithets to his captors. He encouraged others loudly after they were beaten too. His fighting spirit was an inspiration to all. *Now it's your turn.*

b) Get more human support

McCain said of being in solitary: "Without someone encouraging me, right away I started doubting myself." Despite being punished when caught talking to the prisoner in the cell next to him, Air Force major Bob Craner, he would wrap a shirt around the enamel cup each prisoner was provided and speak through the wall. He described his neighbor as "my dearest friend...the closest friend I ever had." And throughout this time they *never* saw each other. Having this support "saved me from going nuts," says McCain!

Who's cheering you on? **You need people who will support you *unconditionally*** (and sometimes we don't get that at home). Seek them out. See Key 10 in the next chapter.

c) Visualize what you want and keep your mind positively occupied

"He spent most hours reenacting stories from favorite books and films," wrote Salter. McCain admitted: "I'd get so wrapped up in them some days that I'd get pissed off if something interrupted me."

You want to keep your mind focused as quickly and as often as possible on positive thoughts that keep steering you back in a better direction. You face your challenges by taking proactive actions that are your best effort at a solution. Everyone needs to keep their head in an empowered place. I am no different. Each of us needs this more often than we realize.

The advanced level is to spend time picturing what you want. Darren, a recent client of mine in Washington DC, said he got through his tough early days as a new financial advisor responsible for bringing in business by "visualizing the success I'm going to have in five years. That only happens if I do the right thing now." – see Habit 4, Key 2 on this: Elevate Your Beliefs.

d) Get more divine support

As I shared in chapter 3, McCain's religious beliefs were a key factor in his ability to survive the ordeal and, according to Salter, were "never more potent than during his years in Hanoi. He spoke of religious experiences like they were epiphanies."

Even if you feel like quitting, remember you don't have to do this alone. Join the company of many great achievers and leaders who, throughout human history, have leaned on God (with the faith of their choice or no religion at all).

e) Stay true to your values

The prison camp leadership were always looking to invent positive publicity to shame the US troops who had been bombing them and attempt to present themselves to the global media in a positive light.

McCain's father was a high-ranking military official who at one point during the war was the Navy's CINCPAC – commander in chief in the Pacific. Having read this in the US newspapers, the camp commandant offered McCain early release several times ahead of other POWs who had been in the camp longer. In return, McCain had only to say favorable things about his captors. Despite missing his wife and young child terribly, every time McCain was asked to do this, he would refuse to be released because there were other US POWs who had been imprisoned longer than him and because he would not compromise his values by telling the world media that his captors were humane and kind when they mostly abusive and brutal.

Why did you decide to do what you're doing now in the first place? If it still aligns with what you value most in life – as you identified in Chapter 7 - stay the course and keep on keeping on. Dawn will break.

Why is it so common to give up when you're so close to a breakthrough?

"Effort only fully releases its reward after a person refuses to quit."- Napoleon Hill

In Weed 3, I wrote about Christopher who committed suicide about 18 months after he gave up on his job in sales. About a year after Christopher left his position, one of the key relationships he had been developing in Chicago with Richard, a trust and estate lawyer, had a referral for him for a $30m opportunity. Richard called me because he couldn't get a hold of him. I introduced Christopher to a lot of people and whenever people asked after him, it was clear he had made a strong positive impression and was on his way to turning some of these relationships into revenue opportunities. It was a matter of time. He just had to stay in line and keep doing what he was doing.

At no point do I pretend commission-only sales or being self-employed is easy or that it is for everyone. Life is seldom easy. It can be hard to pull the weeds and plant the flowers at any age. Christopher was in his mid-50's. So much of it requires persistence and being able mentally to bounce back. One of the craziest parts about achieving a breakthrough is that part of the process includes living with a period of discomfort that causes many people to quit. I've been tempted to do the same more times than I care to admit. Sometimes it feels like there's no one out 'there'.

Napoleon Hill wrote about the phenomenon in *Think and Grow Rich* in 1938 that many people give up when they are in fact very close to a breakthrough and, ironically, the rewards are just around the corner. Why is that?

I remember once quitting a personal development course I was taking – I can't even remember what my 'reasons' were - but I do remember feeling really uncomfortable with what I'd committed to do – and that was to finish writing my first book (*Fearless Referrals*). If the leader of the course had not phoned me one Saturday while I was walking my dog to challenge my decision, and if I had not journaled that night to unearth a pattern I had of abandoning certain things in my life, who knows when I would have completed that book?

I'd already spent three years listening to the neurotic voice in my head telling me that writing a book wasn't necessary and wouldn't make a difference – and did I really have anything useful to say anyway?

1. **The alarm bells are going off inside your head and you feel out of sorts**

   Interpret this alarm as merely your internal GPS telling you you're changing direction.

I described this in chapter 11 – Understand Your Garden. What makes it hard is you genuinely feel 'off' and out of sync during these periods. It can cause you to doubt your progress and talk yourself into stopping what you're doing differently that's actually helping you to make positive change.

The internal protest happens because of the change you're experiencing. You might not be sleeping as well or have some psychosomatic physical ailment. I get cold sores on the upper left side of my lip.

The key is to remember what Steven Kotler calls the "Challenge-Skills Sweet Spot" and know how far to push yourself outside your comfort zone without freaking out and giving up! I've made this mistake. **It takes practice. It is full of trial and error.** We all have a different risk quotient muscle to develop.

2. Your positive changes may sometimes have loved ones around you protesting.

This can put you on a slippery slope to quitting. This is where your people pleasing trait may sabotage you from your own success.

Perhaps your partner doesn't like you getting up earlier, going to evening events, or adopting healthier eating habits. This is a really tricky one because they are taking your change personally in some way. They might be somewhat threatened by the improvements you're working on because they are not growing in that area. At a minimum, you are threatening their comfort zone. This has nothing to do with you and do not take this personally!

If you've not yet achieved your breakthrough, don't give up on any of the changes/positive actions you've been taking. In all likelihood, you don't want to give up on them after your breakthrough either! And, yes, I have absolutely experienced these challenges myself and know how protracted such difficulties can last. You only have one life to take your best shot. If you want better results, don't be cajoled by someone else. Keep your eyes on the prize.

Remember, doing the work and doing the habits is the victory. As Ryan Holiday insists, *"Discipline is the win. When you are just about the work…you won. When you know you put your best into it…you won. When your self-worth isn't predicated on things outside your control…you won."*

3. The ego voice in your head will try to convince you that you've done enough

It's very common and very easy to abandon a best practice by convincing yourself that "I've got it now". This is self-deceit at its worst because the ego voice in your head convinces you that you don't need to keep doing something that has been really helpful in helping you make the positive change in the first place.

High achievers know their weaknesses enough to know that they need certain uncomfortable activities in their life and that they need certain accountability. They actually fear that they may not do something on their own. It's like working with a personal trainer. Yes, you might exercise without one, but with a trainer you know you consistently push yourself harder, get better results, and save your mental energy and daily quotient of self-discipline for what you're best at. It can be the same with some coaches. Seek out more accountability!

4. **You've had an epiphany or mental breakthrough about one of your obstacles, so it's tempting to give up on a best practice even though you have not reached your goal yet**

Be very careful about giving up on something that has been part of your success recipe towards breakthrough – especially if you've not crossed any obvious finish line. It's true that what got you here won't get you there, so once you've reached a certain milestone, it's wise to reassess as you may well need to make new uncomfortable adjustments.

Just hold off on that until you've proven your breakthrough – even if you've had an epiphany about one of your obstacle areas. This is partly because you might have other obstacles in the way too! Life has a strange knack of throwing numerous challenges our way when we get closer to our most treasured targets, because there are lessons we've not been open or ready to learn yet.

Everyone is tempted to quit sometimes. Almost all of the time, ignore these messages from your scared ego.

In concluding Habit 3, my wish for you is to take a breath and be kinder to yourself. Every human mind has plenty of weeds in it and many of them were programmed into your brain long ago. Do not be discouraged. I realize that we all crave simple explanations to solve problems and make change.

While life can put all kinds of weeds in your garden, remember that you can pull almost all of these weeds AND you can also put all kinds of flowers in their place too.

Do your best to feel empowered by knowing what the enemy looks like. Make love your purpose. Refuel from Habit 2. **PULL THE WEEDS FAST, pull them over and over, and focus on all the positive areas you can control...**

HABIT 4:
ELEVATE YOUR CONTROL

5 Mindsets of Worthiness

You are born worthy

You are enough (already)

I've worked really hard to get here.

If not me, then who?

Are my goals worthy of me?

CHAPTER 14

Elevate Your Control

Plant Your Garden

This is the fun part. *Now that you've pulled some weeds, made some room in your mind*, released some of the negative emotion and weakened some of the old neural pathways:

What empowered and inspired thoughts do you want to plant in your subconscious so you can mine your gold?

Habit 4 is about all the areas of your life you can exert control over and elevate in the same way a rising tide raises all boats.

It's not about perfectly elevating every area at the same time but knowing that when you do positive work on one area, it will benefit you and those around you in multiple ways and have other positive knock-on effects.

I believe that many of our challenges stem from not understanding self-worth and that is why it's the first key to address.

Key 1: Elevate Your Worthiness

"Becoming someone else was my drug of choice," declares musician, writer, and activist Antonio Michael Downing. "My personas were the cure for my self-loathing," he explains in his book *Saga Boy*. Raised in Trinidad by his grandmother, he was abruptly hauled away at the age of 11 when she died to live with an aunt in Wabigoon, a rural part of Canada, where they were the only black family.

A year later he was yanked on stage by the singer of an Alice Cooper cover band and came to believe that performing could be his salvation – "to sanctify all the awful away. To redeem my life into something worthy." After tracking down and being again rejected by his birth parents, the shame and the desire to run away from a family he describes as "a patchwork of broken things," leads to a journey of increasingly extravagant musical personalities. "I threw myself into my aliases one after the other…I wanted those disguises to digest the frightened immigrant boy and spit out someone worthy." He craved achieving 'success' so that he could feel good enough. One of those highlights was being the lead singer of a band that opened for Beady Eye, which was the famous Brit pop band Oasis minus Noel Gallagher on their 2012 UK tour.

Back in Toronto working in sales and his next music persona, he cheated on his long-standing girlfriend Eryn, the one solid person in his life. His best rationale? Lack of worthiness: "when the home, the stability I had told myself I wanted for so long was within my grasp, I sabotaged it so I could run away…She was my last chance to feel fully human."

After his brother relapsed into drugs again and revealed he was molested as a child by neighbors, Downing knew it was time to face his own trauma. He too had been raped as a boy by these same neighbors, lured into the bush with a once-a-year treat of salted peanuts. He went looking for therapy too.

Depicting himself as "a poster child for what happens to adults after childhood trauma: poor impulse control, difficulty controlling emotions, shame and guilt, feelings of hopelessness, sleep disorders, depression, sexual compulsiveness," the therapist told him: "You should be proud of yourself," because he had done much better than most people who had survived what he had.

The therapist commended Downing for pursuing his music and writing because they had saved him. "Art is sometimes the most effective therapy…You needed to do it. You needed it to survive." Downing thought he'd pursued music to hide and let out his anger but adds: "While I was busy hiding from myself, words and music had saved me."

His healing process continued to include times where he tried too hard: **"I ran hard, but I never seemed to catch the thing I was chasing."** He was always trying to be good enough. "I'd spent my life pretending I'd never been raped." He knew he had to face it, grieve for the confused child who was hurt and find healthy ways to let it go.

Downing fought his anger and being "sick of the folly of people who were supposed to protect us but instead left us to the wolves." He started to embrace his Trini roots, to embrace the fun-loving boy he was before his assault, and he started flying back to Trinidad for carnivals. Slowly, it brought him back to life, to feeling "a little more whole, a little more rooted, a little more comfortable in my skin."

He also started to forgive. He acknowledged how hard life had been for the adult generations before him: "They were Caribbean women, mules of the empire, forced to carry the burden of the (British) crown's dreadful legacy, of Black bodies chained to the spines of ships, of broken families, of men disempowered, stripped of their status in the home."

The conclusion he came to about his parents and those who raised him is the same as the one we all have to come to: **they had done their best.** "I, too, was ready to forgive…they had all done their best." He also came to terms with what God was to him (among other things): "God was the song I was always trying to sing, the word I needed to write." And the world noticed Downing, named by the RBC Taylor Prize in 2017 as one of Canada's top emerging authors for nonfiction.

How much success do you deserve in your life? Do you really think you're worthy of the best that life has to offer? Or that you 'belong' at the highest levels of your field? Talk about loaded questions.

You don't need to have been sexually abused to find it difficult to feel worthy of great things in life. Our brains – like Downing's - have been bombarded with mixed messages on that since birth. **We all have wounds from childhood**. Sadly, we are rarely conscious of these and so can lead our lives thinking that we are getting our just rewards. **Scarily, we can get used to feeling how we feel and consider it normal. We risk playing small. We risk not mining our gold.**

There are Five Mindsets to Elevate Your Worthiness:

1: You are born worthy
2: You are enough (already)
3: "I've worked really hard to get here."
4: "If not me, then who?"
5: "Are my goals worthy of me?"

MINDSET 1: You are born worthy

I admit this can be a challenging concept to grasp not least because it belongs to your distant past! But read this slowly: When you're an infant, you are loved unconditionally. You don't have to be, do, or have something special. You are a totally lovable baby who can do no wrong - you cry, drool, eat and produce messes out of both ends yet you are worthy of love and all good things simply by existing. You don't have to get an A grade in burping or demonstrate high proficiency at staring at the mobile above your crib to be worthy enough to aim for the stars. You are born with your vein of gold.

While you can't remember this, you were born with the ability to generate your own happiness and feelings of love and worthiness - they do not have to be generated on the outside. You were fully deserving to spend your time lying down and making gurgling noises.

Then you 'learn' you're only worthy under certain external circumstances...

Unfortunately, not too far along the line, you start to believe that you're only worthy of happiness and higher outcomes when an outside event happens – when someone wants to play with you, when someone compliments you or gives you their attention. As we get older, the worthiness is determined when someone is attracted to you, wants to be your friend, or wants to hire you to do some work. But this didn't impact your feelings of worthiness and happiness when you were an infant. You were born worthy.

You become an imperfect human who makes mistakes, tests boundaries and who wants to do things differently sometimes from those around you because you don't have the same DNA as any other human on the planet. Unfortunately, **this is also typically where you experience conditional love**. And it often starts to derail your sense of worthiness because it suggests you are only worthy of this external attention IF you follow someone else's expectations.

Along the way you upset others for not being exactly what they like best and you don't conform to what makes life easiest for them. You get things wrong at school. In the playground, you notice that some people are faster than you or more popular. In the classroom some of them are better at certain things than you are - or are bigger or better looking. Sometimes.

We notice that certain people in our culture get much more attention than most other people. They're famous and sometimes rich. They have power, money, looks, athletic ability or are portrayed as highly intelligent. Their 'success' stories are typically over-simplified, so we are led to assume that they enjoy levels of near perfection and have it all figured out.

We, however, live in imperfect families that never have it all figured out and have problems we pretend in public aren't there - even though all families have their problems and secrets. Unfortunately, it's not socially acceptable to talk openly about most of these. Different dysfunctions and failings are modelled to us and sometimes we grow up believing these ways of being are 'normal'. It can all lead to feeling less deserving.

If this isn't enough, almost everywhere we turn, we are getting messages from marketers telling us: 'you need this', 'watch this', 'listen to this', 'more people will want to be around you if you buy this, look like that, or smell this way', and 'this will make you happier/healthier/cooler and look successful'. You absorb this world from advertisers who remind you daily about all the things in your life you don't have that would make your life perfect. You can't help wondering if you deserve them.

So, it's pretty easy not to feel like a world champion if you let even *some* of this linger in your head!

It's pretty easy to assume you probably don't deserve as much as some other people and that most people are way ahead of you - even though everybody is winging it more often than they will ever acknowledge!

We compound this by unwittingly spending time with people just like us in an attempt to make us feel better about ourselves. And we try to notice the people that we think we are better than – also in an attempt to make ourselves feel better.

Yet despite all this unhelpful messaging, it's clearly human nature to want more from life: to want better health, more money, more happiness and to feel more successful. And one of the obstacles we hit is **feeling like we don't deserve it because of many of the above**

experiences and buying into the idea that we are different in a lower status way.

Let's start with four FACTS about your worthiness to mine your gold and enjoy more success:

1. *No one* is inherently better than you or more deserving (and no one is inherently worse than you or less deserving).
2. *No one* has it all figured out. Everyone is winging it at times – especially parents (so forgive yours; they did their best with the skills that they had).
3. Everyone has problems. Most people would happily take their pile of problems compared to the other seven billion people around the world.
4. Michael Neill, a bestselling author who's coached many high-profile people, said that most of his uber 'successful' clients had "the self-worth of a gnat". So, you're not alone if you don't always feel great about yourself. Nor is it a requirement for high achievement.

Now, I admit rational facts only go so far on this topic but hopefully it helps to realize **you're in a *much* more similar boat with everyone else – despite appearances.** And, if everyone has plenty of insecurity, you can say to yourself:

'The playing field of self-worth is mostly even and much lower than I realized.

I can play wherever I want. I can mine my gold now.'

MINDSET 2: You are enough (already)

Realize you're born with self-worth, love, and happiness so you can never lose them or find them 'out there'. When you're born, you don't question your worthiness for whatever you want in life.

You're able to feel love and be happy on your own (so long as you're fed and dry)!

It is doubt that builds gradually because you learn that you are not a perfect machine who is the best at everything and can please everyone else all the time when everyone else has their own shortcomings, problems, and unmet needs. The ego shows up demanding attention and the ego is the opposite to your Unconditioned Self which comes from love.

How would you live your day if you knew that you already had enough **self-worth, love, and happiness because these were inherently inside you already?**

Since the thought may never have occurred to you in your entire life, the question may seem almost impossible to comprehend at first.

How would you feel if you didn't have to prove anything to anyone?

These are both beautiful questions.

How different would your life have been if you hadn't felt a need to please your mother or father? It's almost an impossible question, yet *subconsciously* this is a powerful driver for many people throughout their lives - even after their parents have died.

Trying to do certain things because *deep down* you want to please a parent is a dangerous endeavor. Some parents may never be satisfied (because of their own issues); you could devote a lot of blood, sweat and tears into a fruitless campaign trying to fill a psychological need that you have no control over.

I DO want to encourage you to ask yourself more deeply:

WHY am I choosing what I choose now?

This is something entirely within your control.

I want you to contemplate: "To what extent does this activity inspire me?"

"To what extent does this activity align with my strengths and passions?

Or is it mostly something to please someone else?"

Also think about this: **what if you no longer had to prove yourself to anyone?**

Because innately *you are already enough as a human being.*

Sit with this for a while.

"I am enough already"

"I don't have to prove anything to anyone."

You don't *have* to make a lot of money
You don't *have* to make endless sales
You don't *have* to prove yourself at work anymore.
You don't *have* to be triathalon fit
You don't *have* to be picture perfect… to be good enough as a human being.
(and, yes, you *can* if that's something you genuinely value)

If you didn't have to prove anything for the rest of the year, what would you do?

At first when I ask people this question, I can literally see them physically relax and they start to feel less anxious. It finally gives them some permission to be at peace with themselves without feeling a need to change *one single thing*.

We can't pretend this is easy when almost everywhere we look we are surrounded by messages, promotions, and advertisements whose sole purpose is to persuade us that we need what they are offering, that we have a flaw or problem they can solve – that there is something missing or wrong with us. And since none of us is perfect, it's quite easy to fall into that rabbit hole.

When you contemplate the idea that you have nothing to prove, you can stop trying to be someone you are not. You can start to listen more closely to the beat of your own drum and tap back into your vein of gold. And what does it tell you?

It is such a foreign concept that you probably need quite a lot of time and repetition to take it seriously. At first, your response may be a reaction to having stuffed up some of your desires too much. You might need a period of doing much less than you usually do simply to recalibrate because you've been so busy 'doing'. Is your plug in too tight? You might over-do it in the relaxing, eating unhealthy food, or watching television departments.

But once you can feel more centered, then you can listen to the parts of you that are based on what really inspires you.

What makes you feel *alive*?

What have been some of your most enjoyable experiences?

What are some of your fondest memories?

Really where I'm coming from is not to suggest you do nothing with your life, but to do what you *really* want - to unearth your gold - and do it from a place of knowing you're enough already. This really puts you in a more powerful position ironically to achieve more and be less attached to it which means to be more focused on what matters most to you. To feel less needy and unworthy and instead to feel more centered and alive.

How can you keep reminding yourself? I am enough already!

Adopt an increasingly worthy mindset – the same as high achievers I've worked with

You are going to need a mindset that affirms that you are good enough to reach greater heights and silence any voice that tries to talk you out of it.

There are three <u>self-talk</u> keys from people I've coached or met along the way who believed they were 'worthy' to accomplish whatever they wanted:

MINDSET 3: "I've worked really hard to get here."

"… it's okay for me to mine my gold. It's okay for me to experience ever-greater levels of success."

Greg grew up poor in Poland and one day his parents put all their belongings in a car and moved to Germany. He did well in school there and ended up studying medicine. Now he is a plastic surgeon working on Harley Street, London's most prestigious location for high-end physicians.

When I interviewed him in 2019 for my podcast, I asked him whether he had ever had any worthiness issues coming from such humble origins and growing up as an outsider. In his German-accented English he quickly shook his head and informed me: *"Matt, I've worked my face off."* He then went on to tell me how even when he went on holiday, he would seek out well-known peers so he could observe their surgeries and learn from them.

The first time I ever talked to Scott he said: "Matt, my average current client is worth between $1-3m. I want to get that to $5m by the end of the year. Can you help me?"

Scott took *consistent* action to make this goal happen *and* within seven years his average client was worth $50m (no typo). When I asked him whether he had ever had any worthiness issues consistently scaling his business, he replied: *"Worthiness? I'm a hard-working, thoughtful advisor with a great network."*

Amanda went from being a suicidal, alcoholic 20-something in her native Australia to a *three-time* CrossFit Games World Champion in her late 30's. When I asked her whether she had ever had any worthiness issues about her remarkable turnaround in life, she told me: *"I was willing to run the hard yards. When I thought I couldn't go on, I just did the next most important thing. I just kept turning up. I've been constantly testing and pushing and exploring my capacities to discover that there's a bedrock in me which is graft!"*

The moral of the story is this: many high performers are at peace with their outstanding accomplishments because they know they've worked hard to be where they are today, and that's good enough for them!

MINDSET 4: "If not me, then who?"

Many years ago, I coached a disability insurance specialist called Corey. He was very uncomfortable about asking people in his network for referrals. I suggested he think on paper about why others should refer him.

He listed off numerous reasons, then I asked him if he got anything from the exercise. He thought about it and said: *"I'm not sure, but I did come to the conclusion: 'If not me, then who?' I mean someone's going to get the business; it might as well be me."*

Every time I talked to Corey, he would end up making the same comment: *"But you know what, Matt? If not me, then who?"* It took me three months to notice how often he said this until it occurred to me to point this out to him. He said he had written this phrase on a Post

It note, put it on the cover of his work planner, and would look at it several times a day.

He literally rewired his thinking to give himself permission to keep asking and it made an enormous difference to his business and the number of people he was able to help – *and it has every year since.*

This is a common high achiever mindset, and it is not arrogant. It doesn't say "I'm better than everyone else." It simply asserts that **you can be as helpful as anyone else, so you might as well speak up and ask for that introduction!**

A complementary mindset to this is: "I can bring a lot of value to this person. I can be a really useful resource."

"Pull the weeds." Filter the doubt out of your mind as fast as you can

Stacy grew up poor and 'second-class' as an African American in the Jim Crow south of the US and has been a multi-millionaire financial advisor for the past three decades. When I asked him whether he had ever had any worthiness issues, he acted as if the word didn't exist in his vocabulary! How did he do that?

Amanda the CrossFit Games World Champion told me what she had learned from spending an increasing amount of time with other high performers: don't give airtime to whether you are worthy or not: *"Most people bang around life not really realizing that thoughts aren't facts. Feelings aren't facts. I heard it a decade ago and it was a revelation to me because I was a slave to my thoughts.* **I filter out what is rubbish and what are lies."** In other words: pull the weeds fast!

Vincent grew up poor and remained that way until he committed suicide at the age of 37 (what a tragedy!). Despite being completely unappreciated in his lifetime, he is now considered one of the greatest artists who ever lived. In a letter to his brother Theo, Van Gogh acknowledged that he was worthy of success: *"I do not think I am aiming too high. I will make drawings that will amaze some people."*

Then he noted what it took (see Mindset 3 again above): *"Art requires resolute and unremitting industry …constant industry**, as also the power of maintaining one's own point of view against the assertions of others."***

In other words, listen to the voice in your head that wants you to do great work and mine your gold, not the naysayers in your world nor the voice in your own head talking you out of it. You need enough self-belief to keep you in the game and to remind you that you're at least as good as others.

MINDSET 5: "Are my goals worthy of me?"

Should you doubt your worthiness to pursue a big goal, flip the script and instead focus on the merits of what you want. Is your professional goal worthy of you? Or are there loftier goals more worthy of you and your time during this one journey on Earth?

This is the time to revisit your definition of success and your purpose. Listen to your heart. Mine your gold. Who do you want to serve in your lifetime? Is your soul being moved? Revisit those goals with better questions.

The message is clear: **find a mindset that affirms that you are good enough to reach greater heights and silence any voice that tries to talk you out of it.**

THE 5 HABITS TO ELEVATE YOUR WORTHINESS

1. **Let Love Drive**
2. **Fuel Up Often**
3. **Pull the Weeds!**
4. **Elevate Your Control**

5. Be and Do Your Change *Consistently*

So much of what we do and don't do is *unwittingly* influenced by whether we think we are good enough. The most commonplace evidence of that is in the income ceiling almost everybody has – that comfort zone of how much you are comfortable earning. Don't you want to see that change? There are *many* things you can do to shift what you think you deserve.

The five habits in this book are all designed to help you raise your worthiness.

1. Make love your purpose and letting God drive boosts worthiness

This is Habit 1. When you are influenced by love instead of social norms, too many business goals and 'shoulds', it centers you beautifully. When love is your purpose in life, you can let love inspire your actions and desire to help others; love can inspire you to provide a better life for your family – and it will be much better received!

Letting go of trying to control everything and giving some of it up to God (with or without the religion), I started to feel better and more worthy because my center - my heart - comes from the same source as yours. **This centering source of love is full of worthiness.**

Whether it's love or God or both, **when your life has a purpose greater than you, you find yourself rising to the occasion** and filling the bigger shoes.

Remember to focus only on what you can control. A really useful small habit here is:

After I feel frustrated,

I will ask myself if it's something I can control or not.

Then feel good.

2. Finding deeper motivation to get you DOING MORE and doubting less boosts worthiness

This is Habit 2: Whether your drive comes from past pain, a cause, being clear about what true success is for you, or by an exciting future vision, *successful people do more*.

Whenever I think of accomplished athletes, artists, and performers from the past like Shakespeare, Da Vinci or Jesse Owens; they had no knowledge of the science of achievement. *Think and Grow Rich* had not been published! As they got ever better at their craft, it wasn't just their confidence that grew. **Their mindset/thinking had to shift too so that they felt worthy of the accolades they received** and confident enough to write/paint/run again and not psych themselves out.

This didn't happen consciously; it happened because they contin-ued to take a lot of action that proved a self-fulfilling prophecy for their brains: "I am an ever-improving writer/artist/athlete".

REPETITION!!! Feed your own brain the messaging it needs to build your sense of worthiness sp you mine your gold fully. And don't stop.

3. Pulling the weeds boosts worthiness

This is habit 3: There are many ways we make our lives harder that unwittingly reinforce a lack of worthiness: self-induced crises, worry, envy, comparison, people pleasing, and feelings of guilt. Awareness of these weeds can help you not make similar errors or at least do them less.

4. Building your life on what you can control builds your worthiness

These dozen keys make up this habit – Habit 4!

5. Changing your 'identity', focusing on power habits, and doing your best boosts worthiness

This is habit 5!

The other conclusion is this: if you're worrying about worthiness, you're on the wrong path.

I spent much of my life hardwired to question whether I was 'good enough' for this or that and my heart goes out to all those who have the same mental battles. You can spend your whole life trying to feel good enough and never actually feel it. Fortunately, you now have a long laundry list of things you can do that will help.

The easier route is to learn these mindsets from high achievers and do the same:

1: You are born worthy

2: You are enough (already)

3: "I've worked really hard to get here."

4: "If not me, then who?"

5: "Are my goals worthy of me?"

Talk to yourself differently. Know you are as good as anyone else and pull the weeds fast - filter out the unempowering thoughts so you can get on with doing what you were put on this earth to do: make a positive difference.

Elevate your worthiness and elevate your control!

5 Steps to Elevate Your Beliefs

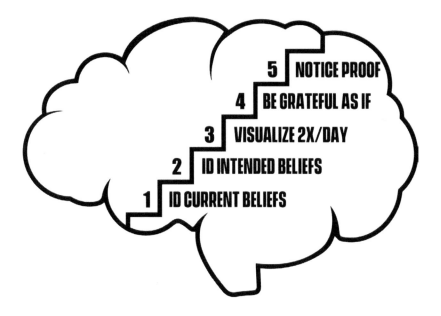

Key 2: Elevate Your Beliefs

"Here's the secret to the quest for deep and lasting self-belief: You can choose to believe anything you want." - Fiona Harrold

"Nurture your mind with great thoughts, for you will never go any higher than you think."- Benjamin Disraeli

Let Big Thoughts Occur to You

When you were 18, what did you most want to do with your adult life?

Not too long ago, Steffen, a coach I was working with, asked me the above question that got me thinking about old dreams of mine from childhood. When I was 18, my 'dreams' were either to be prime minister or a comedy script writer (either help people or find a way to make them laugh!). My understanding of a dream at the time was more of a distant someday 'hope'. I say this because I didn't exactly pursue either of these dreams. I attended a one-day playwriting course with Ben Kingsley in Stratford (who was playing Othello at the time) and did nothing more beyond it.

Looking back, I didn't really believe these things were possible for me. **The thought never even crossed my mind** to take them seriously. They didn't exist in my worldview.

And this is exactly my point. First, you have to think these thoughts and take them seriously.

What big dreams would you love to realize?

One thing is for certain, you are not going to come up with things that are impossible. If you are too old or lack the ability to qualify for the Olympics, you won't make this a dream. You will come up with a different physical challenge. If you can't sing, you aren't going to aspire to perform at the Sydney Opera House. Not sober anyway.

The first thing you have to do is expand what you see as possible in your world. All of us has a limit on the size of ideas we will consider.

The only way you can grow much bigger is to first entertain the idea that something bigger is possible – that you can plant more beautiful flowers in your garden. **This will help to elevate your control of all areas of your life.**

Then start to *do* things in multiple areas of your life that stretch you and your thinking into reconsidering what is possible for you. None of this is easy. You need to embrace a new relationship with change and variety to keep your mind on its toes.

These 'flowers' need planting – then *memorizing*. This is best done in a relaxed, meditative state either first thing in the morning or right before bed, but any kind of mental repetition will make a difference.

First, your subconscious mind must be told what you want. This is something you do with your conscious mind.

5 Steps to Elevating Your Beliefs and Boosting Your Gold Mining

1. **Identify your current beliefs**

This is easier than you might think. **Simply look at your current outcomes to discover what you currently believe.**

If you are out of shape, that's what you currently believe you deserve and expect (I know, scary, isn't it?)

If your marriage is mediocre, that's what you currently believe you deserve and expect.

If your finances are strong, that's what you currently believe you deserve and expect.

If your relationships with your children are strong, that's what you currently believe you deserve and expect.

The most effective way to write this down is to draw a line down the middle of a page and **write the current beliefs on the left side:** "I deserve and expect a mediocre professional life."

"I deserve and expect to feel too busy and stretched and short on time."

At least answer a-d, you can pick and choose the rest depending on how much time you have:

a) Your key relationships: "I deserve and expect…"
b) Your business/vocation:
c) Your finances:
d) Your physical health:
e) Your mental health:
Your self-belief:
How confident you feel:
How much you respect yourself:
Your sense of worthiness to achieve your long-term goals:
How happy you feel:
Degree to which you feel positively challenged:
Degree to which you tune into your intuition and trust your gut instinct:
How constructively you deal with anger and other negative emotions:
f) Sense of spiritual connection:
g) Adventures/fun/hobbies:
h) Contribution and giving back:
i) Living your purpose:

2. **Identify your intended beliefs (the ones you *really* want)**.

These are the ones you want to fuel and engrain in your mind as real.

FIRST: To get a stronger sense of what you really want to believe...

Using the same categories a) – i) above, start by *answering this question for each area of your life:* What do you want?

THESE QUESTIONS ARE ALSO VALUABLE:

*How focused are you on what you do best and love to do (your zone of excellence)?

*Where would you like to make a bigger impact?

*Most importantly, how much are you enjoying your journey?

*If you had all the time, resources, and money in the world, how would you spend your time?

<u>*What would you do if you knew you couldn't fail?</u>

This is my absolute favorite question.

What does a *typical* IDEAL MONTH look like? This is important. Describe or map out a month that is a model of how you want to spend your time month-in and month-out. If it helps, imagine you've just got a long vacation out of your system. Have as much fun with this as you can. And, yes, you do deserve to think this through!

Use these for new targets. THEN you are even better positioned to think clearly about how far you can get along this path in upcoming years.

NOW ELEVATE YOUR BELIEFS!

On the right-hand side, write down what you intend to believe. "I deserve and expect to feel charged and deeply fulfilled by my vocation."

"I deserve and expect to have enough time to do all the things that matter deeply to me."

Put all of your new beliefs somewhere visible to keep reinforcing them. Review them often with love.

Lastly, picture the exact environment you want for and create a vision board:

      a) Your ideal family life and home

      b) Your ideal business

      c) Experiences and adventures you want

Find the pictures that portray this vision and put them on a vision board so you can see it often throughout the day.

As Dean Graziosi writes in *Millionaire Success Habits*: "If you don't have a vision and clarity on the destination you want to reach, you'll simply never get there."

3. **Visualize your gold mining beliefs twice daily**

Repeatedly develop new neural connections through emotionally-charged visualization and positive messaging in a meditative state. You do it to influence your subconscious.

You do it to help you stay in the game long enough to reach your goal. Gareth Timmins explains this brilliantly in *Becoming the 0.1%* which describes the mind-bendingly grueling process to become a Royal Marine commando and earn the Green Beret – a world renowned symbol of excellence. He says that there are times you will lose sight of what you're aiming for and recommends that you "visualize what achieving the end goal will do for you; reinforce how it will alter the trajectory of your life; what opportunities will come after achieving it and, notably, why you are choosing to leave the environment you currently inhabit." (How to face fear of success, remember?)

Use this process recommended by John Assaraf and Murray Smith:

a) Meditate a little to get in a relaxed state

b) Think of an emotional anchor*

c) Visualize the same images of your raised beliefs each time *full of positive emotion*

d) State the most important new belief while in this emotional state.

*The <u>emotional anchor</u> is an experience you had that where you were "on fire" – a time when you played your best-ever game or were so inspired you gave your best-ever presentation. It could be a day that felt like a dream, a day when you were on a roll and it felt like everything was going your way, or a day you were totally in love or were mesmerized by nature. Then from this state, you start to picture what you most want personally and professionally.

Your subconscious mind cannot tell the difference between something you imagine in your mind and something you actually experience. Assaraf describes it as a "magnificent blind spot" that the subconscious has: *"our conscious brain has an amazing capacity to create pictures through imagination – pictures that the powerhouse of our nonconscious cannot distinguish from the "real" thing."*

Then your subconscious brain connects you with the quantum field of infinite intelligence which has access to all knowledge.

Water and Tend Your Garden of Elevated Beliefs

Success at influencing your subconscious mind and changing your beliefs comes over time through constant watering. Yes, this is the part that requires patience and persistence (doesn't everything worthwhile?)

Choose your hard: choose to work diligently to build the beliefs you want or choose to believe something that forever does not empower you

The two keys to conjuring up the new raised beliefs from the inside backed by plenty of action are: **REPETITION AND EMOTIONAL IMPACT**

Remember from chapter 2 and Eckhart Tolle's three ways to do everything? Enjoyment and enthusiasm were two of them. Remember Thomas Troward saying that putting your full spirit into everything was "the great secret to life"? Napoleon Hill learned this too from his research a hundred years ago. If you want your beliefs to shift: *"Your subconscious mind will only act upon instructions that are emotionalized and handed over to it with 'feeling'."*

Lock in this advice as **it's the most common mistake** for people to make: you *must* pump real emotion into the experience. You must FEEL IT in your body. You can't just say to yourself: "I am wealthy," you must FEEL WEALTHY TOO – otherwise the body gets a mixed message. *It's your emotions that get you to take action,* not soulless rhetoric.

Gradually tune out the inner critic ego voice that will come up at times and replace it with an increasing belief in what you want. Remember not to aim for perfection with this.

Your job is to convince the subconscious and your belief center through vivid and emotional visualization that your future dream is your current reality. It is to create a new automatic steered towards what you want. Joe Dispenza explains that you want to "memorize a new feeling in the body so that nothing in your outer world can move you from it."

I followed this process religiously in 2009-2010 for many months. Every morning I would relax into a meditative state, picture my emotional anchor (which was a cold January afternoon at the Memorial Park in Coventry when I scored a hattrick during a rugby practice; that day I felt completely unstoppable) and then picture images of things I wanted to have happen in the near and farther future.

I was very disciplined about doing it morning and night partly because at the time I was feeling quite low. That pain and frustration drove me. I took the leap of faith that it would help me. I pictured speaking to large audiences, making love to my girlfriend, I even pictured our two children running around the Field Museum pointing at the dinosaurs. (Keep in mind we had only just started dating). I pictured speaking in an English castle.

The results were hand-on-heart astonishing. Just eight months later, a UK firm invited me to speak at an event hosted at Britain's longest-inhabited castle. Three months after that I got engaged. I had my best ever year of business. Five and a half years later, my two-year old twins went on the rampage at the Field Museum. My life completely transformed, so I know this can work for you too.

4. **Be grateful *AS IF* = Be grateful for what you want *AS IF* it has already happened.**

This matters because it causes a change inside you: from somebody just waiting for a change to somebody who changes something inside of you that produces an effect outside of you. Remember the Law of Action. It also helps you build faith.

ACT AS IF the great things you want are part of your current reality. Have no worry or fear. Just look forward to it.

When you write down what you are grateful for AS IF, you write. "I am so happy and grateful that I feel charged and deeply fulfilled by my vocation."

"I am so happy and grateful that I have enough time to do all the things that matter deeply to me."

Author Gregg Braden explains that when you accept your raised beliefs and future dream as current reality and do so **in a way "that your body believes is happening 'now,'** you discover how to set into motion a cascade of emotional and physiological processes that reflect your new reality. The neurons in your brain, the sensory neurites in your heart, and the chemistry of your body all harmonize to mirror the new thinking and the quantum possibilities of life are rearranged to replace unwanted circumstances of your past with the new circumstances that you've accepted as the present."

Think for a moment: what have you got to lose by trying this for some time? Either way you'll feel good. That can only be good. Joe Dispenza adds:

"The quantum mind is like a big mirror - it reflects back to you what you accept and believe as true. This means your outer world is a reflection of your inner reality. The most important synaptic connection you can make is to know that IT IS REAL."

5. Notice proof

This might sound like a mixed message. I've frequently said don't keep pulling up the roots of your efforts expecting quick results and detach emotionally from your efforts. On the other hand, your optimistic side - your faith - should be on the lookout for all signs of proof that your new belief is true and you're increasingly on track to mine your gold. This is partly because your new belief already is partly true in some respects (you wouldn't choose a belief that's totally impossible); it's also very likely you have had an unempowering or mostly irrational belief in the past that has slowed you down.

Elevating your new beliefs is aligned with **noticing what you are doing right**. For example, I was raised in a household that had a scarcity mindset about money: there was never enough. This can be really hard to shift when it's reinforced often first by your peer group, then by your self-talk, and *especially* when *you* are always noticing the proof that it is true! The problem is you *don't notice when it's not true*. Or you write it off as a freak exception. Also, you're more likely to twist experiences or unwittingly influence them towards scarcity because that's what you believe and expect. It's all you deserve – or so you believe.

This is not a one-off exercise. I've made that mistake. Every so often, I'd write a list to prove there had been abundance in my life, but I'd do nothing with it after that. I'd put no emotion into it. You want to be looking for proof often with the best positive expectancy you can – without feeling negative about it. Some beliefs are incredibly stubborn. They can change. If they haven't yet, keep giving them more love. Don't give up.

Keep tending your garden to raise your beliefs and your control. None of this is easy. Weeds grow back and your garden always needs water.

Rather like clearing your stuff about God, there is an element here of taking a leap of faith, *and your ego is going to protest consistently*, so do your best to remember your true self is love and keep re-focusing back to the ideal you that you're becoming. Remember! Nothing can change until you change your thoughts, feelings, and actions. Fuel the beliefs you want. Water the right flowers!

Elevate your beliefs! Elevate your control.

Key 3: Elevate Your Self Awareness

What Lesson Have You Not Yet Learned?

There's a line of thinking that says that life is always trying to teach us something and it will keep trying to teach us this lesson until we do. If it's an important lesson, it will make us uncomfortable.

The problem is we can spend our whole life finding a way *not* to face and learn this lesson because it feels uncomfortable. And we can even convince ourselves how intelligent we are that we have outwitted it...until we don't.

We run from accountability. We don't do the things we know we need to because they are somewhat uncomfortable. It's too easy to say "I don't feel like it. I'll wait until *some day* when..." - and that 'someday' rarely comes. And we mostly unwittingly find ways to make sure of that by not making the money, losing the weight, changing the job, or leaving the relationship.

The misnomer we often use to mask our pain is 'coping strategy' – we eat when we're not hungry, we pour another drink, we escape with a movie; we work even more; we over-exercise, we shop, we scroll on social media, or we just get 'busy' to divert our attention. We are experts at this.

And life tries again to wave at us in some way (e.g., the death of a loved one) and say 'pay attention' – this is an important lesson! **Life usually gives us this lesson in a painful way** - probably because we keep ignoring it. And when the pain strikes, we have to avoid our autopilot 'coping strategy' and, instead, *relax* and ask a better question, such as **'what is life trying to teach me here?'**

Confront What Life is Trying to Teach You So You Can Better Mine Your Gold!

Oprah Winfrey had an eating problem for decades. It was her way of stuffing uncomfortable feelings and memories. She was sexually molested as a child and teen. Much later in life, her painful lesson in life came when she found herself in her father's kitchen making breakfast for one of the men who had molested her! The perverse, extremely painful nature of this situation was what it took for her to realize she had repressed difficult feelings and avoided standing up to people like him all her life. Her only liberation was to start confronting such people whenever they appeared. **She said she broke open and broke through and hasn't stopped.**

What lesson has taken you the longest to learn? And, more importantly, have you *really* learned it, so you act on it consistently? Maybe it's a lesson you haven't yet actually learned or applied.

Most of us are poor at applying the difference between what we KNOW and what we DO.

Knowing isn't doing. Knowing isn't doing. Knowing isn't doing!!

It finally hit me when I originally wrote about this for my newsletter a few years ago:

1. The previous night a client had texted me a video about a '20-point system' – a way to measure your daily prospecting and business activity to make sure you thrive.

2. That morning, the audio book, *The Wisdom of Sundays*, raised the question: What lesson has taken you the longest to learn? I thought about it and had this uneasy feeling that I knew the answer but that I wasn't living it fully. I could not put it into words. I hadn't honestly 'learned' it yet.

3. Later, another client emailed me wishing me a '20 Point Day'. This had never happened before. Ever. I meekly replied that it was on my to-do list – even though it has been on and off for about 15 years and it had never been done or executed.

4. Then a prospect texted declining to work with me. I was really stung for many reasons including my over-confidence that he would say yes as it had come from a slam dunk referral. When I asked him what a rival firm had offered, he wrote back about a points system called the 'Automatic Revenue Machine'. (Who wouldn't want something called that?!) Remarkably quickly, instead of feeling resentful, I felt relief and said to myself: "Thanks. Yes, that's what I'm missing."

    I think I was so criticized as a child, that as a coach I had been erratic about accountability for myself and others because I never wanted to make someone else feel badly like I did as a child. So, I was too nice too much of the time. I was very encouraging – which fortunately helped some people thrive – but too nice to help many people progress.

5. Then I 'suddenly' remembered a business venture that failed for me five years prior that I concluded had lacked enough metrics to give it the credibility it needed. I'd made excuses for not coming up with any rather than making it happen.

6. I thought about my discomfort with calling people and my endless excuses over the years about how my business model was 'different', other sales models were 'old fashioned' and so metrics didn't apply; there wasn't a textbook for my business because it was new, that I could figure out a better way to avoid the discomfort of the things I didn't feel like doing. And on and on.

You get the point. I got my big lesson to execute on; now, what about you? It's reasonably comfortable to read about other people's challenges.

What are you stuffing inside and not learning? What lesson does life keep trying to teach you? Or maybe you know it but could be putting it into action better.

What truth needs to be uttered into the mirror?

What truth needs to be uttered at home or at work?

We all put our heads in the sand from time to time. What can you do?

a) **Journal about your current situation**. It is a great way to gradually raise topics and think them through on paper. Not all of them have to be jugular topics; plenty may be minor challenges that need to be resolved. **Build up a repertoire of great questions to ask yourself, e.g., What is life trying to teach me right now?** How satisfied am I with my ripple – am I impacting people enough and am I impacting enough people? What would you do if you knew you couldn't fail?

b) **Meditate.** Entire books have been written about this so I will defer to them. The benefits are considerable and quieting the mind can help you be clearer about what matters most.

c) **Choose a topic to reflect on while you drive, commute or go for walk.** This time to think can be incredibly helpful at processing something important. Sometimes I carry it on paper as a reminder to keep my brain on point.

The more aware you are of your own reality, the easier it is to adjust. While this may not be a new revelation, I'd wager that most of us are not good at this because we feel too busy to take the time and too tired to do it when we do have a spare moment.

You know better: running blindly through life is unwise.

At least do a Monthly GPS

This is a really useful way to quickly monitor key areas of your life for change and to make small shifts like a GPS does to keep you moving in the right direction as life events frequently interrupt and/or throw you off.

In his book, *The Art of the Good Life,* getAbstract co-founder Rolf Dobelli finds the most effective people in our culture are not overly stubborn about plans and change: *"The most common misunderstanding I encounter is that the good life is a stable state or condition. Wrong.* **The good life is only achieved through constant readjustment."**

Once a month, I recommend you create your own check-in on your progress. You can successfully make small changes on a monthly basis. You can assess different areas of your life and 'catch' them from slipping far or slowly turn the ship around on a challenging problem when you stop and think once/month.

Many of us struggle with acknowledging what's really the truth about one or two areas of our life and then do something about them.

1. **Rate different areas of your life on a scale of 1-10 each month**

Every month rate yourself on a scale of 1-10 in these four foundational areas to help avoid being 'blindsided' by a big problem.

a) Key Relationships

b) Professional/Vocation

c) Financial

d) Health – physical and mental

It's a really quick and simple yet useful way to keep frequent tabs on the key basic areas. We should not have blindsiding events in these areas 98% of the time. Relationships, professional success, health, and finances rarely go from a 9/10 to a 3/10 overnight. Decline usually is a slow, unobserved process. The problem is we are either not paying attention or living in denial. Or we are too focused on something else.

A) Health

On a scale of 1-10, how would you rate your health?

1-10: While there's common sense about exercise, nutrition and sleep and listening to your own body, there's also a lot of misinformation driven by our quick-fix culture. Get guidance from people with long-term, proven results *that work for MANY people like you* - not just for themselves and especially for people your age. And be willing to experiment outside a basic recipe. (I've personally seen several instances where an overly-enthusiastic 20-something personal trainer or health coach has pushed a 40-something client too hard and they've hurt themselves badly – even if the client wanted to push themselves hard).

Having an annual physical, training for strength, cardio and flexibility are all wise. Interestingly it's nutrition that makes the biggest different to weight loss.

B) Key Relationships (or Feeling Connected to Others)

On a scale of 1-10, how would you rate your key relationships?

1-10: Start with your partner if you have one, then your children. It's up to you if there are other key loved ones to include. I score myself on connection with 'friends' too.

1-10: What we all need – and the Pandemic really brought this to light – is we need to feel a sense of connection to others. A lack of this can quite easily lead to depression (see Johann Hari's brilliant *Lost Connections* for more on how to combat this epidemic).

C) **Professional/Vocation**

1-10: How pleased are you with your trajectory? Either you're living your purpose and trying to fulfill your potential or you're not.

D) **Financial**

1-10: How pleased are you with where you're heading? You can modify this if necessary. Sometimes there is short-term progress and long-term progress to measure separately. It's okay to focus on one area of your life at times – that's likely necessary. It's not realistic to beautifully balance all these out. But at least keep an eye out and not put your head in the sand. If your high achievement and happiness are part of the 'home' you're building, this is one way to make sure the foundation stays strong. When you do this monthly, most of the time if an area has dipped a bit, you're just getting a small nudge about it such as 'let's be a bit more diligent about…" – and that's the way you want it. Then hopefully a tiny habit can get you quickly back on track.

2. **Check your goal progress each month**

I like the timeline of a month. It gives you plenty of time to sink your teeth into change and make pleasing progress or not get too far off track so you can make adjustments as you look over your goals.

In addition, take a look at the **list of breakthroughs** you want this year to chart progress and consider modifications. Lastly, it's also helpful to have a **list of identities** that answer the question: 'What type of person do I want to be this year?' and to review this gently. I say this because we can only truly focus on a couple at a time, but it never hurts to refresh on the big picture or re-confirm our priorities.

3. At the end of the month complete this: "**Next month here's what I need to**":

Stop (doing)
(Do) Less
Keep (doing)
(Do) More
Start (doing)

- **Accept** (about my life – especially consider what's changed that you have no control over e.g., new debt or an ailing parent or something that requires a lot of patience e.g., rehabbing an injury)

I notice that when we make monthly shifts, they are more achievable than trying to adapt daily or weekly; and cumulatively add up to a better year. They build our ability to be flexible and better handle change in general which is often unexpected. It's also a relief to notice changes before they can get any worse.

I remember going month to month rating my relationships with my children typically about a 9/10. Then early into the Pandemic and after a month of awful home-schooling where I was impatient with my kids, and resentful that I had to wear the hat of teacher and run my business and be stuck at home all the time with everyone, I rated my relationships with my children at a 6! It was the first time I'd paused to notice what was happening and I was shocked at the rapid decline. But at least the monthly review made me aware so I could try to course correct.

It is important to preserve a LOT - even if this feels less exciting. Accomplished people already have a lot of good habits (but are often tempted to make changes by the concept that change always equals progress).

4. **"What did I learn this month?" "What skills did I improve?"**

    This can be a useful reminder about books you've read or listened to, courses you've taken – even life lessons you want to remember.

5. **If you're in the second half of your life...**

    Consider these powerful questions from Harvard professor Arthur C. Brooks' book *Strength to Strength:*

    a) If I had one year left in my career and my life, how would I structure this coming month?

    b) What would be on my to-do list?

    c) What would I choose not to worry about?

    d) I also added this to give me the opposite perspective: "If I have 40 years left in my life, how would I structure this coming month?"

    Even if you only do points 1 and 3, you will keep much closer tabs on what you're doing right and how to make slight adjustments as you go. It will help you keep your comparisons focused on your recent past self and what you can control and away from the social cancer of comparing yourself to others.

    Elevate your self-awareness; elevate your control!

Key 4: Elevate Your Health

"What surprises me most is "Man" because he sacrifices his health in order to make money. Then he sacrifices money to recuperate his health. And then he is so anxious about the future that he doesn't enjoy the present; The result being he doesn't live in the present or the future; He lives as if he's never going to die, and then he dies having never really lived." - Dalai Lama

"Self-care is so profound: Our bodies retain information from our mind. We like to call our bodies separate from our minds but if you sense pain, your brain's providing it and trying to alert you. Our bodies are not getting the repair they need and are under constant stress." – Sue Hitzmann, founder of the MELT Method

You don't need a chapter in this book to tell you to honor your temple. You probably already know a fair amount about what healthy choices are. What you might well need is a book that helps you with the *doing* part. You've come to the right place!

Physical health is the only topic in this book that has always been a relative strength of mine. I know that's not helpful information for you other than as a reminder that you too have a few great strengths that have always come quite easily to you. These may well be the ones you build on even further to play absolutely full out on (see chapter 9 for more on this). It's easy to take these for granted but you've also lived long enough to notice that most other people do not have those same aptitudes.

When I look back, I think I got lucky in the sense that I enjoyed playing sports at school and that required being fit. Either I ran around the field in practice, or I didn't get to play my favorite sport, which was rugby. I think I played sports just long enough in my life to help hardwire the mostly subconscious feeling that I felt better in my head after I had exercised. I remember riding my bike home from the gym once after I'd left school. I was no longer playing sports because of too many knee injuries. While begrudgingly accepting that I was never going to be Arnold Schwarzenegger – my body type didn't seem inclined to want to be particularly strong or muscly - **I noticed how good I felt mentally**. And it was all natural! No artificial additives or preservatives. Like falling in love.

This was mostly luck. But because I liked feeling good, it was generally relatively easy to talk myself into exercising. What also developed as a mindset as an adult was realizing that I am no good to anyone if I don't take care of my health – that at some point if I neglect my health, it is going to decline and dig me a deep hole that I might never come out of. If I took care of my health, I'd get sick less often and I'd have more energy to work harder pursuing my dreams. If I stayed in shape, I could play games with my children (if I ever had them). If I take care of my health now, hopefully I can be an active loving grandparent (although they will probably have to replace my knee first!).

The same is true if we neglect or make unwise decisions with our professional development or financial lives. Oh, and our relationships aren't much different although, unlike our bodies, our careers, and our savings and investments accounts, some humans are capable of forgiveness! It's not something to count on though.

As I acknowledged, this isn't very helpful to most of you reading this other than to take a moment to reflect on what your equivalent area of strengths are because you're definitely a natural in some areas. You've had luck in other ways. Not everything is hard work and in need of a lengthy mining process. Sometimes there is low hanging fruit that you can be grateful for.

In terms of physical health and honoring your temple if it's not been one of your strengths, you're going to apply the 5 habits of this book (as I had to do with everything else including your strength areas)!

The ingredients are the same for everyone in any area you want to improve:

Habits 1 and 2: Tie health to your purpose - do it for love: Love of your yet unborn children or children's children, love of doing more of the things you love to do with more of the people you love – whatever gives you positive fuel. Or leverage painful fuel - face a regret you have from your life about physical health, fitness or missing out some cool activities and do something about it while you still can. Or look at the Ghost of Christmas Yet to Come – what happens if you stay on the same trajectory for the next 20 years?

Habit 3: Pull all the weeds fast that tell you that you can't do this! Keep pulling them. Your ego loves you for buying into all the fear and excuses it's fed you that you've bought into listening to the wrong voice in your head. And the success block that being healthy is hard? Being unhealthy is hard and it gets harder and harder. Whatever source you use to identify leading causes of death around the world, heart disease comes first; and several of the other top causes can be avoided by honoring your temple better. Choose your hard.

Habit 4: Elevate your control in multiple ways and your 'HEALTH' will start to rise too. When you start to make more effort taking care of yourself, you won't want to sabotage the helpful things you've done by reverting to old unempowering habits that make you feel badly about yourself. So long as you apply Habit 5.

In Habit 5 ahead in this book **you decide you need a new 'identity' around health**. You want to see yourself as the type of person who is *increasingly* healthy. **This requires you to then take action to prove to your brain that you're becoming healthier.** You take advantage of what's called cognitive dissonance: the more you tell your brain something, the more obligated it feels to follow through on that message. Then start small with your plan. **Make small commitments that are easy to keep and gradually build from there. Work on ever better habits and routines.**

Every chapter in this book is committed to the process of helping you mine your gold wherever it needs mining. Good physical health is one of them.

Just stick to the steps in this book! Lean into finding fuel, pulling weeds in your head, seeing yourself in a new light and taking small steps *consistently* that can lead to bigger ones.

Here are the main areas to start small with:

What's the first thing I can do to improve my cardio?
What's the first thing I can do to improve my strength?
What's the first thing I can do to improve my sleep?
What's the first thing I can do to improve what I eat and drink?

Active Recovery and taking breaks

Since there are many tomes written on health by people with far more expertise than me, the only other health-related topic I would like to address that relates to mining your gold is active recovery and taking breaks. *These are no longer a nice to have for the high achiever.* Your body can only push so hard for so long and you become increasingly unproductive. You have to let it recharge, just like your electronics.

Take more mini breaks during the day so your battery doesn't run down too fast. Make the time to allow your body to recharge physically with a hot Epsom salt or ice bath, sauna, massage, walk or stretching (not TV and alcohol: TV stimulates the wrong brain waves and alcohol messes with your sleep).

Make Time for This

One August, I took a couple of days off to celebrate my wedding anniversary and my wife's birthday. I had planned over three hours of spa treatments for her so was curious what I'd do with this window of time in a nice hotel. They had a great gym, sauna and steam bath and I thought for sure that's where I'd go after I dropped her off.

But I was still full from breakfast so I went back to our room, sat on the bed with some light non-fiction and looked out at Lake Michigan in the summer sun. And I lay there and listened to my body and it sent me a resounding message: "Don't move. This feels delicious!" So I read, texted a few friends and family, and took a nap.

The following week we had a holiday on the beach planned. I'd been intending to bring at least a couple of professional books to read but after my experience at the hotel, I decided against it.

Crazy Busy. Over-caffeinated: We all feel busier than ever. We are all too easy to reach and too connected to communication sources. We act as though we are computers connected to a power source that can perform at a consistent level all the time. And we aspire to be ever more like this because of the benefits to productivity (as if this is our only reason for living).

But we are human beings not 3D printers. 3D printers don't have to deal with children who need to come home from school because they're sick, bad weather, clients who need to cancel, running out of milk or cat food, their partner having had a terrible day at work, inept governments, reckless drivers on the commute home, bad nights of sleep, or their favorite team losing… again.

Our culture has been rapidly speeding up and extolling the virtues of always being on the go. That faster always means better.

There is a stigma to taking breaks and of having a day completely free of work email or anything work-related.

There is a stigma to having a holiday longer than one week.

There is a stigma to recharging.

Great client service is often defined as responding to someone when you're on a holiday because it shows such 'above and beyond' care!

For many, it is socially unacceptable to suggest you are anything other than crazy busy.

That's how silly things have become.

As if the only thing we want on our tombstone was "Kept Busy" and "Got back to others the fastest." As if that's our ultimate definition of success.

The other big problem is energy depletion. The biggest mistake we make is we don't notice that our productivity wanes gradually down-hill when we are constantly on the go and never slowing down long enough to let our bodies recharge. We run the likely risk of slowly becoming ever less effective without even noticing.

Then we look for quick fixes like caffeine and artificial or sugary energy 'boosters', crash harder and repeat. It's what it does to us over time where the damage is being done.

My prescription – at least one day/week – is:

Don't check your email
Take a nap
Don't do anything work related
Read something fairly mindless
Sit in a hot bath, hot tub or sauna
Go for a walk
Don't do a single thing

And if you need to loosen up a little (like me):

Overindulge to balance out all that self-discipline you typically use
Eat a bit too much – especially dessert
Have an extra glass of wine
Play your favorite tunes louder
Sing, dance or pogo

People wiser than me recommend three day breaks every month and a week off every quarter.

I realize that there's nothing earth shattering about this. But I know that almost all of us are brushing off the topic of constant busyness too lightly partly because of our cultural norms. This is a mistake. We're not listening to our bodies, not listening to common sense, and increasingly behaving as though our bodies are machines that need little rest and minimal maintenance.

One more piece on how I'd almost forgotten the importance of experiencing a proper break after a 17-month Pandemic with no time off. My wife and I took the family to Florida one week somewhat wary that it had the highest Covid death rate in the country at the time!

The best moments in no particular order:

Being on a plane again for the first time in 21 months.
Being in the ocean, looking out into the ocean and seeing nothing but water and sky – no people, no buildings, no boats, no planes - just 100% Mother Nature
Not checking email for a week
The wind blowing in my face on the fishing boat as we sped back to shore
Watching the kids play in the pool.
Sitting outside a food truck eating ice cream – more than once!
Drinking cappuccino at an outdoor café
Seeing dolphins playing in the water
Watching the children catch fish for the first time and catching a 35-inch fish the very first time I ever picked up a fishing rod
Walking barefoot in the sand every day

Giving my self-discipline and habit tracker a week off
Reinforcing that kids especially need these memories of their childhood

My biggest concern was whether to read about Sergeant Jim Chee and Officer Bernadette Manuelito chasing an attempted murder case in Navajo country or to see how Elizabethan investigator John Shakespeare was getting on chasing down a conspiracy to assassinate Sir Francis Drake.

My son's toughest decision was where to cannonball into the pool without landing on anyone.

The hardest thing my daughter had to do was decide which floatation device to try next.

My wife's biggest dilemma was which restaurant we should go to.

I could not get back to 'normal' for a few days and I hope you have the same problem soon too. Important lesson learned. Coming at things refreshed matters! Take a break!

"Slowing down is sometimes the best way to speed up" - Mike Vance

Elevate your health; elevate your control!

Key 5: Elevate Your Gratitude

*"The two most powerful feelings for quickly man-
ifesting your goals are appreciation and gratitude."* – Jack Canfield, *The Success Principles*

Jack Canfield grew up poor with an alcoholic mother and a physically abusive step-father. He has gone onto live a remarkable life,
touching millions through his workshops, books, and *Chicken Soup
for the Soul* series.

What finally persuaded me to at least 'try' having a daily gratitude
practice - after many years of hearing it recommended - was listening to billionaire Oprah Winfrey talk about how pivotal her gratitude
practice was in helping her achieve such stunning success. She too
came from really challenging beginnings growing up not only poor
and lonely, but through the trauma of sexual molestation and result-
ing teen pregnancy from a 'trusted' family friend.

When Robin Sharma writes about the billionaires he has coached
for the past twenty five years in his latest book *The Everyday Hero
Manifesto*, he says: *"They understand that **what you are grateful for
grows**. And all you appreciate expands within your consciousness.
Start celebrating all that you have been granted, however small or
large – from food on your family's table to a job that allows you to
make a difference...and what you applaud will be magnified. So even
more of it will flow naturally into your days."*

Want research? Steven Kotler has been studying and coaching
peak performers for thirty years. In his seminal 2021 book *The Art of
Impossible* he notes that *"Unfortunately, to keep us safe, the amygdala is strongly biased toward negative information. We're always
hunting danger. In experiments run at the University of California,
Berkeley, psychologists discovered that we take in as many as 9 bits
of negative information for every positive bit that gets through. Nine-
to-one are lousy odds under the best of conditions – and peak performance rarely takes place under the best of conditions."*

He then explains that **we need a daily gratitude practice to change our brain's negativity bias. This will make gold mining easier.**

As I mentioned earlier, Joe Dispenza, one of the most popular spiritual influencers of the present day, believes that **you have to take gratitude one step further and not only be grateful for what you have *but also for what you want.*** That way you can send your intentions out to the quantum field and change something within you before you can see it turn into physical reality. What helps me with this is I mix together what I have with what I want to have, and this helps (or confuses?!) my brain to blend them both together as real.

He explains: *"When you are in a state of gratitude, you transmit a signal into the (quantum) field that an event HAS ALREADY OCCURRED. Gratitude is more than an intellectual thought process. You have to feel as though whatever you want is in your reality at this very moment."*

What's also going on here is you are planting these thoughts into your subconscious mind so it can go to work on making it happen. This is so crucial because – remember what John Assaraf shared in his book *Innercise* - *"only about three to five percent of what's happening in your brain occurs at the conscious level of awareness."* In other words, 95%-97% of the actions you take are made subconsciously during your day, i.e. with no thought put in at all.

As you influence your subconscious mind more by being grateful, you continue to attract in more of what you want by focusing on it more and then gradually taking ever more ACTION to make it happen. Make sense? It's not an accident.

The Useful Part: What is an EFFECTIVE GRATITUDE PRACTICE?

What has to happen is you have to FEEL REAL GRATITUDE in your HEART. This is where I went wrong for years. I would go through the motions. I'd often feel in a hurry and I would scribble down some things I was grateful for but seldom would I let them sink in deeply enough to genuinely FEEL GRATEFUL.

There are two ways to have a gratitude practice. Make sure it lasts at least 5 minutes and preferably 10. Start with 30 seconds if that's too hard and scale up.

1. You can list out things you're grateful for but you have to feel really, really thankful as you do it otherwise it's a waste of time.

2. If you can, try writing full sentences for TEN MINUTES. Begin your thoughts with the words:

   a) I am really grateful for…

   b) I so appreciate …

   c) I feel very blessed that….

      I would add that listening to and reflecting on some of Joe Dispenza's meditations has helped me speed up the process of rewiring my head.

I had written about this topic a few times in the past, but I can honestly say that absorbing and practicing the above methods was the first time I felt it made a noticeable difference to my brain and my life. I started to feel things changing and much more often I felt waves of gratitude.

Having a gratitude practice attracts more good things – just like the experts all say. You do have to get granular and appreciate all the little things too. This practice also reduces the social cancer of comparing yourself to others so much. You're reducing your negativity bias. Feel it. Feel it. Feel it. Then first your subconscious brain and then your conscious brain will get you to make it all happen.

Elevate your gratitude; elevate your control!

Key 6: Elevate Your Peace

> *"If the mind is disciplined, the heart turns
> quickly from fear to love."* John Cage

Mining your gold requires clarity and focus. No one would argue that we live in a world full of what Robin Sharma calls Weapons of Mass Distraction. One of the practices that elevates your altitude is to find more quiet in your life. Your mind has only so much capacity and you need every bit you can source to help your most important causes. Fight for all the peace you can find!

How do you currently seek out mental and emotional quiet? Besides responding "not enough," (!) what works for you? And, on a deeper level, when do you connect to what moves your soul?

Epictetus remarked: "Most of us would be seized with fear if our bodies went numb, and would do everything possible to avoid it, yet we take no interest in the numbing of our souls."

What about re-connecting to your heart? Don't dismiss these things as first-world concerns and nice-to-haves. Raising peace will speed up your journey to wherever you want to go by tapping into your deepest sources.

1. **Meditate and Pray**

   I touched on meditation in chapter 11 to help you grow your awareness of your inner dialogue and to slow it down. Raising your peace brings more calm that allows you to better pursue your purpose. A daily practice is great, but this is not about perfection; it's about using strategies that bring you peace. Put together your own recipe.

   Prayer can raise your peace too. Talking to God can help you connect to something far greater than you. Almost every day, I ask God to make me an instrument of love. This requires a clear, peaceful connection. It helps me steer in a better direction.

2. Spend time in nature

It is natural and grounding to be around trees, grassland and bodies of water that aren't trying to be anything but their imperfect seasonal selves in their sometimes-imperfect seasonal weather. It raises peace by centering you. It's a snapshot of how life works: old, new, beautiful, messy, chaotic, organized, alive, conflicting, sleeping, real. It can help bring perspective to our noise. No frenetic drivers. No harried parents. No self-imposed crises. Just birds in the trees and a few flies – none of them in a rush. Maybe a deer if you're lucky.

3. Go for a walk – anywhere – is surprisingly helpful.

Walking puts your body in motion and raises peace by reducing stress. You don't have to dress up like an Olympic cyclist or get up at 5am to do it best. Just walk.

Danish philosopher Soren Kierkegaard was a familiar sight to the locals in Copenhagen. He explained its importance to his sister-in-law in a letter once: "Above all, do not lose your desire to walk: Every day I walk myself into a state of wellbeing and walk away from every illness; I have walked myself into my best thoughts, and I know of no thought so burdensome that one cannot walk away from it."

4. Sit in front of a fireplace or firepit

I love to do this at my local library because it raises my peace. I used to go camping a lot before I got married and moved to the city; my favorite thing about camping was building the fire without any paper, cooking on it, and staring at it in the dark.

The quick version of this is to stare into a burning candle. It's peacefully hypnotic.

5. Declutter

"If a cluttered desk is the sign of a cluttered mind, what is the significance of a clean desk?" - Laurence J. Peter

Got too much stuff? Hanging onto it "just in case" – for years and years? Because you spent good money on it? Having clear surfaces and rooms only with what you need can raise a surprising amount of peace and the opposite raises a horrible emotional burden that tugs you down every time you see it. Small steps are the way to do this effectively (see Habit 5 of this book). Three minutes here. Three minutes there.

6. Go to a museum

This is a different kind of peace that focuses the mind on inspiring or really interesting artifacts. Focusing on something other-worldly or so different from what you normally lay your eyes on can leave you with a sense of peace, wonder and help you raise your tide. My favorite place on the planet for this is the Field Museum in Chicago. I spent many days there working on this book. Their café sits in the atrium where there is currently a Titanosaur, several pterosaurs overhead, and two African elephants for company. It's a magnificently peaceful experience.

7. Elevate your wisdom

Learning has been esteemed by all faiths and throughout the ages partly because the more you learn, the more you realize how much you will never know: it makes you humble. Tolstoy expressed this beautifully when he said: "I cannot understand how some people can live without communicating with the wisest people who ever lived on earth."

This isn't peaceful all the way. As Ryan Holiday points out in *Stillness is the Key*: "Wrestle with big questions…Treat your brain like the muscle it is…It might even make things less clear – make them darker before the dawn…But that's okay…Because on the other side is truth."

8. **Listen to classical music or nature sounds on headphones**

   This is a useful one when you're in a busier place like a noisy coffee shop or airport where peace is hard to find any other way. Plug sounds into your ears that bring peace and creative generation that do not distract you from raising your level of peace.

9. **Let go of bottled-up anger and frustration**

   This was a key focus in chapter 12: Weed Your Garden.

You never know what benefits will come from slowing down and elevating your peace…

One Saturday morning I was doing *absolutely nothing*, trying to be at peace with waiting, and I am 98% sure I saved someone's life. I was waiting outside a London Underground station. A man was engrossed in his phone and about to step in front a speeding taxi. It was a death trap of a street (in my opinion) because it was paved to look much like a pedestrian walkway different from the road it intersected. This explains why his normal sixth sense about danger was absent. If you were only vaguely looking down, the street looked like a traffic-free walking area.

I'd actually noticed him standing there already. This is most unlike me but, as I said, I was doing *nothing*. I was being present. Normally I am embarrassingly oblivious to details around me. I would make a hopeless crime-scene witness. But this man was about my age and, inexplicably to me, I had even temporarily put myself in his shoes and wondered what my life would have been like if I had stayed in

England my whole life instead of emigrating to the USA. From the waist up he could have been me (he was a little heavier than me). Then I noticed his shoes and they were pretty eccentric. And he was wearing lime green socks. "He must be gay." I said to myself. "Good for him!"

Then he stepped out to what would have been his likely death had I not been standing there. That taxi would have hit him so hard that his head would have bounced straight off those street cobbles. And my day would have been very different standing right in front of a grisly, horrific scene that would have given me nightmares and thinking "that could have been me."

I was turning my head frequently in *four* different directions waiting for my friend, Melissa, a lady I'd interviewed for my podcast who had some important news that she couldn't share with me in her office setting the day before. So, at the last minute, we set up this coffee that neither of us had intended to have less than 24 hours prior.

My head could so easily have been pointed in a different direction and probably was two seconds prior. Had I not been looking for her, I probably wouldn't have turned my head to the right and noticed the taxi barreling down towards us.

It was the THIRD spot I had stood in to wait for Melissa. I had pre-ferred the previous two spots but both times someone had come along nearby and lit up a cigarette, so I had moved away.

The strangest part of this whole experience was that I can take NO CREDIT for saving his life. When I met up with my friend a few minutes later, I explained that I was feeling a bit shaky; "The weirdest part is I didn't even think about it. My mouth just opened and shouted "CAREFUL!" and jolted him to freeze.

I can even contrast it to an incident I experienced the day before on an Underground station when two people looked about to start fighting. They were shouting and swearing right in each other's faces, and I was sure a fight would break out. But as this happened, I had a moment to think. I wanted to break it up and calm them down, but they were much younger and bigger than me and so angry I was sure I'd get clobbered, and I am not an experienced fighter (this is quite the understatement!). I walked away from the intense negative energy and remarkably one of them decided to do the same.

The man who was not supposed to die that Saturday was mostly embarrassed afterwards. I tried to make him feel better by saying how unclear and dangerous I thought the street was: "I've seen several other people walk across this street not knowing it was for traffic."

He said, "I shouldn't have been looking at my phone" and walked on. He probably thanked me, but I honestly don't remember. I was so alarmed by how unsafe the street was.

It was after my coffee meeting that my brain went into high gear on all the variables that had to happen for me to be in that place at that time. And on the bizarre control I felt about the incident. For a split second that man's life was in my hands. I felt like the conductor of an orchestra. Briefly.

Later my wife said on the phone; "You witnessed a near accident." And I said, "No, I wasn't a witness: I prevented an accident." Only as I write this now do I realize she was exactly right. I was only the witness. I had no control over my mouth opening at that moment. It was like a reflex action. Isn't that crazy?

The good news for the man who lived was that my mind was empty and at peace. I was doing nothing. Had I been looking at my phone or engaged in a conversation, I would not have been in a peaceful state.

The 'what-ifs' blew me away too:

What if Melissa had told me her news briefly in the office? She could have.

What if I hadn't asked her about her work when chit chatting briefly before my Mastermind meeting that she had provided a conference room for?

What if those two people hadn't had the urge to smoke - causing me to move 20 yards to wait elsewhere? Or that I have a very low tolerance for being around smokers – my dad, a non-smoker, died from lung cancer and shared an office for many years with a chain smoker?

What if I had turned my head to see where my friend was – as I had done so multiple times before in the prior minutes?

What if I hadn't been staying at Victoria (I've never stayed at a hotel there before on my previous dozens of times in London) which prompted Melissa to suggest the specific location we did meet near there?

She'd suggested a 9am coffee but I preferred 9:30. I could have acquiesced and met her earlier.

What if I'd been staring at my phone? I'd be lying if I said I wasn't as guilty as the rest of the world on this addiction.

And this doesn't even account for:

The what if's in the taxi driver's life

The what if's in the taxi driver's passenger's life that prompted such fast driving

The what if's in the man's life. I don't know why he started walking when he did other than (also weirdly) I saw him standing at a bus stop a few minutes later (why didn't he go there right away? We weren't standing by a bus stop).

You may think I'm stretching this story with all these scenarios but since I was there and arguably saved someone's life, it sent my head spinning. Somebody could easily have been getting buried a few days later surrounded by crying friends and family. Instead, these same people were probably most concerned that week about what they were going to have for dinner or who they were going to vote for in the UK's General Election. When I think about all the infinite possibilities of things that could have happened otherwise, it's beyond comprehension.

And, for a couple of weeks anyway, that man was probably on a London street somewhere wanting to check his phone but thinking twice about it!!

What could be learned from this experience?

On one level, you could explain this whole event as complete chance. It might sound like the premise of a film you've seen. I certainly don't know; you may well be right. I bet you've had close experiences like this while driving on more than one occasion and forgotten about some of them because they happened so fast.

On the other hand, given how serious the consequences were to the man who didn't die that Saturday because I was so unoccupied that my mouth opened, it made me appreciate a few things more:

1. **The only thing we can control at any given time is answering this question: How do I want to be in this moment? And to BE PRESENT rather than distracted: that elevating your peace is a worthy endeavor.** You can choose whether to do something that makes a positive difference, no difference, or a negative difference – all day long.

2. **Everything you do *can* make a difference** yet how often do we rush through tasks even with family and clients?

   Epictetus pointed this out 2,000 years ago when he wrote: "The contest is now: you are at the Olympic Games, you cannot wait any longer, and that your progress is wrecked or preserved by a single day and a single event."

   Your actions and words can make a big difference: In Habit 4, Key 10 I write about a friend who got in my face many years ago urging me to start dating again. I followed his advice, got married two years later, and had twins two years after that. **His words that day totally changed my life**. Stefan and I had been out of touch for most of those years when I updated him not that long ago. He responded by saying: "I'm glad I inspired you. Most would not have done anything with this advice – it was you who took action and succeeded."

3. **Details clearly can matter.** Why do some people pay such a premium for business class travel or five-star hotels? All hotel rooms provide a bed and bathroom contained in a walled room. All passengers land at their destination at the same time. Why do we remain loyal to certain service providers or remain friends with certain people? Sometimes it is because of the details they care about enough to remember.

In an age of empty 'likes' and high *quantity* online so-called 'connections', we could all benefit from elevating our peace, slowing down in our relationship quotients, and going deeper on the detail. We could all benefit from reflecting further on a few 'what ifs' and seeking more meaning in our hyper-paced world. And odds are that those deeper relationships and thoughtful services will be your most rewarding and most profitable ones.

P.S. One friend of mine texted "divine intervention" after I explained what happened. I have to say it really felt that way because while I determined the outcome of this event – I saved this man's life – 'I' really didn't.

Elevate your peace; elevate your control.

Your Home of Confidence

Key 7: Elevate Your CONFIDENCE

Much of my life used to consist of two experiences around confidence: it was often either shaky or - even when I did feel confident - I couldn't explain why. This undermined me because it caused me to think that I probably wouldn't be able to sustain the confidence I was enjoying or replicate it when it waned.

For me, confidence was a fickle friend that I couldn't rely on, understand well, or - much more worryingly – had little control over. Motivation, although also erratic, came easier for me because that could be traced to purpose, to addressing my childhood powerlessness and wanting to make a difference in the world. But confidence seemed much more intangible.

I know there's a wise adage about keeping things simple, but as I reflect on how to keep high levels of confidence, it's not simple. There are too many little things that can cumulatively knock us off our game and bigger ones (see point 15) - at least at certain times of our life - and we're rarely immune to global events like economic downturns and wars.

I'm also reminded of the Haitian proverb: "**Beyond mountains**, there are **mountains**," which means that as you solve one problem, another challenge presents itself. This can really test your resilience and deflate your confidence. Hopefully you go on and solve that problem too, but you can likely remember times when you caved in for a period of time.

It's been a very long, painful journey for me – painful because I was so desperate at times to find more confidence and better answers. Here's what I know now about confidence, and it is good news: there are MANY things you can do to feel more confident right now. Even one next step from this list will make a positive difference for you today:

1. **It helps to have a visual of what building confidence looks like:**

    a) **See it as building Your Home of Confidence (see visual)**

    It's a process. You work at all times on having a good foundation and gradually you add more bricks. It's an ongoing experiment as you and your life change, so sometimes the bricks need swapping out with more important ones. And the roof of the home consists of the mindsets that empower you to be an ever-better version of yourself.

    b) **OR treat your confidence as piecing together your own 3D mosaic**

    When I interviewed Amanda Allen for my podcast, she had had an upbringing laced with depression, suicidal tendencies, and alcoholism. In her early 40's she became a three-time World CrossFit Games champion. Winning it is an incredible lifetime accomplishment, but repeating that feat twice more is even more astounding. When I did CrossFit five times/week, I wound up in hospital after five months unable to move with a herniated disc!

    Her philosophy of life was that – akin to building a home – 'success' (however you define it) was a mosaic. And you had to piece together your own mosaic 1% at a time. Every detail: from all the things you put in your body, to the thoughts you had, to who you spent time with, even to the soap you used and the clothes you wore. You could piece it together by getting the best ideas for you from as many different sources as you wanted. And no one could prescribe all the pieces for your mosaic. You had to do this on purpose yourself.

Since then, I've noticed the mosaic is 3D because there are multiple layers to change and progress. Have you ever thought you'd learned a lesson in life only to discover there was more to it? Whether it's letting go of trauma, building a business, or, yes, building confidence, these things have varying degrees of depth to them and adding 1% may only be the first of several layers.

For the Foundation of Your Home of Confidence:

2. **You need consistent basic maintenance - all the important areas of your life** *at all times* **to sustain good habits and avoid problems**

   Confidence fluctuates like interest rates. It is not a static process that you 'achieve' and then coast into the sunset. **At frequent intervals, you'll be challenged by a problem with a foundational area, and it's normal for it to shake your confidence.**

   Key relationships
   Your vocation/professional life
   Financial life
   Physical and mental health

   If you hurt your back, business is slow, get hit by a big tax bill, or even when your partner or one of your children is having a significant problem, it can undermine your overall confidence quite easily sometimes.

   Have proactive daily/weekly habits for these areas to avoid being blindsided by a big problem that creeps up on you. Also use the Monthly GPS Review in Key 3 to keep eyes on this.

And when something does go awry in one of these areas, lean on other points in this section and use the Setback Plan (Weed 3).

On the ground level of Your Home of Confidence:

At the Front Door, it reads: DO YOUR BEST. This precedes EVERYTHING YOU DO (See chapter 25 for more on this)

3. **Start your day with an empowering routine that energizes you physically and mentally. Ideally, bookend your day**

"Having a morning ritual has really helped me evolve and develop disciplines by focusing on nothing but me for 90 minutes every morning," Adam, one of my first UK clients told me. I cannot say enough about the power of this advice. It is a fantastic way to start the day feeling centered and inspired.

Any one of exercise, meditation, journaling, or reading can be great ways to start your day off on the right confident foot. (For more on this, see Chapter 21: Start the Day Strong)

4. **Be as consistent as you can with daily/weekly habits that *boost* your confidence on your Habit Tracker** (inc. health habits = a must for long-term confidence)

It's important to build integrity with yourself. When you do the small things daily that improve your life long-term, you are keeping your word to yourself and this builds confidence. These are all things that either help sustain a good life or make it better.

List out: 20 Things That Build My Confidence and 10 Things That Reduce My Confidence.

This exercise is a really helpful way to get clearer about what helps and hinders you. This can give you some practical ideas to take action on quickly. Do you feel better about yourself after you've exercised? What else elevates your mood and confidence quickly – certain songs? Comedy? Fussing your pet?

When you get up early, exercise, eat nutritious foods, remember the loving niceties with your family such as the hugs and goodbye kisses, they add up. This is the easiest place to start – what already works for you? Make the time for these things.

5. Get out of your head and live in the present

No apology for any repetition on this crucial and sometimes hard-to-live topic: Your ego does not want you to feel confident or be at peace right now. You may recall from Chapter 2; your ego loves to resent reality and thrive on unhappiness – on there never being enough. Eckhart Tolle writes in *A New Earth* that you "don't know that you are creating hell on earth…this is the essence of unconscious living; this is being totally in the grip of the ego."

He adds: "The ego says: Maybe at some point in the future, I can be at peace – if this, that or the other happens or I obtain this or become that. Or it says: I can never be at peace because of something that happened in the past." I hope don't mind these reminders; I know I need them!

He believes that being at peace and being yourself are the same thing. The boldest statement in all his writings is this: **"The secret of all success and happiness (is being): One With Life.** Being one with life is being one with Now." In other words, accept and live in the present and you can feel confident because you are not perseverating about past frustrations or future worries.

Take ownership (Chapter 5) for how you feel on the inside. Check in and ask: **"Is there negativity in me at this moment?"** Tolle maintains that once you're *aware* of your thoughts and emotions, you have shifted from thinking to *awareness* and that allows you to separate from your ego and your past 'stories'. This helps you be present and One With Life.

This helps you get out of your egoic mind and refocus on what builds your confidence.

6. Be well prepared

This doesn't sound powerful, but it adds layers to building your confidence. You've probably heard the leadership mantra: Failing to prepare is preparing to fail. When you feel fully ready for meetings – or even to try a good recipe for dinner – you feel a sense of peace. And being unprepared is the quickest way to sabotage your confidence and unnecessarily increase your stress.

Being well prepared also allows you to tune in and **TRUST YOUR DEEP INSTINCTS – *these instincts know what's possible.***

John Wooden, one of the most successful basketball coaches of all time, added another layer to preparation: "Failing to prepare for *failure* can prevent success." Since a team would miss at least 30% of its shots even on a good night, he taught his teams that how they capitalized on mistakes made all the difference, that what happens to you after a missed opportunity or failure is vital.

Details matter: One of Wooden's assistant managers described this routine from 1942: "Practice was in the YMCA in downtown South Bend. Managers had to be there at 5:30am. Coach Wooden wanted us to inspect each player's locker for clean practice uniforms, four pairs of socks – two sweat socks and two light pairs of socks. Prior to practice we had to paint the bottom of players' feet with a protective solution to protect and toughen their feet and then apply foot powder. After practice vitamins were given to each player. *The little things were big to Coach Wooden*."

7. **Have a sufficiency mindset: Know there is enough and remind yourself: *"I am enough"***

When you feel like there is never enough time, money, and energy to do what you want or need, it saps your confidence. Tune into knowing there is enough for what matters most. For more on this, see Habit 4, Key 9: Elevate Your Sufficiency Mindset.

8. **Confident humility – reminders from elsewhere in the book that all have a big effect on your confidence:**

   a) **Take full responsibility for and focus on what you can control.**

   b) **Do *everything* with either acceptance, enjoyment, or enthusiasm.**

   c) **Detach emotionally from the outcomes of your efforts.**

   d) **Have humility and grace with everything you *can't* control.**

9. **Don't fuel the wrong fires that will undermine your confidence**

See Habit 3 for more on this.

10. **Build your professional competence/skills**

The better you are at something, the more confident you feel. For crucial roles in your life that you want to see thrive in the future, it serves you to spend time on boosting your competence. This is a process, so if you're in a new field, you have to give yourself some slack and time to develop your skills.

11. **Surround yourself with people who want you to succeed and *recognize what it takes to be successful.***

It's hard to notice the effect others have on us. You need to get a little distance from them to have a more accurate impression. You need to tune in internally and gauge the effect. (See Habit 4, Key 10: Elevate Your Support Team)

"I pay attention to who I surround myself with. People who can't see hope for the future are no longer in my inner circle," said Myah, a wealth advisor I interviewed early in the Pandemic. How you spend your time is who you become.

12. **Be kind to yourself. Progress not perfection.**

Achiever types are notorious for being too hard on themselves. Somewhere along the line, we learned the erroneous belief that it is effective to be hard on ourselves, and that we should never toot our own horn or praise our own efforts.

Being British, I understand the cultural norm and modest virtue of self-deprecating humor, but often this leads into self-criticism. Beating yourself up is seldom helpful.

13. Act without waiting to feel confident - stop thinking and believe you already know what to do and how to do it

One of the biggest mistakes that you can easily get lulled into thinking is: "I'm going to hold off on doing this until I feel more confident." This type of thinking belongs on Someday Isle (which is a living hell I remember spending time on when I was single in my 30's because I believed I had to be earning a certain amount of money before I could date): "**Someday I'll** start that business, write that book, start dating again, re-join the gym…"

Your confidence will grow much more quickly from taking action NOW whether you feel like it or not. It is self-initiated rather than waiting for something you hope will show up.

The best mindset habit for this is:

After I find myself stalling,

I will tell myself: "Don't think. Just act."

On the upper level of Your Home of Confidence:

14. 4% growth. Do the things that *nudge* you outside your comfort zone.

Confidence can be built through small acts of courage – being bolder. Building the courage muscle by doing things that are 4% outside the comfort zone boosts your confidence and makes you more open to try new and more challenging things. This has exciting knock-on effects. It helps build the resilience muscle when challenges come which helps you have reserves of confidence on hand to tap into. (See Chapter 24: 4% Growth and Feeling Alive)

Remember these immortal words from the Reverend Doctor Martin Luther King, Jr.

Courage is an inner resolution to go forward despite obstacles;

Cowardice is submissive surrender to circumstances.
Courage breeds creativity;
Cowardice represses fear and is mastered by it.
Cowardice asks the questions, is it safe?
Expediency asks the question, is it politic?
Vanity asks the question, is it popular?
But conscience asks the question, is it right?
And there comes a time when we must take a position
That is neither safe, nor politic, nor popular,
But one must take it because it is right!

A great way to stay out of your comfort zone is to get an accountability partner or coach.

15. Spend more time on your zone of excellence and get more flow state

The more time you can spend doing what you do best and love to do, the better. This creates flow state which has a powerful ripple effect on your days and your confidence. (Go back to Chapter 9: Unearth and Max Out Your Zone of Excellence)

16. **Trust your instincts and intuition.**

   Then you have increased confidence in your gut to take prompt action and navigate the hard road to get there. Believe what you know about yourself.

   A relentless instinctive drive to do whatever is necessary can get you to the top and help you stay there. No need to go further than Oprah Winfrey:

   "Every right decision I've ever made has come from my gut, and every wrong decision I've ever made was a result of me not listening."

17. **Fuel the right fires (and quiet your inner critic) - reminders from elsewhere in the book that all have a big effect on your confidence:**

   a) **Turn up the volume on the voice that wants you to be better – your inner hero – you become what you think about**

   b) **Fuel your blessings** - Appreciate what you have

   c) Fuel your new identities **(on your habit tracker** – chapter 19)

   d) **Fuel your ability to say no a *lot* more** (Weed 5)

18. **Solicit and follow through on constructive feedback**

   If you're not making mistakes, you're not making things happen. Getting feedback from others is a crucial – yes, not easy - step to growing. Others can spot things you can't. (See Habit 4, Key 8)

19. Be aware of the (positive/negative) 'vibe' of your surroundings at all times

This helps you to avoid external surprises and get caught off guard in ways that severely undermine your confidence. Tune into the energy vibration of where you are. Does it feel good or does it feel rather depressing and lifeless?

20. *Scale up* if it healthily builds your confidence and you're not mindlessly chasing 'more'

There's no doubt that it can feel good to make more prospecting calls, do more workout reps and go for a longer run. It feels like you're making progress and that is always a wonderful feeling. I am inspired by it too.

Just keep an eye on what 'more' you're chasing and if something more important has to give as a result. Ever more and bigger business is wonderful until it isn't because you find yourself struggling to make time for other important priorities like your children or your health.

21. Be persistent and keep building.

- Brian Tracy wrote: *"Your persistence is a measure of your belief in yourself."* If you want to build your confidence, don't ever give up on yourself. Keep building. When the storms come, you may well have to focus on shoring up the foundation, but you never stop. You just remind yourself that it's a season that will definitely pass.

On the roof of Your Home of Confidence:

22. Elevate your beliefs and seek proof that your empowering beliefs are true

We believe what we believe because we seek and notice proof that we are right – even if our belief is ridiculous, e.g., all people who drive pick-up trucks/Porsches (insert your own bias here) are obnoxious or rude. As discussed in Habit 4, Key 2: Elevate Your Beliefs, to build your confidence, make extra effort to notice the things that feed what you want to believe but don't quite yet. Otherwise, your brain is going to lapse back to its old way of thinking – something less empowering and confidence- enhancing.

23. **Decisiveness. Commitment. Action. Success. Repeat.**

    Decide where you want to be. Ask yourself what you're willing to do to get there.

    Make a plan. Act on it. (Feel free to add any of these to Your Home of Confidence!)

    In addition, stay focused on <u>your definition of success, your consistency and Journey mindset and above all, you make your purpose greater than your fear.</u>

- When you can approach confidence as if you are building and sustaining your own beautiful 'home' – and doing your best to avoid messes - you can address it effectively and, finally, not rely on luck or things beyond your control to enjoy a lot more of it! Most importantly: take action on one step now.

  Elevate your confidence; elevate your control!

Key 8: Elevate Your Ability to Ask Anyone for Anything

For many years it drove me crazy that only about 15% of people who hired me would get great results from following my referral process. While it's true that you can't do the push-ups for someone else, I still felt badly that I couldn't help more people get out of their own way.

After years of seeking solutions to this and learning about mindset and the power of small habits, I decided to look much more closely at what the 15% did differently than everyone else. And I was quite shocked to see that this 15% had NOT made that many changes to mine their gold; they were not superheroes who needed to stay on the pedestal I'd unwittingly put them on.

In fact, for the most part, they only made two significant changes – *and you can do the same.*

They shifted a key mindset around asking and they developed a power habit. But before I go further:

<u>Let me start with what NOT to do when it comes to asking any-one for anything:</u>

> a) **Stop putting your self-worth on the line when you ask for something!**
>
> > One huge mistake we make is we (UNWITTINGLY) put our need for approval and acceptance at stake when we ask. We act crushed by a 'no' – even a 'not now' and let it ruin our day or week. We feel rejected personally as if our very professional survival is threatened by the other person's response.
> >
> > You can stop this when you…
>
> b) **DON'T TAKE IT PERSONALLY when people say no or flake out on you!**

"Taking things personally is the maximum expression of selfishness because we make the assumption that everything is about 'me'." – Miguel Ruiz

When people don't come through for you, it's because of **completely impersonal reasons**. Accepting this is not easy when you need to bring in new business. You have to be somewhat impatient and persistent, and the waiting part can be infuriating.

However, it's crucial to understand that people say no because:

* Of their own fears and insecurities

 * They don't understand the benefits to what you're asking

* They don't want to – but again – for their own reasons.

Often the timing is wrong for the other person – they don't need or want what you're offering or there are other life events going on that take higher priority *at least in their own minds.*

'Never Take Anything Personally' is one of *The Four Agreements* in Miguel Ruiz's excellent book: *"Nothing others do is because of you. What others say and do is a projection of their own reality. When you are immune to the opinions and actions of others, you won't be the victim of needless suffering."*

That's why you want to have a power habit, consistent prospecting recipe, or points system to follow so that you can build faith that the results will come from high enough activity. You fret less when one day or week alone does not produce the results you want – and when certain people don't get back to you on your timeline.

c) Don't get psyched out by others - Notice only your common ground

Unfortunately, all too often you can get intimidated (unwittingly) by the people you are asking depending on whether they:
Make more money than you do
Went to a better college or have more formal education than you
Are taller/bigger/physically stronger than you
Are better looking than you
Have more experience in their field than you
Are older or, (as you get older) younger than you

Even having all the apparent advantages above in their favor can still leave someone feeling like a failure on the inside and unhappy with their life. If you really want something, don't buy into the judgements that whatever culture you live in makes about who is more important and 'valuable'.

The solution is to remember that no one is better or worse than you. We are all equal souls. Focus on what you have in common: you are as human, you both have your own aspirations and goals, flaws and failings, unique strengths, and both of you have people in your life that you love.

When you focus like this, you can build a deeper connection with almost anyone and, in time, ask more for what you want that can help you mine your gold.

What the 15% did to get great results that you can do too:

1. Mindset shift (over time)

Each of the 15% told themselves something that empowered them to ask anyone for anything. Here are a few real-life examples:

1. **I'm a hard-working, thoughtful advisor** with a great network.

2. A client with $100m has to choose someone, **why not me** and my team?

3. *I now have **a process** to get consistent referrals that are turning into business (now when I ask, it WORKS!)*

4. ***Successful people want a younger advisor** who will be there for them long into their retirement*

5. ***My clients get THANKED** by the people they refer me to*

6. I know *my "One Thing"* - get **8 appointments/week**

= With a mindset like this, you can ask anyone for anything

There is no rule about *what* you say to yourself other than:

a) It empowers you

b) It is something you *increasingly* believe to be true.

The power of this is that instead of talking yourself *out* of making a big ask, your brain chooses a thought that helps you talk yourself *into* it. Ironically for others this may include not thinking at all and having the mindset:

I don't think, I act

One final example that I love was a 63-year-old I coached a few years ago whose shift was: *"I used to think 'I am an old financial adviser.' Now I believe: 'I am a WISE financial adviser who is proud of being in business and my clients are lucky to have somebody with 40 years' experience.'"*

It's crucial to understand that mindset shift *usually* takes weeks, sometimes months. It depends how hard-wired a competing unhelpful belief is, how much positive emotion you associate with the new belief, and how often you repeat it.

Other helpful mindsets:

MINDSETS:

a) Believe you're just trying to help others – make the focus of your asking *not about you* **but about helping others**. When you ask, don't come from a place of neediness but of helping others.

b) **Believe that asking for help is essential to get where you need to go and stop thinking it makes you look weak. High achievers ask.** I can't emphasize this enough.

When I interviewed high achieving advisors on my podcast in 2019 about what they attributed their success to, I was taken aback at how many of them made a comment such as: "Don't be afraid to ask a lot of people for help." Then they would often add: "I can't say I love asking for help but it's definitely part of the recipe."

I heard it so many times that a light bulb finally went off for me where I said to myself: How interesting. Many low and medium achieving advisors I've coached felt that asking for referrals made them look weak and were afraid it suggested that their business wasn't doing well, but the highest achievers – while they don't necessarily relish asking – accept that it's one of the rules of the game. If you want great results, set your ego aside and ask often.

You would think it were the other way around. You would think that the high achievers wouldn't need to ask for what they want. That it's just something everyone else has to do. In fact, it's exactly the other way around. We've got it all wrong. In other words, the recipe for you getting what you want is: get out of your own way and don't be bashful about asking often.

When you're running a healthy business, it's normal to have a sign outside saying: "I'm open for business, and that I'd like to help other people you care about."

One last thought: when you see a company advertise on television or online, do you ever think it makes them look desperate? Weak? No, you don't. You accept it as a normal part of what businesses do. You asking for what you want is exactly the same. I acknowledge that you are doing the marketing yourself when you ask, but that's all you're doing. Marketing activity to help people. Nothing personal.

> c) Accept help – don't let a lack of worthiness cause you to block opportunities or mess them up. Be prepared to get what you want!

Now it's your turn: **PICK ONE** of the above to get you started or come up with your own

Next, create a small habit for your new mindset so that every time you feel discomfort about asking anyone for anything, you can catch your old way of thinking that typically stops you.

After I worry about asking anyone for anything,

I will remind myself "why not me?"

Then feel good.

2. Develop a power habit

Because the aforementioned past clients made their asking a habit, they did it consistently day after day, month after month and that got them the big results. The other 85% were inconsistent with following habits and didn't do them long enough to see outstanding results.

What did the 15% DO? What did they ask for?

1. 5 'upmarket' asks/week

2. Ask 3 people/week to help me with something (test the waters)

3. 3 specific asks/week

4. 3 'stretch' asks/week (out of comfort zone)

5. 3 specific asks/week

6. 8 appointments/week

For more on this, see chapter 18, The 'Money' is Here: Power Habits

3. Overcome the biggest obstacle: yourself

The new mindset can be enough to help you ask anyone for anything. It was for the 15%. I wish I could claim everything was as simple as this for everyone. I've coached well over 1,000 people in the past 20 years and, while the right mindset truly is enough for some people, it's not enough for everyone. You may still find that you have some awkwardness about asking for what you want, so you will need to work on your worthiness and build yourself up. Dig a bit deeper on the inside to face down your asking reluctance. Here are a few tips:

In his book *Supercoach*, Michael Neill says: *"You can ask anyone for anything if you don't buy into your own thinking about it would mean if they said no."*

Really think harder on that one because it's completely true; we are the ones who make up the stories and this only hurts us. If you didn't worry at all about the reaction you were going to get from people, you wouldn't hesitate to ask. You've nothing to lose from asking because you don't have what you're asking for now anyway. So therefore, if you ask and you don't get it, you haven't lost anything. What we lose in our own self-talk is the interpretation that we give it, and that's what inflates it into something scary.

Create a mindset habit to address it:

After I feel uncomfortable about asking (specific person),

I will remind myself that **_success for me is "I'm facing my fears not living scared anymore"_** *(regardless of what they say or whether they respond)*

(And you can word the "I will" statement in any way that inspires you. **Experiment with this until you find the right words that get you to act**.)

Once this helps and your confidence grows, change the I will statement to:

"I will ask anyway and expect a yes."

You might find a wild celebration after your difficult ask will give your brain the dopamine hit it needs to encourage it to do it again. Try this *at home* a few times ☺

Ask yourself this daily question: "On a scale of 1-10 today, did I do my best not to be psyched out by anyone?"

Face the uncomfortable and you will find it wasn't anything like as bad as you thought it would be, you will feel GREAT about yourself, AND even more aware that you have far more potential to fulfil. That's exciting. That's being fully alive!

4. Implement a process to ask anyone for anything

The 15% needed the right mindset and power habit to get great results. They did even better because they also used a referral/asking process. I outlined a 6-Step process in my first book, *Fearless Referrals*, and then simplified it further to four steps/ five words and here I apply it to asking for what you want:

4 Step Fearless Asking Process: Earned; Who; Ask How; Control

Step 1: EARNED: Do you have enough water in the well in the relationship to be able to ask for what you want? Fortunately, most people like to help others, however, asking total strangers for big favors isn't likely to work out well terribly often. Most people are not going to stick their necks out if it feels too risky to them.

It helps in business to show that you *genuinely* care about someone as a human being vs. as a source of possible revenue or help (to earn the right to ask).

Provide help first if humanly possible to the other person before asking for what you want. At least inquire about how you can be helpful (and not just in passing; ask multiple questions). Put as much water in the well as you can – this also makes the asking easier. The more you come from a place of love, the more comfortable you will feel. The acts of kindness and thoughtfulness that I wrote about in Chapter 1 all apply here. The more you believe in what you're asking for, the easier it gets. This is not a technique! It's a way of being.

Step 2: WHO: Be so clear about what you want that there is no room for confusion. This is the most important step and one that most people do ineffectively. Don't ask for more time or money. Be specific about exactly what you want. If it's an introduction you want, identify the exact person you want to meet. Don't ask someone to refer you to 'anyone who could benefit from my services'; ask so that only one-two specific people come to mind.

Step 3: Ask How: Make sure the person you ask can help and feels *comfortable* and *competent* with what you're asking them. If you're asking for an introduction, get their opinion on the best way to go about helping you with your request. Always assume that this person could benefit from some guidance in the best way to go about helping you. Assume the person does *not* know how to introduce you effectively because this is not a skill most people have. Offer to write the introduction for them and give them permission to make any changes they want.

Step 4: Control: Firstly, do your best to get a follow timeline suggestion from the person who agreed to help you. This helps them think through when they are going to do it. It's effective to ask: *"When should I get back to you to see if (name) is open to talking to me?"*

Persist with your follow up. Only give up when, in your heart of hearts, you no longer want what you're asking for or no longer believe you can help the person you want to meet.

The other tips on follow up are between your ears and I've covered them elsewhere: don't take people's lack of responsiveness personally (above in this chapter) and detach emotionally as best as you humanly can from your efforts when you follow up and hear nothing (Weed 6).

What to say:

Develop wording that works for you to ask anyone for anything.

Here's a template to start you out if you're asking for an introduction to someone:

"It looks like we've got about 10 minutes left. Before we wrap up, there are a couple of things I wanted to ask you about.

Firstly, I would love to help more people that you care about.

I'm curious: of the people you work closely with, who do you get along best with that you'd be most comfortable introducing me to?

Thank you! What would be the easiest way to connect us?

And when should I get back to you to see if s/he would like me to get in touch?"

Also, when you ask, expect a yes.

You will ask with increasingly more confidence.

The Other Ask to Make is For Feedback

> *"Taking on board constructive criticism…however uncomfortable these encounters may be, if we are to reach our full potential, then it is a fundamental process that must be undertaken."* Gareth Timmins, *Becoming the 0.1%*

Face your fear of feedback so you can mine deeper

I've not found it easy to solicit feedback over the years. One of the most stunning lessons I've learned over the years from truly *thousands* of people across dozens of countries is how almost no one is ever asked for face-to-face open-ended feedback. It's a question I've posed many times to audiences around the world for a show of hands and it's mind-boggling how rare it is that someone has been asked to give feedback face to face.

Since business books have been espousing that "feedback is the breakfast of champions" certainly since the early 1990's, I can only conclude that most people feel too threatened to ask for feedback. Sure, online surveys can be easy to fill out. But I'm talking about YOU looking someone in the eye and asking. I think it's fair to say that since almost no one does it, that most people feel like it's too hard to stick out your neck and hear what others have to say about your work. Presumably we are too scared and fear that someone might say something that hurts our fragile self-concept.

Why should you care? Let me start with Elon Musk: *"I think it's very important to have a feedback loop, where you're constantly thinking about what you've done and how you could be doing it better. I think it's the single best piece of advice: Constantly think about how you could be doing things better and questioning yourself."*

And on the rare occasion when the feedback isn't positive: "Failure is an option here. If things are not failing, you are not innovating enough."

Troy, one of my most accomplished clients (he added $44m to his pipeline the WEEK I first wrote about this topic), always tries to get feedback when he loses a prospect because he usually learns something that makes him better next time. Julz, another past client of mine, is one of the best at her firm because after every meeting when she collaborates with a colleague, she asks: "What could I do better next time?" And she will ask again and again until they realize she means it and give her useful feedback.

What can we learn from people who have found ways to get comfortable requesting feedback?

1. **Find a way not to make it personal**

    Create a barrier between you as a human being and you as the professional/salesperson in that one situation. You are not your company name. That is a business entity. That is what is getting feedback for that specific business meeting or business relationship.

    In a weekly Clubhouse room I once hosted on *Tiny Habits and Confidence*, someone who coaches keynote speakers said: "I only allow a few people to pull my chain. I take the rest with a grain of salt."

    It is our ego that gets hurt and so the trick is to separate yourself from it. See it as feedback to your professional 'suit', not to you personally.

    Mindset can play a huge role:

    "Feedback is designed to help my life/business."

2. Reduce the impact by soliciting simple, constructive feedback

Part of the challenge with feedback is that many people are not skilled at giving helpful feedback so try to make it easier for them.

For example, ask: "What's one thing you think I can do better?"

This way you can receive the feedback as designed to help you, not hurt you. One of the things I always liked about Toastmasters was that for every presentation, one person was designated to give you feedback and only point out ONE thing you could do to improve (rather than demoralize you with multiple things).

That way, when you spoke next, you could focus on addressing one specific area (at a time) such as eye contact or gestures.

Two small habits for feedback:

After I feel uncomfortable about asking for feedback,

*I will remind myself that the feedback is for **my business**, not me as a human being – and it may give me ideas to make my business even better*

After I feel uncomfortable about asking for feedback,

I will remind myself to ask for one thing I could do better in the future

Good luck making inroads here that will help you grow!

Elevate your ability to ask for what you want; elevate your control!

Key 9: Elevate Your Sufficiency Mindset

As I wrote in Habit 4, Key 7 on Confidence, when you feel like there is never enough time, money, or energy to do what you want or need, it saps your morale. It is your ego that has to have more and, according to Eckhart Tolle, has you "condemned to seeking and never finding."

I do not pretend this is easy to address when our entire culture bombards us with how we should have more and that we are lacking if we don't always want more. But it is a recipe – a life sentence - for endless unhappiness and shaky self-confidence.

In *The Soul of Money*, Lynne Twist masterfully explains that we have been brainwashed by three "toxic myths of scarcity":

There's Not Enough

More is Better

That's Just the Way It Is

Her antidote is Sufficiency:

1. Know that there is enough and that you are enough

There are enough resources for everyone; it's just that they're not distributed. There has been enough food to feed the world's population since the 1970's. The fact that thousands of people die every day from hunger is an indictment on world leaders, human greed, party politics and a reflection of thinking focused on the three toxic myths.

When the Pandemic was in full swing, I did a webcast on this topic and interviewed various high achievers I know. Several of them referenced a turning point in their lives when they realized that there was more than enough to go around. One MDRT Top of the Table producer said that once he adopted this mindset, *"leads, referrals, opportunities – I started to see these things showing up more in my life."*

Another commented: *"I believe there is LOTS of money out there - more than I could ever need."*

a) The easiest place to start is to *seek proof* of abundance. Deepak Chopra recommends starting with nature. **Notice** abundance. As discussed in chapter 11, part of our problem is we look for proof to support all our beliefs (including the unempowering ones). If you always notice evidence for where you are in life, nothing will change. Nature can easily show you abundance.

b) **Start a list of things that prove abundance in your own life**: blossom out the list from just money so you can feel the positive effects: include good health, energy, and enthusiasm for life, fulfilling relationships, creative freedom, emotional and psychological stability, a sense of well-being and peace of mind.

Your ego and your inner critic will not want you to do this, so notice it talking you out of it. Most of the high achievers I'm talking about started from humble origins. They *chose* to believe something different. You can do the same.

As you see more evidence of abundance, *gradually* it will start to feel more normal. Depending on how deeply hardwired you are for scarcity, this can take time to shift – usually longer than you wish.

c) **Tell yourself: "I am enough."** Each of us is born with skills and talents to be developed. *This crucial reminder from Habit 4, Key 1 is one we all need regularly.* When we come at everything from a place of not being enough, life is always a struggle and never brings happiness and we only notice what we lack. We are never satisfied, never content. We never have enough and never feel like we are enough. What a perverse way to torture ourselves.

d) Don't make all your goals and dreams about your need to accumulate more – otherwise you stay trapped in the same rat race and, by default, the same shaky confidence.

The indigenous people Twist describes in her book have a different dream for the world: *"They see a world that is totally sufficient, animated with spirit, intelligent, mystical, responsive, and creative - constantly generating and regenerating itself in harmony with the great diversity of resources that support and collaborate with one another through the mystery of life. They see human beings as part of that great mystery, each human being having an infinite capacity to create, collaborate, and contribute."*

2. **Make as big a difference as you can with what you have.**

"If somebody offers you an amazing opportunity, but you are not sure you can do it, say yes - then learn how to do it later." – Richard Branson

a) Be more resourceful. Tap into your deep inner resources. **It's so easy to complain that you don't have enough money to do various things.**

What most people are guilty of is not being resourceful enough, of brainstorming or tapping into their creativity to find ways to be, do and have what they want in life. You become just like the hamster running on its wheel if your only thought is "I need more money. I need more time. I need more money. I need more time."

Stephen Covey saw this clearly: *"Your economic security does not lie in your job; it lies in your own power to produce - to think, to learn, to create, to adapt. That's true financial independence. It's not having wealth; it's having the power to produce wealth."*

Ask a better question: How can I make this happen? Who might help me? Who could I partner with? Who's done this before and how did they do it?

Part of feeling more resourceful is understanding your value proposition:

Who is your ideal client and how do you serve them best? Think deeply on this and be able to communicate it clearly.

b) Help others get what they want – give what you most want to receive.

This can sound like a platitude you've heard a million times but think about it: If you want friends, does everyone magically intuit this, or do you have to be a friend to one person first? If you want love, you have to be loving first. If you want success, you have to help others be successful first.

You can't stare at an empty fireplace and yell: "Warm me up!" You have to put the wood on the fire. Before you can have anything in life, first you must BE that thing. AND helping others - for the right reasons - makes you feel ever better (worthier) about yourself.

Forging a path for others can often open all kinds of doors for you too. In one sense perhaps you 'earn' the worthiness (even though you can argue that we are all equal souls with this earned by birth; if you don't *feel* that way, this argument may be harder to appreciate).

The easiest small habit to introduce is to find a quick way to add value to one person per day. This could be a text wishing someone well, sending someone information useful to him/her, or making an introduction between two people in your network. The key is the degree of thoughtfulness you put into it.

c) Enough is boosted by living your purpose.

Steve, a financial advisor I interviewed for a webinar during the Pandemic, told me that his purpose was to help others plan for a secure future: *"If I am living my purpose, I am happy, full, and fulfilled. When not engaged in those types of activities, I feel a bit lost. Hint: Lifting others up lifts me up as well!"* Return to Chapter 8.

d) Create a business plan based on your highest goal.

If your highest business goal is recurring revenue, increase your clarity on how you get there with everything you do.

e) Think bigger to make even more of a difference with what you already have:

You can apply this to any area of your life by elevating your expectations whether it's for your health or for more respectful relationships.

From a financial standpoint, Steve Siebold shares 100 contrasts in his book *How Rich People Think*. For example, he argues that rich people generate money through ideas that solve problems whereas middle class people generally trade time for money. He points out that rich people know that leverage creates wealth while middle class people think hard work does.

In other words, re-consider how you look at parts of your life where you want to raise the bar and be resourceful about the questions you ask yourself so you can shift your paradigms. When you change the way you look at the world, the world you look at starts to change. See the questions in Habit 4, Key 12 on Elevating Your Dreams and Goals and Chapter 18, The 'Money' is Here: Power Habits, for more on thinking bigger.

3. *"What you appreciate appreciates."*

When you plant and water seeds directed towards your highest ideals, ever better things will blossom (compared to focusing on how there's never enough). Respect, preserve and honor what you have.

You can find a new freedom around money with a sufficiency mind-set when you appreciate and develop what you have. It will expand as well as deepen your experience of yourself and your **true** wealth (which includes all you have to contribute to the world: money is only one of MANY resources we have to offer). Revisit Habit 4, Key 5: Elevate Your Gratitude.

What higher commitments stir your heart?

4. Collaborate, partner, share, and reciprocate.

This is about sharing and using resources wisely together. It requires generosity and openness.

When preparing for one webcast, a business consultant said to me: *"Being vulnerable with people…may not seem like it could bring abundance, but it's amazing to me when we live and speak our truth and are vulnerable, it can bring out the best in others and in ourselves."*

Lynne Twist adds: *"In our relationship with money, collaboration frees us from the obligatory chase to acquire more in order to feel we have enough and becomes an opportunity to make a difference with what we have."*

Chase a nobler cause than MORE. From this, grow new and greater possibilities and you can break through old limits. You can have a different dream for yourself and your family and a new relationship with money and what is enough.

"If we tend the seeds of sufficiency with our attention and use our money like water to nourish them with soulful purpose, then we will enjoy that bountiful harvest."

Elevate your sufficiency mindset; elevate your control!

Key 10: Elevate Your Support Team

Elevate Your Network to support your efforts to mine your gold: Battery Chargers and Battery Drainers

When Tim Ferriss, the famous podcaster and entrepreneur, was 12, an unidentified caller left a message on his family's answering machine: "You are the average of the five people you spend time the most time with," which is a quote from Jim Rohn. Ferriss was hanging out with the "bad" kids from his school at the time. He knew it would lead to trouble sooner or later, so he asked his parents to send him to a private school. Surrounded by a new peer group led him to a high school year in Japan where he studied judo, 4 years at Princeton, where he became an all-American wrestler, a national kickboxing champion, and eventually starting his own company at 23.

John Assaraf has built 5-multimillion-dollar companies, written two New York Times bestselling books and featured in eight movies, including the blockbuster hit "The Secret" and "Quest for Success" with Richard Branson and the Dalai Lama. He grew up poor in Montreal and also fell in with the wrong crowd as a teenager. What started to turn things around for him was thanks to a job he had at the gym at the local Jewish community center. After his shift ended, he would relax in the men's sauna. As it happened, night after night several local businessmen would unwind there too and talk about all their successes and failures. For him it was like getting a free education on what do and what not to do in running an effective business.

Tony Robbins tells a story of working on a project with the marines. When he met with those in charge, they wanted to know why marines who had excelled in the military often would underperform once they returned to civilian life and not maintain their great habits.

Robbins explained that "who you spend time with is who you become." Many of these marines would return to challenged neighborhoods with few opportunities and those marines would ultimately start to fit in and become like those around them - exactly as they had done as marines only with very different outcomes. You live up or down to the key people around you.

One challenge we all have is we don't realize how influenced we are by the main few people we spend most of our time with. We think we are independent thinkers who make all decisions on our own with no consideration to anyone else – except the minute we think that thought we know it's not true. We do consider who we live with and who we work closely with. We consider their feelings and preferences. We do consider what our family might think. And friends.

So then maybe we eat the food they want even though it doesn't support our health goals. We stay up late watching Netflix to make them happy even though that makes us less effective at work the next day. We spend time with people they like to keep them happy who aren't exactly lighting up the world, who complain quite a lot and aren't scaling new heights – and on and on. These are moderate and subtle things but cumulatively it can add up to years of under-achievement and mediocrity.

This isn't such a straightforward topic, is it? If nothing else, I want to raise your awareness of it. It's a curious blend of fear of success – that we might lose our friends and family – along with some people pleasing and ignorance.

You've likely heard of the concept that you are average of the five people you spend time the most time with. Few people take this literally enough. I remember reading years ago a comment from Mark Victor Hansen that if you wanted to make $1m, you needed to spend time with millionaires. And that once he made his first million, he started hanging around multi-millionaires.

I admit it doesn't sound very loyal (!) but for the principle to be valuable, apply it however you want to your one life. To be fair to Hansen, he wasn't talking about making friends. He was alluding to the concept that there are basically two types of people: battery drainers and battery chargers.

To use a different example, I remember when I played rugby. Every year we'd have a different teacher coaching us. My desire to impress tended to vary in these teen years depending on the coach. In my third year of secondary school, we had a maths teacher for a coach that I didn't respect entirely and didn't particularly trust either (many years later he was jailed for child pornography charges!), so I didn't push myself as much with him. But the following year we had Geoff Courtois, our PE teacher. I really liked him and did everything I could to gain his respect. I worked really hard under his tutelage. In other words, being surrounded by a different person (even with the same title) made a huge difference. The same is true in your own life. There are energy generators and energy vampires.

Don't wait to be cajoled by a friend!

Rachel had shown up excited for her meeting with the head of her department. She thought it was going to be a discussion about a promotion because her sales numbers had been so strong. The prior Saturday she had even been looking at a new car to buy as a reward. Once she arrived, this single mother with a young daughter could sense the discomfort in the room but was still completely blindsided and gutted when she was told that the university had to slash its budget and had to let her go from her fundraising role.

She cried so much as she drove home that she had to pull over. Her eyes were so full of tears she couldn't see well enough to drive. "At first, I felt lost. My mind went into a negative spiral as the (2008) economic crash hit harder. I was convinced I would not get another job and be able to put food on the table."

The turning point was when a friend came over to see her. He heard her out, then got in her face and said: "You can't afford to feel sorry for yourself right now. You need to step up and take as much action as you possibly can. And you don't stop until you've found yourself another job. Your daughter is depending on you."

This tough love, this friend getting in her face was like a bucket of cold water and it snapped her back into action.

At 28, ue had been dealing with a year and half of debilitating foot pain that turned into bodyside fatigue and ache. She had been active in the health industry since leaving school but faced a life situation that she did not know how to deal with. While at home one afternoon, her friend James stopped by to check on her and his dog jumped up and whacked her so hard on the nose that she thought it was broken. A colleague had been telling her many times to see his craniosacral therapist to get her foot looked at, but she had resisted because she'd already seen so many acupuncturists, bodyworkers, and doctors. But now that her face was out of whack, his cajoling paid off.

"She worked on my nose and I had a somatoemotional release, recalling a moment in 11th grade where my coach threw a windmill pitch at me that I wasn't ready for and the ball tipped my glove and whacked me dead smack into my face. It knocked me unconscious," recalled Sue when I interviewed her for my podcast. Her father pushed her nose back into place telling her "Don't worry. It will build character." But she never got her nose properly treated by doctors so had to face an entire school year of humiliating big nose jokes.

When Sue saw the therapist and she worked on her nose, the memory popped into her head like a flash. "The next day, my *foot* pain was gone and for the first time in nearly 2 years, I felt overall, more like myself. Like a cloud was lifted." That's when she realized, muscles and bones (the musculoskeletal system) is just one facet of the human body that we can help return to balance. Pain isn't just a muscle and joint problem and that was a huge revelation that veered her out of the fitness industry and into the healing arts.

Since then, she's developed a hands-off bodywork program called the MELT Method that has been featured on numerous national shows in the USA including the Dr. Oz Show, Rachael Ray Show, Good Morning America, and Live! With Regis and Kelly.

In 2009 I was at a birthday party. My friend, Stefan, had just moved in with his girlfriend. He and I had had numerous conversations as single men in their 30's and now his life had changed, and his happiness was so evident.

Part way through the evening, we were talking. I don't remember how the topic came around to my single status. I expect I'd congratulated him on his relationship and then made a couple of fatalistic comments about dismal dating experiences I had had that year and that I'd pretty much thrown in the towel. He got extremely impassioned, leaned in, and very directly said: "Matt, you need to get online again and meet someone."

I was so taken aback at his candor and was so unable to handle it, that moments later I remember thoughtlessly grabbing my jacket and driving home. I don't even remember trying to process what he said. He spoke with such care and conviction that without questioning him at all, I went online and filled out the application for e-Harmony.

The next day I did a favor for some friends by driving their son to his grandparents so they could go hunting together. I didn't take my laptop or give my application another moment's thought. When I returned, I logged in and saw I had a response from a woman near Chicago called Erica. Two years later we got married. And we're still married.

Sometimes we need a friend to kick us in the backside and say: "Get on with it!"

The problem is: ideally you don't want to wait for that!

Maybe you have a friend who needs you to do that for them!

That's what a good support team does.

Find someone who believes in you!

When Beata first came to the USA from Poland with her father, she really had no idea what she wanted to do professionally. The day it changed was when she offered to help her dad out by going with him to sign some mortgage documents. His English wasn't that good, and he needed her help translating. The lender was so impressed by Beata that he asked if she would like to interview to work with him. Thirty years later, Beata makes a seven-figure income as a mortgage lender.

"My mentor believed in me before I believed in myself and helped me see that everything I need to succeed is within me."

While I suspect Beata always had the drive to do well, she is certain that the man who hired her and mentored her in her early days made a huge difference in her life because she knew he believed in her. It's impossible to know the power of having someone in your life who believes in you when you don't really believe in yourself.

Scott, one of my former coaches became quickly estranged from his parents after he left home at 18. Raised by a hostile and unhappy mother and an emotionally distant father, he was only too glad to move out from his east coast upbringing and campaign for civil rights in the southern United States in the 1960's.

Looking back, he attributes all his key learning and positive direction in life to a mentor who 'adopted' him at that time and helped him find his own way to make a powerful positive difference in the world. The proof in the pudding is hearing the esteem Bill has for his mentor almost fifty years after the fact.

I can see the challenge if you're in this scenario because when you don't believe in yourself, it's even less likely you'll seek a mentor or someone who will believe in you. You may not even know it's what you need more than anything else.

If your self-worth isn't strong, it's also possible that you might disregard someone who tells you "I believe in you" because you might not think you really deserve it anyway.

Let me get practical.

1. **Write down the Top 5 people in your life. Then list out each person's strengths and flaws.**

   "Until you reach the point in your self-development where you no longer allow people to affect you with their negativity, you need to avoid toxic people at all costs."- Jack Canfield

   Are they negative and toxic (dream stealers) to you in any way?

   What percentage would you say each person is positive and nurturing?

   Severely decrease time with the former.

   Become more aware of the subtle influence this has on you.

   "There are two types of people – anchors and motors. You want to lose the anchors and get with the motors because the motors are going somewhere and they're having more fun. The anchors will just drag you down."   - Wyland, world-renowned marine artist

2. **Identify other people who would be uplifting to spend more time with**

   "Surround yourself with only people who are going to lift you higher."- Oprah Winfrey

   This might be something that takes place gradually. Increase your interaction with certain people because of the positive influence they have on you.

You might be asking yourself: how do I meet more people like this? You might want to join a new professional or civic group or business/country club. Or a new networking group. It's one reason entrepreneurs join YPO or EO. The same can be said for workshops and courses that help you develop your skills and knowledge – you meet like-minded people. That's one of the reasons I like to run coaching groups: the rising tide raises all ships.

A more radical measure would be to move house and live in a more affluent part of town. It is not as crazy as it sounds, and most affluent areas have some housing that is not high priced. You just have to go there and seek it out.

I can speak to this personally because I've done it. Even the 'elevating' effect it has on you is subtle and you don't notice how it changes you until you go to back to those former haunts of yours. I'm not for a minute talking about becoming 'better' than anyone, I am talking about raising your 'normal' to one where expectations are increasing and this forces/ encourages you to think bigger about what's possible.

3. **Ask the top people in your world to share their best strategies with you.**

   Avoid Weed 9 - Resisting a Proven Process and apply the process shared in Key 8, then experiment doing the same things, thinking like them, and reading what they read.

   These things will also help you raise your game and, as you do, you will meet people at higher levels and be able to rub shoulders with a new crowd.

   Jack Canfield summarizes this best in his book *The Success Principles*: *"You need to be surrounded with those who have done it; you need to be surrounded by people with a positive attitude, a solution-oriented approach to life – people who know that they can accomplish whatever they set out to do."*

4. **Support yourself better by noticing what you do right every day**

Notice what you do right – be kinder to yourself.

In my life experience, achiever types benefit from *some* task mastering; we all do better with some accountability. But frankly what they seem to need more is to be kinder to themselves. Not so they achieve less, but so they enjoy life more and, ironically, in so doing, often end up achieving more – just look at Richard Branson. His way of living has been focused on making a difference but only doing it if it can be fun.

I also think of a few athletes who manage to perform at high levels and do so at times with a smile on their face. I think of England's Jack Grealish and former Green Bay Packer Brett Favre. You might think of a favorite musician such as Sting.

For Steve Plewes, who used to run his own financial planning firm, the kindness and the magic happened after he identified his target market, clarified his value proposition, and delegated out more of the work – he gave up the control. These three things helped springboard him to focus on what he loved to do and do best.

In terms of being kinder to himself, it gave him permission to stop trying to be all things to all people, to live by his values, attract people who aligned with that and repel people who didn't. He would tell people that he was not available if his child had an event he wanted to attend. If someone looked put out by his priorities, he knew they weren't a good fit for his business. The clarity and outsourcing gave him permission to say no more often and for him to feel like he was being truer to himself.

Why are so may achiever types so hard on themselves? There's a funny saying: "the beatings will continue until morale improves." This is what I've experienced time and again with my clients: frequently beating themselves up for not hitting all the outcomes when they want them. Perhaps it's because we have had some success along the way and know we are capable of strong results. Perhaps deep down we felt most loved when we were recognized for an accomplishment – or it's really important to us because we feel that we didn't get a lot of recognition or encouragement growing up.

The mistake we make is that we tend to set the bar too high. Then we experience disappointment because our high expectations have not been met – even though we may well have done our best. We may well just have an unrealistic timeline. It can easily lead to a cycle of almost always feeling 'less than'. And on the days we do hit a target, we tend not to celebrate it enough but write it off as "well I expect nothing less!" or "that's good but you should be doing that all the time," – perhaps like a tough love parent or coach once treated you. So you can't even feel good about the win! That's misery.

Another mistake we often make is not expecting what Marshall Goldsmith calls the "high probability of low probability events" – all the unexpected things that pop up most days and throw us off track.

I hope you can start to see how this could be holding you back. It's why I love working with small groups of achiever types so they can see themselves in the mirror and see that everyone has off weeks and bumps in the road. They realize that they are not alone - that hurdles are a normal part of the journey and they don't need to be so hard on themselves.

Most of our self-talk is so harsh and so equally unproductive. Telling ourselves:

Why haven't I done that yet? What's the matter with me? I know it's important!

I am so lazy! I haven't done that yet. I am such a coward. I never made that ask!

Having self-discipline is great - doing the things we need to do whether we feel like it or not is great. But don't forget that your best ideas and most positive energy comes from multiple sources. You enjoy life more and are most productive when you're feeling inspired rather than feeling that you are constantly underachieving.

Do your prospects respond better to you sounding serious and anxious or to you sounding light and animated?

Do your prospects respond better to you sounding frustrated and impatient or to you sounding upbeat and energized?

When you're kinder to yourself, you're going to have better outcomes. How can you fail with activities that inspire you, relax you, invigorate you or recharge you more often?

We have too many 'have to's' and 'shoulds' in our day and not enough questions about 'what would I love to do right now?" or 'how can I make this fun?' or 'how can I accept, enthuse or be excited about what's happening right now?"

What do others do to be kinder to themselves?

We're all guilty of dropping the ball in some areas that would serve us better. I've gone years without journaling and have sacrificed my self-awareness as a result. I've gone years without slowing down to smell the roses in my race for 'success'. It feels like I may have gone decades without being as consciously present as I'd like. I've gone many months on numerous occasions where I skimped on getting enough sleep in an attempt to 'get ahead' faster.

What can you do to be kinder to yourself?

322

a) **Pause:** Reflect. Commend yourself for doing something right and taking care of yourself. Realize that *you are no good to anyone if you don't take care of yourself*. If you're sick or moody, you bring nothing of value to anyone. If you can't be present, you're just taking up space and letting real life pass you by.

b) **Journal:** You might start with journaling and becoming more self-aware. The benefits to journaling can be enormous if you go beyond your to do list. You can reflect on what's on your mind and explore it in greater depth. You can problem solve or brainstorm. You can unload pent up emotions and process them thoughtfully. It can help you unravel what's confusing you. Even when you can't resolve something on paper right away, you feel lighter for having expressed it – you almost feel 'heard'. And it's very easy for us to fool ourselves about things going on in our lives or our heads that we don't process.

c) **Talk to a trusted friend:** Talk to someone with whom you can simply think out loud, unload or get stuff off your chest.

d) **Breathe:** Or meditate to center your day. There's an adrenaline rush to constantly running and putting out fires all day, but it's exhausting and when you hit your wall, you are 'done' for the day. By pacing yourself better, you can be more effective throughout more of your day and be more present later in the day rather be a zombie or on autopilot.

e) **Exercise:** Stretch or do some yoga poses to be kinder to yourself. This can be done in small doses to incorporate your physical needs and keep you feeling more whole and engaged. It could be as simple as adding a short walk in after a meal or five minutes of stretching.

f) **Stay hydrated:** My wife's workdays can be so hectic and in numerous locations that she often finds it hard to stay hydrated. Being kinder to yourself includes making sure you are eating and drinking in ways that nourish your body. This is crucial fuel. It might include taking certain supplements to round out areas that need shoring up. These small things add up.

g) **Get enough sleep:** There is an increasing body of compelling research that speaks to how important it is not to skimp on this. If you're in a relationship where your partner negatively impacts the quality of your sleep, I urge you to confront this and discuss what compromises can be made so you take care of this essential need. I remember years ago my wife counseled someone who could not sleep much because her husband watched noisy TV in bed. The constant flashing of the screen in her eyes and volume of the shows kept her awake for hours. At some point he would eventually fall asleep with the TV on, but in her fitful attempts to sleep, yet more time would go by before she would get up and look for the remote to turn it off. Frankly that's at best selfish to the extreme and borderline abusive given how much our bodies need to rest.

h) **Reward yourself:** In being kinder to yourself, enjoy that glass of wine, beer, or fine scotch. Most people love chocolate. *In moderation* we all want to enjoy the smaller pleasures in life. It's usually unhealthy to have the plug in too tight. The odd donut is not going to kill you. It reminds me of a funny comment former Navy Seal Mark Divine makes in one of his books, that 80% of the time he is extremely careful about everything he puts in his body but that for the other 20% he "cheats like hell."

On another level, it seems almost perverse that I'm listing mostly basic needs under a heading of being kinder to yourself as if this is 'special' treatment. Most of what I've listed above should be givens in our life so that we function effectively. But we're all guilty of dropping the ball in some of these areas.

i) **The Mirror Exercise:** I first heard about this on an audio program by Jack Canfield. The principle is the same as the 5 Things I Did Right Today which I wrote about as a solution to Habit 4, Key 2. While looking at yourself in the mirror before bed, go through your day and compliment/acknowledge yourself for all the little and big things you did well. Then once you're finished, maintain eye contact with yourself and, using your name, tell yourself: "I love you."

This is more confronting to do. I remember when I first did this in 2006 it felt too uncomfortable and strange to handle. But when I revisited the exercise several years later, I found it helpful and affirming. Now it's time to address them by tiny steps. You need a great support crew. Spend time with idealists, visionaries, and people who: Believe in you; Encourage you to go after your dreams; Applaud your victories and

Focus on what's possible for you.

Elevate your support team; elevate your control!

Key 11: Elevate Your Persistence Muscles and Mental Toughness

"Talent is insignificant. I know a lot of talented ruins.
Beyond talent lie all the usual words: discipline, love,
luck, but, most of all, endurance." - James Baldwin

Amanda Allen started drinking when she was 14. While not the victim of any overt trauma, she took on the parenting role for her two younger siblings as they bounced between living at the hotels that their divorced parents owned in Australia. "Nothing was consistent," she wrote in her autobiography, *The Time of My Life*. She felt she didn't belong anywhere, and it slid into self-loathing and thoughts of suicide: "I was weak-willed, fat and just not right in the world." Drink became an escape from the mounting evidence she built in her head that she was "a fraud and a failure...For many years I just wished I could die."

She did sense, however, that she had a vein of gold in her: "I'm forever grateful that *a glimmer of hope inside of me refused to die*."

This was reinforced by some of her reading: "These books assured me that suffering was ultimately transformative, an essential part of the hero's (or heroine's) journey. **I believed it.**"

She was also frequently taking courses and learning from others. Most of the time, what she learned did not hit the mark for her: "Not that," she would say, but she persisted.

What brought her the consistency and the chance to build herself up - literally - and prove herself was checking out a CrossFit gym and starting to show up each day. She had always been a talented athlete but her mental health, inability to persevere, and her nasty inner critic had prevented her from mining her own gold for long and staying at the top.

She became willing to do the "grimy hard yards," she told me. "When I thought I couldn't go on, I just did the next most important thing: I just kept turning up." Gradually, she took ownership for everything in her life: "I got well one day at a time, leaving depression further and further behind me: one action, one thought, one meal at a time, one run at a time." Her workouts were a way for her to find out what she was made of and to keep building on what she called her "bedrock."

When I interviewed Amanda for my podcast in 2019, she said: "That bedrock is built by acts of integrity and learning to trust your own word and intention…that builds toughness." This is what struck me more than anything when we spoke – her ever growing desire to take one more step away from her painful past and toward a stronger future. She described her bedrock of graft as her "greatest strength" and "greater than any obstacle I've ever confronted."

At the age of 41, Amanda won the CrossFit Games and became a bona fide world champion. As remarkably, she went on to win it twice more - three years in a row – and even more remarkably after her second gold medal, she battled cancer and had 4.5 kg of fibroid tumors removed from her abdomen before going on to win her third gold medal!

"Every 1% of my life is the answer to being well. It's built a foundation." The 1% includes everything from what she eats, to what she watches on TV, to what she thinks about. "Even the soap I have in the shower is part of my 1%. It may not appear to have anything to do with depression or being a world champion, but it does."

She does nothing in her day by accident. Everything is there for a reason and found its way there by trial and error. "I put them there because I failed so greatly. I was in such a state of suicidal depression, and I never want to go back to those places again. Ever."

She used her past pain as fuel: "For decades I felt like I was a failure. I wonder why we think suffering is such a terrible thing. It is not comfortable but it's fertile ground for incredible positive change **if you choose to use it that way.**"

She learned to filter out the negative thoughts – to pull the weeds: "Most people bang around life not really realizing that thoughts aren't facts, feelings aren't facts. I heard it a decade ago and it was revelation to me because I was a slave to my thoughts." She now sees many unempowering thoughts as lies. "I filter out what is rubbish and what are lies."

Instead, she focuses on "the thoughts and feelings I have that are driven by my priorities and values for myself." Clearly, next to none of us is going to win the CrossFit Games: "It's not for everyone to be a World Champion. **Everybody has their purpose and whatever that is for you, you never flinch with it**. It doesn't matter what the context is, the principles are what are powerful." I couldn't agree more with this. I'm a very average athlete but my purpose to complete this book has driven me to put in quite grueling hours at time and not flinch about it.

Routine and habits have also allowed persistence and consistency: "Every morning is structured…and that gives me freedom to achieve all that I want to be."

When she describes grit, she believes that: "mental toughness is like motivation. You're not born with mental toughness. We all have capacities within us and it's up to us to harness them…My demons may be different to you, but the desire to overcome is universal."

Based on this story alone, to overcome your demons and build your own grit and persistence muscles:

1. Trust your vein of gold is there.
2. *Choose* to believe that **your past can be used as fuel** now to be who you want to be and that you can go on your own hero's journey.
3. Keep learning
4. *Just show up* – regardless of how you feel. Then test yourself and see what you're made of.

5. Build your bedrock/foundation 1% at a time. Your race, your pace.

6. With every action/thought/product, ask: **"Is this a 1% I want in my life?"**

7. **Thoughts and feelings are not facts. Pull the weeds fast.**

8. Keep your thoughts and emotions focused on your values, purpose, and priorities. Elevate your control and purposeful journey.

9. Achieve freedom through positive routines and habits

10. Never flinch with pursuing your purpose

What is grit anyway? University of Pennsylvania psychologist Angela Duckworth defined it in her 2016 book, *Grit*, as "determination and direction. Perseverance plus passion. It's consistently pursuing excellence towards an overarching goal or vision for your life." Former Navy SEAL and bestselling author Mark Divine describes it as "a non-quitting spirit" that has to be earned.

You want more grit to be better prepared for the inevitable challenges life throws at you.

What are the four psychological assets that people with grit – like Amanda - possess?

1. Passion - a strong interest in what they do

Amanda knew that beating her demons could be done by focusing her passion on developing both her physical health and her mental health by following a proven recipe, becoming a student of nutrition, and testing herself one step at a time.

Worldwide only 13% of adults are "engaged" by their work. The challenge is that many people are not clear about their passion or how to pursue it. It can take years of exploring followed by a lot of development and a lifetime of deepening. It is rarely a sudden discovery but usually a longer, less dramatic story or journey.

A good place to start is to dream big dreams (see the next key!). Tim Grover was Michael Jordan's trainer for 15 years and worked closely with other basketball legends like Kobe Bryant and Dwayne Wade. In his book *Relentless*, he endorses dreaming big because your instincts will not steer you wrong. You're not going to dream about things that are not possible for you: *"Everything you need to be great is already inside you."*

2. A capacity to practice and a desire to improve

All gritty people aspire to improve continuously and grow by *deliberate* practice (not just repetitive hard work).

It starts with the growth mindset that you can get grittier and that your past life script doesn't determine you. Amanda had that "glimmer of hope" that the hero's journey story just could be hers too.

Here's what it involves:

a) Clearly defined stretch goal

b) Full concentration and effort

c) Immediate and informative feedback

d) Repetition, reflection, and refinement

The second half of this process includes:

Make a mistake/fail; get help; determine what went wrong and what needs to be done differently; take new action – get back on the treadmill!

The mindset you need is: Do the things you need to do, when they need doing, whether you feel like doing them or not. Olympic gold medalists all know that it was not talent that got them on the podium: rower Meds Rasmussen sums it up well: "When it's not fun, you do what you need to do anyway. Because when you achieve results, it's incredibly fun."

3. Purpose – a growing conviction that your work matters to you and others

What you most want is an overarching goal or vision for your life that can give you your sense of purpose. How do you most want to make a difference in the world? Part of finding your purpose is connecting your own dots to how you make a difference now and to what you value. For Amanda it became helping others as a personal trainer and lifestyle coach. Revisit Chapter 8: Discover More Purpose.

Below this purpose/life goal are potentially several layers of goals that range in importance from low-level daily to-do items to medium level steps that fulfil the larger purpose. Small steps, one at a time – see Habit 5! One valuable skill set is to be aware of your different goals at different levels to make sure they keep you on purpose.

And be aware which goals should be abandoned because they distract your focus and send you in the wrong direction. Grit does not always mean "never give up on every goal" or "work even harder". Improving includes adapting as you learn and progress.

What's the value of all this grit? Big results and mining your gold can take years.

When Simon Wiesenthal was tracking down Nazi war criminals after World War Two, it was not unusual for an investigation to take 10-15 *years*.

Josef Mengele, Auschwitz's 'Angel of Death' who tortured thousands of children in medical experiments, was pursued for 34 years before the man was known to have died hiding in Brazil.

He hunted Adolf Eichmann, who was head of the Gestapo's 'Jewish desk' and responsible for transporting the Jews for the 'Final Solution,' for 15 years before he had information that got Eichmann abducted from Argentina and ultimately tried and executed in Israel in 1962.

4. **Hope - optimism to handle failures and persist with your gold mining**

Duckworth defines hope differently from many. She argues that hopelessness is caused by suffering that comes from being in a situation where you think you have no control (hence the importance of Habit 4).

Hope is taking charge of the future you want to create. Amanda told me: "When I finally admitted to myself that I was an alcoholic, then I was willing to do whatever it took."

Hope = having a **growth mindset** that leads to **optimistic self-talk** that leads to **perseverance over adversity**.

Amanda's self-talk shifted towards the optimistic too: "We just have dark nights of the soul, and - you know what – that's okay. It's normal. We need seasons to grow. Plants have got to be savaged by storms to grow stronger. It's the same for us…Failure and suffering have extremely negative connotations in society and it's a mistaken identity. The more and greater the failures, the more you move to success."

Advanced Ways to Develop Grit

In Steven Kotler's *The Art of Impossible*, grit is defined as one of the traits you need to build because no matter how much fuel you have, it's never enough to sustain you every day to succeed at a challenging endeavor. **These gritty exercises also help to build flow and leverage the crucial neurochemicals we need to improve our performance levels and mine our gold**. He makes it part of his recipe for peak performance. Here are some recommendations to developing more grit:

1. **"Do the Hard Thing First."**

   This is akin to the Navy SEALS motto of **"Embrace the suck"** or the phrase Brian Tracy coined 'Eat That Frog' first thing in the morning. Whether it's exercise you don't relish or some big prospecting calls you need to make, get the most challenging thing or the action most outside your comfort zone done as early as you can.

   Your willpower wanes as the day goes on. This includes your self-discipline to do the things that are in your best interest (exercise, tough prospecting) as well as losing the self-control to avoid the things that can sabotage your goals (e.g., making poor food choices or drinking too much as the evening goes on).

2. **Learn to adjust to change quicker**

   Gareth Timmins was 20 when he signed up to be a Royal Marine Commando. While he describes his 32-week training as a "nightmare," he gritted his way through to be awarded the coveted Green Beret. In his recent book, *Becoming the 0.1%*, he concludes that: ***"Nothing is more fundamental for 'sustained' personal growth, productivity, and effectiveness than one's ability to adapt to change quickly."***

This is supported by London Business School professors Lynda Gratton and Andrew J. Scott in their global bestseller *The 100-Year Life*. They argue that a multi-stage life of living close to 100 is upon us (not the old three-stage life of education – work – retirement) that requires ever better handling "significant uncertainty". Some of the ways to adapt better are by having great self-knowledge, building diverse and dynamic networks, and a growing willingness to ACT (not think) your way to change through continuous learning and new experiences to build additional skills. (I created a tracker/planner specifically for this: *My Breakthrough Tracker* which helps you accept and adapt to change better. You will find it on my website and Amazon etc.)

This is no small point. The advances made in the past 100 years are astonishing compared to the rate of change over the rest of human history. No wonder so many people are stressed, and educational institutions struggle so much to keep up preparing their students for jobs that are either becoming extinct or have yet to be created.

Build this muscle or you will get left behind.

3. Have a low energy grit exercise to build perseverance muscles

For the days when you're running very low on fuel - such as when your toddler or a pet has kept you up half the night – have something testing for yourself that doesn't completely write off your day: 100-200 leg squats or push-ups/press ups might check this box. Why push yourself like this? Kotler has found that: ***"The grit that matters most is learning to be your best when you're at your worst."*** On this other side, we discover new reservoirs of energy - the second or third wind.

Mark Divine wrote about this third wind in *The Way of the Seal*. When he went through Hell Week to become a Navy

SEAL and got to Day Five (of six) without sleep, he was shocked to "notice my body getting stronger. *Maybe I am capable of twenty times more than I think I am. What are my limits?* I wondered. I'm still wondering to this day, as I have repeatedly blown past my own expectations and seen thousands of others do the same."

Even if it's 'just' your mood that's not feeling like it. Gareth Timmins learned that: ***"What we do behind closed doors, when the spotlight is not us, matters the most. It is the investment, commitment, and self-sacrifice (or lack thereof) that we do without hesitation, when nobody is watching, that makes us either incredibly average or furiously unstoppable."*** By the end of their training, they were as fit as Olympic athletes.

Next time you say to yourself: 'I don't feel like doing it now – and no one will notice anyway' when you are supposed to be something difficult and valuable, catch yourself and remind yourself: 'I'll never get great outcomes if I don't take action.'

The moral of the story: Don't place limits on yourself and your gold mining.

Stop playing it safe.

4. **Treat failure as just one of your teachers**

One experience I used to be ashamed of was how I gave up on being self-employed about five months after I started. My initial experience starting my coaching business in 2002 was a time when my emotions ranged from euphoria to near terror. There were exhilarating moments landing my first few clients and speaking to groups - once I even sang a song to introduce my business at a chamber event and won an award for it. There was the thrill of going to my first

Toastmasters meetings to improve my speaking skills; every time I drove down the hill towards the restaurant where we met for lunch, my mouth would literally dry up in anticipation of having to stand up and speak.

I remember the joy of sitting in coffee shops helping people create goals that were not just 8/10 goals but ones they were really, really excited about. I had left my teaching job in Wisconsin, returned to England, and moved to Albuquerque – where I knew nobody. At times it felt vindicating to frequently discover incredible views from the top of the Sandia Mountains and explore a completely different city in the desert rich with American Indian culture.

I recall driving around town listening to *Networking with Millionaires* by Thomas J Stanley on repeat and feeling like I was learning about a world I never knew existed growing up around schoolteachers. I was fascinated. I remember walking into a large corporate building for a meeting at a New York Life office and marveling at what on earth I was doing – how I had literally walked into a new world I never thought I'd experience. Just once I recall treating myself to a meal at a restaurant after landing a new client and sitting outside looking up at the sunset over the mountains and feeling, for a few moments anyway, that I had "arrived", that my big risk was worthwhile.

But the stark contrast was not just living outside my comfort zone: I was living in a frequent panic zone - trying to make ends meet as a business novice in an industry nobody had heard of (what was then called life coaching before it got itself a bad name) with no network or friends in one of the poorest cities in the country with a high crime rate to match.

For a week I washed dishes at a Route 66 diner. I got a part time job at a book shop and taught an improv comedy class in the evenings. I had no health insurance and when

I walked my dog on the trails, I was in constant fear she would either clumsily shove her nose in a rock crevice and get bitten by a rattle snake or pick up the bubonic plague and transmit its fleas to me (yes, that really did kill a handful of people each year in New Mexico at that time – no idea whether that's still the case). I lived in a cheap apartment with no furniture except a desk and I slept on the floor. And I spent money on two high quality suits so I could look the part of the successful coach at networking events.

After five months I was $2000 in debt and felt completely ashamed. I had never been in debt before. I had even cashed out my small teacher retirement money at high expense. I remember sitting on a concrete parking block by my car outside a fast-food restaurant feeling that I had completely dishonored my deceased father who had always taught me financial frugality. Not long after this, I got back in my car with my tail between my legs and drove back to Wisconsin where I had lived before and started picking up substitute teaching work.

It took me several months to pay off my debt and was the following summer when I chanced across a book in the career change section called *Road Trip Nation*. It was a collection of interviews with high achievers in various fields done by two travelling college students who had rented a mobile home for the summer. I was inspired by what the contributors had to say and took copious notes.

When I went back through these interviews – and I did this unwittingly as it wasn't something I usually did – I actually decided to pay attention to which piece of advice was mentioned the most. I've no idea why because I'm not normally that detail oriented. When I tallied everything up, the most frequently mentioned point by far was that **failure should be expected and that it was simply part of the journey.**

That everybody failed. In fact, *the people who got the furthest had failed even more than everyone else.* The only difference was that they hadn't given up.

This was a complete revelation to me. "It's normal?" I thought to myself. "How is this possible? How did I not know that?" I had found the going tough early on with my business and, when it wasn't an almost immediate success, I had truly come to the conclusion that "this must not be for me" and that "I wasn't destined to ever be good in business."

I wondered: How come I hadn't learned growing up that failure was normal? Did nobody teach me this or did I just manage not to pay attention to this? I reflected on my sporting experiences and how we certainly didn't win every rugby game and, while this was always disappointing, it wasn't shameful. "Wait, that means I can try again!" I said to myself. "I don't have to put up with a life I don't particularly enjoy. Wow!"

This was such a foreign concept: Everybody fails.

It's crucial to have a healthy way to handle 'failures'. You can decide what true failure is. You can come up with your own definition. We all make mistakes. No one is perfect. When we are younger, it's common to define some failures or losses as earth shattering and final – professionally and personally (yes, I made that mistake too!)

Some people don't use the word failure at all. They reframe it as 'a lesson learned'. It may be one of the biggest cliches, but we all learn far more from our failures than our successes. That's really the message. What did you do right? What do you need to do better or differently next time?

Then regroup and go out and do it again - also aware of the Haitian proverb: "Beyond mountains, there are mountains"

– in other words, don't be gutted to see more mountains after you get to the top of your next mountain. (I know almost none of us wants to digest that, but it's for the best).

The bottom line is really this: don't give up on yourself. And when you fail – because you will – how do you bounce back? How quickly do you get up after you've been knocked down?

Do whatever works for you so long as you continue to mine your gold.

Remind yourself: Everybody fails. It's part of *everybody's* journey. It's on everybody's recipe for success. You can decide how to define failure – not anyone else. Sometimes it's the only way you can learn an important lesson - It's just one of your teachers. And the highest achievers fail *the most*.

5. **Toughen your mind through controlled positive focusing**

   Doubt and disappointment are constant. Even when you have top producer habits and routines, there is inevitably some boredom and frustration. These five strategies from Mark Divine will help develop more empowering neural pathways in your brain to keep you in the game:

   a) **Control your response:** When feeling stress, learn a deep breathing technique that can calm your mind and your body. Divine likes Box Breathing where you inhale for four counts, hold your breath for four counts, then exhale for four and hold for four more counts.

      Mindfulness – Be interested *in the gap* between thought and feeling because you want to develop the FREEDOM to choose your reaction so you can halt negative thoughts. 5-20 mins/day.

b) Control your attention with positive self-talk:
International speaker Mohammed Qahtani, a Saudi Arabian engineer who had a stuttering problem and went on to win the Toastmasters World Championship of Public Speaking tells us: *"Words have power...Your mouth can spit venom, or it can mend a broken soul."*

Your amygdala is biologically biased for negative thoughts on a scale of 9:1! Negative thoughts are constrictive thoughts. They increase stress and crush innovation. Fooling your brain with hyped-up affirmations will not work. It knows whether you're a multi-millionaire, Iron Man athlete or not.

Kotler's research has found that our brain needs three positive statements to erase every negative thought. **Turn up the volume on your inner hero voice versus your inner critic.**

c) Develop emotional resilience: First, remind yourself: "I am not my thoughts or feelings." Shift your emotion from anger to determination or from doubt to curiosity. Divine adds: "Note how you feel physically with each shift."

A gratitude practice will also alter the brain's negativity bias. Remember: *Feel* it when you do it. 5-10 mins/day. Go back to Habit 4, Key 5.

d) Effective goals: The key word is 'effective' – the right goal can help you focus on what's most important at any one time which can reinforce your mental strength. Navy SEALS train for ONE mission at a time, not ten – so avoid having too many goals. For more on this, see the next key, Key 12: Elevate Your Dreams and Goals.

e) **Visualize powerfully:** I covered some of this in Key 2: Elevate Your Beliefs. There are three forms of visualization: guided meditation, mental projection, and mental rehearsal. The latter two forms are best for building mental toughness. You can picture yourself achieving a goal and practicing a skill or upcoming meeting/presentation.

By running through these events in your mind in an empowered way, you can manage and reduce your fear better when it happens in real time; you will feel more capable.

6. **Lean into what scares you most**

Fear is okay. Normal. Find a way to leverage your fear and look at fear as excitement, a focusing tool or a playmate.

Everyday Tony Robbins jumps into a tub of cold water as part of his wakeup routine. "There's never a morning I jump in cold water and want to do it. I say "GO". I've done it so many times so often, that it helps me have less fear. You do it whether you feel good or not." This shows me his humanity. He still feels fear.

Nelson Mandela never claimed to be fearless. "The brave man is not he who does not feel afraid; it is he who conquers that fear."

And this isn't all about macho tasks and jumping off cliffs. It is all relative to what's outside your comfort zone.

Fear is, well, scary. When we push ourselves hard - physically or mentally – the pain induces fear. **The first key is to turn this into focused determination and the benefits you're getting.** Mark Divine noticed: "After my mind and body regained balance, the experience made me stronger and wiser. There was nothing to fear from the pain but the fear itself. This happened repeatedly during my time in the SEALs, and it has become a habit since." (Sensible caveat: you want good pain that makes you stronger, not bad pain that leads to injury or regret. I've made that mistake a few times!)

If you can dig deep and find the funny side, laughter at crazy times like this can help: "It's incredibly empowering to find that you can change your story simply by taking control of your facial and verbal expressions." Divine adds: **"Connect the pain of the moment to your purpose and goals and know, deep inside, that you are travelling the upward spiral to success."**

"Fear is an illusion of the mind," is what Gareth Timmins found. *"Nothing is ever as bad as the mind projects it to be."* Given how many life-threatening situations he encountered as a Green Beret in Iraq and later as a private Maritime Security Contractor in Somalia, it adds huge reassurance and credibility on the topic for me. Break tough situations down and visualize better outcomes that you can then take positive steps on.

Focus and flow come when you rise to bigger challenges. This is exactly what you want more of! But the MOST INSPIRING PART is this observation from Steven Kotler:

"The even larger lift comes afterward, with the discovery that our real potential lies on the other side of our greatest fears."

Amanda Allen shared this with me too: "I pushed myself to be as good as I could be – to give everything. It's like holding yourself in a fire, literally a furnace and you've stepped closer than anybody else and held yourself to that fire. And what I found is I didn't flinch." She learned to thrive under pressure.

7. **Taking risks is a flow trigger too that also produces dopamine**

   Risks could be physical, emotional, intellectual, or creative. It can include presenting on a topic that's quite new to you or asking a client a tougher-than-usual question that puts you outside your comfort zone. It might include dancing at a conference social. This is definitely on my list where I tend to feel really awkward! And that's the MAIN GOAL: **get used to being uncomfortable**. You can either desensitize to this slowly OR flood the area by going all in. See avoiding fear as more uncomfortable.

8. **Get gritty about recovery**

   We are not machines, and we cannot run all day every day. Especially A-types resist taking the time to recover, but I remember Amanda Allen, a three-times World CrossFit Games winner once telling me that *recovery* **was her secret weapon.** For more on this, see Habit 4, Key 4: Elevate Your Health.

9. **The even better ingredients for ferocity**

   Kotler finds that: *"Excellence, no matter what level, will always take everything we've got."* The three core characteristics set the highest achievers apart:

   a) **You have to dream big** (again, do the exercises in the next key)

   b) **Lots of flow to sustain long-term perseverance**

   c) **Habit of ferocity – *"this is the habit to immediately and automatically rise to any challenge."* You need gritty training and fuel to do the impossible. You**

need to automatize your instinct to lean in to the hard.

10. **Mental strength, resilience and smiling in adversity can be learned.**

One of the most interesting observations for me *Becoming the 0.1%* was Timmins revealing that he thought the Commando training would remove his fear, anxiety, and self-doubt *"and ultimately strip me of all emotion."* To his "surprise" and "horror", it didn't. But what it did do was teach him how to identify and manage his emotions, *"and that is only possible when you undertake something large enough that it allows you the opportunity to explore the innermost workings of your being, and to find resolve."*

What's a project or goal you could pursue that would obligate you to step up this much?

And, if you don't hang onto your mental strength, Corporal Rickards reminds the recruits before a key endurance test, *"you lose it upstairs, you'll lose it your heart, and then quitting will become easy."* I'm sure you can relate to that process when you gave up on something. I know I can.

There are plenty of useful ideas here for you: do the hard thing first; pick a grit exercise for days when you feel 'off'; get feedback on your greatest weaknesses and work on them gradually; a 5 minute gratitude practice; meditate for 5-20 mins per day; have a tiny habit to shift experiencing fear into excitement; take more risks to see who you're capable of becoming and get used to the feeling; schedule active recovery so you're ready to go tomorrow and lean into the hardest things automatically!

Experiment, have some fun with it and above all, persevere in that, well, gritty way.

Elevate your persistence muscles; elevate your control!

Key 12: Elevate Your Dreams and Goals

> *If you're an entrepreneur, you've got to dream big and then dream bigger.* - Howard Schultz, CEO, Starbucks

> *My parents are both massive feminists and always led me to believe that I could dream big and do anything that I wanted in my life, almost to a delusional degree.* - Jennifer Hyman, CEO, co-founder, Rent the Runway

Before you get back to sprinting too fast each week from one place to the next, when was the last time you dreamed? While it's socially acceptable to talk about goals, it seems that talking about 'dreams' has a bit of stigma to it. It can come off as sounding a bit fluffy and naive.

When I first started in business, I had this cassette tape by Brian Tracy called *The 21 Success Secrets of Self-Made Millionaires*. I listened to it endlessly in my car. The very first 'secret' was to "Dream Big Dreams". This sounded rather fanciful to me as I desperately attempted to stay afloat financially, but it *always* inspired me. I was in my mid-30's and didn't know I was allowed to still dream. Later it was Matthew Kelly's *The Dream Manager* that I loved. He reminded me that **we all need dreams to chase if we are to avoid empty, flat lives.** And these dreams can be in any area of life.

It's a terrific reminder that everyone needs:

    a) Meaningful work

    b) To feel that they are making progress

    c) "The belief that they are moving toward the fulfillment of their dreams"

Yes, we will get to goals later, but I urge you to find up to an hour, if possible, on your own in peace to do the following.

a) At the top of a page, write: "I would love to…" and have at it! Make a list of dreams and, notes Kelly, **"if you find yourself putting it off, ask yourself why."** Add to it over time.

b) Then, work through these terrific questions compiled by Clark Kegley in his e-book, *11 Questions That Will Change Your Life*:

1. How can I do my 5-year plan in 5 months?
2. How do I get paid to do what I love?
3. If I had all the time and all the money in the world, what would I do?
4. What would make me most excited to wake up in the morning to another day?
5. How has being "realistic" or "responsible" kept me from the life I want?
6. What three things am I most proud of?
7. What have been the three most defining moments in my life?
8. What has been my greatest lesson learned from failure?
9. When do I feel most myself? When do I not feel most myself?
10. What's the one thing I believe is true that others think is crazy?
11. What would I do if I knew I couldn't fail?

This last one has always been my favorite question. The mistake we make is to only answer these questions once and then not do it for again for years. Make a note to answer these questions quarterly – use *My Breakthrough Tracker* to keep them top of mind.

c) My favorite question in *The Dream Manager* is this:

"Isn't one of the primary responsibilities of all relationships to help each other fulfill our dreams?"

This begs the question: are you clear not only about your dreams but your partner and your children? Your best friends? *What about your clients?* I suspect some of us fall at the first hurdle here (ourselves!).

The Dream Manager makes a very compelling case to run this as a program for your employees. Move past initial objections to doing it because it won't be a quick fix and understand that this will be far more effective than offering simple financial incentives. Kelly argues that we all need a dream manager to hold us accountable and that we can all play the role of dream manager with others.

It is really important to keep dreaming. It's not just for the children and the ultra high net worth. You deserve to do this too AND it will take you further.

Once you've got some loftier aspirations, then it's time to turn towards goals. Since goals is a topic a lot like health – you don't need another in-depth chapter explaining what they are, **let me start with five reasons goals matter so much:**

a) Best benefit: **we know where we're going.** When we do, we get there more quickly. Goals provide the steps to be in business and satisfy our needs.

b) They help with FOCUS: Our brain can only handle 7 bits of information at once.

c) Goals help you realize your ambitions

d) Goal-orientated people put more effort into accomplishing their goals

e) Goals make decisions easier and help you avoid whims and moods

I find it easiest to break down goals into areas of my life: Health, relationships, professional, financial etc.

You will start to notice that as you do so, you ask yourself the question: what type of person do I need to be to reach this goal? You may find that who you become is more important than most of your goals. Because if you increasingly become this person, you will be full of self-respect, confidence, and happy with whatever progress you make - so long as you do your best - as life continues to throw the unexpected at you most days!

Set SMART Goals most of the time: Specific, Measurable, Achievable, Realistic, Time-Bound

> I earn $x by Dec 31, 20xx
>
> I weigh x lbs./kg by June 30, 20xx
>
> I enjoy x date nights with my partner/children per month
>
> My favorite goal to set does not meet all the above…

1. **Set a breakthrough goal.**

   If you want a large increase in motivation, big goals lead to the best outcomes (challenging but attainable). Jack Canfield defines one as:

   *It's an *ambitious stretch*
   *It produces a *quantum leap* in one area of life

   *It's something you can accomplish in one year
   *It should be very compelling for *you*

   ***It scares you somewhat**
   *You aren't exactly sure how you're going to reach it

Caution with setting goals that are very hard to attain – for *most* people (in my coaching experience I'd say about 98%?) these backfire and can lead to frustration and dissatisfaction.

To stay in the race, you will need strategies to keep your head in the game with a goal like this because it is so far beyond what you have reached before.

2. **Set goals for 3 Years – 1 Year – 90 Day – 30 Day** (where it serves you)

3. **Tread carefully about who you tell**

   There are two opposite camps on this one – you decide!

   a) Keep them to yourself because telling others can give you the feeling it's already been achieved. It might dilute your efforts or open you up to naysayers who fill you with self-doubt and prompt you to talk yourself out of it.

   b) Tell the whole world and you'll be too embarrassed not to achieve it – you've stuck your neck out and committed yourself.

   I've seen this work on social media with a former client who wanted to lose a lot of weight. I do not know if he kept the weight off!

4. **Set clear goals for each day**

   Have a well-crafted daily and weekly to-do list of tiny missions. Stack little wins each day and build big confidence over the months.

   I hope you can make this a fun exercise and don't forget you can always modify goals. The journey does not go well for perfectionists and will always be a curve that goes up and down. These steps can set you up for success on your terms, give you the focus you need and the inspiration to make this your best year yet!

Elevate your goals; elevate your control!

As I conclude Habit 4, I realize that on any given day, you can wake up feeling like there's little fuel in the tank, unexpected events can throw you off, and weeds can appear in your garden, including ones you thought you'd pulled enough times never to see again. This is when you want your brain to think about Habit 4 and focusing on what you can control.

Fortunately, it's a long list: remind yourself of the worthiness mindsets and what it takes to emote new beliefs into your garden; do a monthly GPS and journal – ask better questions such as 'what is life trying to teach me?' or 'who can I make a difference to today?' Use *My Breakthrough Tracker* – find it at www.BreakthroughBound.com

Get the endorphins going again by getting some exercise; write out and feel what you're grateful for; find peace in the woods or pray; pluck an idea from Your Home of Confidence such as taking action on a to-do item without waiting to feel confident; ask for something you want; revisit the sufficiency mindsets and go somewhere that gets you into a more resourceful state of mind; seek support from someone who shores you up or offer to shore up others should they need it – get your head off you and onto serving others; build your persistence muscles or do some active recovery, and look over your goals again.

Choose your hard: taking another step forward is hard at times; giving up is hard. Work further on what you can control, and that circle will grow remarkably over time. I doubt this is news to you! Be patient and persistent and be amazed over the months and years about what kind of gold you can mine.

HABIT 5:
BE AND DO YOUR
CHANGE CONSISTENTLY

So far in this book, what's been reinforced deeply is to source as much fuel as possible to help you mine your gold (because motivation is inconsistent), to pull the mental weeds that derail you, and to focus on taking action on the many areas of your life that you can control. But if you want new results, change requires doing something differently. The good news is it doesn't always have to be hard especially once you understand how.

It is normal to resist change and it is also normal – for you too – to need some change. Ease into this chapter at whatever pace feels right. Remember: "My race; my pace."

CHAPTER 15

The Three Mindsets for Mining Mastery

Before you kick off into action, you want to make sure your head is pointing in the right direction, so you set yourself up for success. It is our thoughts that that determine our emotions. Our emotions determine our actions. Then our actions determine our results.

Mindset 1: The Half Marathon Mindset - The Mindset You Want to Succeed at Almost Anything

If you had to step outside right now and run a half marathon – 13.1 miles, could you do it? Most of us could not come even close.

If you want to mine your gold, the first thing you need to do is to adopt a 'Half Marathon Mindset' – truthfully about how you see the world. Why? Because there's rarely a quick and easy way to accomplish something big and substantive. **You need to get your head in the right place**. **You want to manage your own expectations** and not set yourself up to fail by giving up too soon because the results you want simply take time and likely will require you to overcome setbacks. It's important to acknowledge now that there will be ups and downs along the way.

Virtually the only way you are going to mine your gold is to take the many small steps and do them consistently. From 20 years of coaching many hundreds of people, **inconsistency and not staying**

in the race are the biggest reasons people don't get the results they want.

The vast, vast majority of people I've coached over the years had the ability, the intelligence, competence, and the people skills to achieve certainly very good outcomes, but most did not stay in the race long enough and even fewer were consistent, especially once the coaching ended.

Recently I heard an interview with a star player from the Las Vegas Raiders. He came from a Division 2 college, was not a high draft pick, and he was asked how he had done so well and continued to get better. His response: "Mindset and consistency."

You might be a little disappointed to read such a non-sensational revelation. Even I wish I could tell you that after my obsession with reading 'success' literature for over 30 years, I had found something 'sexier' to share.

Mindsets 2 and 3: The Journey Mindset and the Consistency Mindset

In 2010 I hit my first business peak and it still gives me chills to think about. Just a year prior in 2009, the economy had tanked, and everything looked grim and surrounded by scarcity for me. I was single, living in a low-end condo with no couch or TV, just a dining table and a furnished bedroom and office. Every penny I made went into the business. But I did four things right in 2009: I stayed in business – kept coaching and building my network, finished and self-published my book, I joined an online dating service, and I made a trip to the UK before Christmas to meet Nick Cann, the CEO of the UK's Institute for Financial Planners (IFP) in London.

The following year these seeds (plus some I'd been watering for a few years) blossomed and I had a week-long speaking tour across Louisiana (home of the best food in the US in my opinion), I spoke at the annual IFP Conference in Wales, the Million Dollar Round Table in Vancouver, met someone there who invited me to speak in Dubai that October, spent two weeks in the summer in the UK where I had some unforgettable workshops including at Britain's oldest inhabited castle (and haunted if you ask me), introduced my girlfriend to my family, helped my brother in law out for a few days when my sister was unwell, got engaged at the Grand Canyon and made by far my biggest income to date.

It went so well that I was breathless and felt it greedy to want more. I didn't know where to go next! And gradually some of my best habits started to wane as I subconsciously wondered if I deserved so much success. I didn't notice any of this happening.

Two other mindsets I wish I had understood and applied were the Journey Mindset and the Consistency Mindset. One Hit Wonders don't know about this either. Some child actors don't know about them nor do some athletes who achieve remarkable things at young ages. I'd had plenty of adversity before 2010 but the year was so overwhelmingly amazing that I didn't know how to follow it and I didn't understand **the Journey Mindset** that says:

Life is a journey: you have to think about your life as going to the 'gym' forever – not just to have consistently good health but to pursue strong long-term habits in all areas of your life. This mindset will help you recover quicker from the inevitable setbacks and lifequakes *and* help you sustain and build on your successes.

And many of those habits can get, well, monotonous. Think about it: have you ever heard an Olympic athlete or your favorite sports star say: "What I love most about my sport isn't the thrill of the big game, the millions of dollars I make, the fame, the attention, and the lucrative advertising deals; what I love most is how exciting my practice drills are – how every day as a (fill in the blank sport/position), I get to practice exactly the same (fill in the blank sport/position) day-in, day-out, from dawn to dusk just as I have ever since I started playing when I was 5!"

What **you have to come to terms with is the routine (i.e., often** *dull***) nature of your powerful, productive habits.**

You have to go to the gym forever if you want to mine your gold to the best of your ability.

Do your best to focus mentally on the outstanding outcomes you get from doing the right thing day in and day out whether you feel like it or not. These reminders are really important because it isn't easy to show up almost every day.

The mindsets that help you do this are the Half Marathon Mindset, the Journey Mindset, and the Consistency Mindset because, for most of us, running 13.1 miles would take a lot of small, consistent actions done repeatedly over a long period of time before we'd be able to accomplish this. And the journey of life is, hopefully, a long and rewarding one.

(BTW: If you're the rare bird who can run a half marathon handily, feel free to call it something else, such as the Master Chef Mindset or the Guitar Great Mindset - something that would require a lot of effort for you to achieve.)

The Consistency Mindset is you becoming the type of person who is increasingly consistent - someone who shows up whether she or he feels like it.

The only way to prove this to your brain is to do it - to take consistent action and become a consistent person.

This is where you go from:

The THOUGHTS (I am becoming increasingly consistent)

And feelings (I feel good when I am consistent)

To the (consistent) ACTIONs that get you

The RESULTS (you increasingly mine your gold)

As you start to believe increasingly, over time, that you are consistent, you are going to take action that is congruent to this – you are going to do the right things week-in and week-out most of the time. I know this sounds easy enough, but until I taught this explicitly, I found 85% people were not consistent. **Inconsistency is many people's biggest problem to getting the results they want in most areas of their life** and I'm sure you see this with some of the people in your life too. Most of us don't have a knowing problem; we have a doing problem.

What should you be consistent about? Developing ever more productive habits including the five in this book!

The moral of the story is: if you want to mine your gold, you must have a mindset that reminds you to stay in the race and to be consistent whether you feel like it or not.

From a practical standpoint:

a) **Keep the mindsets in writing and highly visible**. I have the Half Marathon Mindset printed at the top of my daily Habit Tracker.

b) **Set calendar reminders for future months** to check in with yourself and ask:

Am I still in the race on this January goal?

How consistent am I being with the actions I need to take?

It's easy to be nonchalant about this now or in early-January, but in mid-March? August? Early November? No offence, it must be human nature, but this is where most of us struggle and fail. I don't want this to happen to you. Reading this chapter and 'knowing' this is not enough. Your brain needs frequent reminders: 'These actions may not be exciting, but they will get me some exciting results once they become habits and I do them long enough.'

- **BE and DO Your Change *Consistently***

CHAPTER 16

What Type of Person Do You Need to Be?

When Blair hired me ten years ago, he said: "My clients average net worth is $1-3m and I want to get that to $5m by the end of the year. Can you help me?" I asked him what type of person he needed to be so that he could achieve such different results and he said: "I need to go increasingly upmarket. I need to focus on bigger opportunities."

Once he was clear about his new identity, he committed to making five asks per week for opportunities in the $5m+ market. His success came because he was consistent about this week-in and week-out and, happily, by year-end he reached his goal.

When I called him seven years later, his average client was worth $20m. He explained, *"Honestly, it was <u>a progressive evolution</u> where I went from focusing on anything to then >$3m to >$5m, etc. With your help, I continued to develop my skillset and decided to focus on the Ultra High Net Worth (>$10m) where my skillset resonates."*

What Blair did was to start his goal where we all need to begin: with IDENTITY (how you see yourself). Einstein was the one who said you can't solve a problem (i.e., expect new and better results) with the same level of thinking that created it. You have to use a higher level of thinking and see yourself as becoming a different person (which you are perfectly capable of).

All change starts with thought which determines your feelings which determine your actions which determine your results. Remember? You weed your garden of unempowering thoughts and feelings and replace them with the flowers you want.

Before you can have your gold, first you must BE something.

Question 1 = Based on the past 12 months, what type of person do you NOT want to be?

Question 2 = What type of person do you need to be to mine your gold?

    a) Brainstorm a list first.

         Think about character traits such as bold, consistent at prospecting, focused, resourceful, or confident. One of my favorites is 'willing to ask anyone for anything'.

    b) Then pick **no more than two** to focus on first otherwise you are chasing too many rabbits and it will dilute your outcomes.

    c) I URGE you to always precede your trait with the word "INCREASINGLY". Your brain must buy into the change you are making. If you have an ambitious identity that is not very close to your current reality, your brain will be quick to talk you out of what you're trying to change. This is the main reason new year's resolutions fail so soon. If you struggle to run a mile but decide you want to become someone who is an 'Ironman athlete', you must precede your new identity with 'increasingly'. That way, even when you make small incremental changes, you can tell yourself you are on your way – however long it may take you.

d) Word it positively and in the present tense. Instead of 'stop procrastinating' or 'stop over-thinking' write 'I AM increasingly quick to act'.

e) *You can always revisit your list and make a change* if you feel confident that one identity has been addressed or something else has become more important to you. What you will find is that as your confidence grows, you will be willing to take on loftier identities.

   Other useful questions to help you decide your two identities:

   What do you most want and what's your biggest obstacle?

   What would you do if you knew you couldn't fail?

   Which area of your life is causing you the most pain and how can you step up?

   e.g., Inconsistency; You are too hard on yourself; Your sense of worthiness for much bigger success; You doubt your abilities to achieve great success.

   What are you afraid of by mining your gold? Failure; Not being good enough; Not looking good; Rejection/Being criticized/Getting hurt; *Imagined* responsibilities of bigger success – revisit Habit 3, Weed 1: Fear of Success for more.

   Lasting change comes from a paradigm shift:

   What do I mean? The real purpose to these questions is to uncover that how you see yourself is probably your biggest obstacle to mining your gold. Addressing this includes identifying and facing

down some fear. It includes changing a way of how you label or look at yourself that currently does not empower you to grow and breakthrough.

Your destination is to change how you see yourself, to change your identity, and move away from your old labels of "I am the type of person who isn't…" to "I am an increasingly healthy/focused person," or "I am an increasingly effective and consistent prospector." Remember: since the turn of this century because of fMRI technology, neuroscientists have been able to physically *see* neural pathway change - your brain has plasticity so it can change whatever your age; it just may take longer for something more engrained.

If you embrace this process *and back it up with consistent activity*, you can make the shift to: "I am the type of person who can change," and "I am the type of person who can mine his/her own gold." It's pretty amazing. Have some fun with this. It's the best place to start…

Easy Start: List out some answers to this question first: *Who do you NOT want to be in the next 6 months?* Then reverse them into the opposite quality that you can increasingly become. Final point: revisit this question most months because your answers will probably change as your priorities and life changes. As you excel in one area, another will need your attention. It will definitely help you adapt to change.

BE and DO Your Change *Consistently*

CHAPTER 17

How to change and be consistent

"Don't wait for the muse…He's a hard-headed guy who's not susceptible to a lot of creative fluttering. This isn't the Ouija board or the spirit-world we're talking about here, but just another job like laying pipe or driving long-haul trucks…Above all else, be consistent." - -Stephen King

Problem One: Until 2020, I always considered myself change-averse and someone who believed that change was hard. I made the same mistake we all do with a belief: I only sought evidence to prove it. I noticed all my clients who struggled to change; I noticed the ones who did change but then couldn't sustain it for more than a few months, but I managed NOT to dwell on the ones who transformed themselves. I remembered the times when change was hard for me and failed to remember the times I adapted to change remarkably easily – other than to discount these times as good fortune or the exceptions.

While each of us varies in how well we handle change *today*, I now know that we can all learn to adapt better and change. You need to learn how to make it easy to get started, believe you can change, and notice the proof.

Problem Two: When my business first peaked, my newsletter would go out like clockwork every week. And, every Sunday, I would go through my prospect list and write out who I needed to contact that week. During my 'wilderness' years when my morale dropped because I couldn't figure out how to help the 85% of my clients getting underwhelming results (even though they got the same content and coaching as the other 15%), this newsletter would go out very sporadically. Sometimes a few months would go by, and I wouldn't send it out at all. Then I'd have an 'up' burst and send it out for a few weeks. Then it would stutter, stop for a while, re-start, and repeat. For years. My weekly prospecting habit happened (at best) every other month.

A few years ago, I recall getting a very excited referral to a woman who I was told had a brilliant business idea. My friend Michael said, "You've got to meet her. Try to figure out how to work with her." I thought I'd heard it all, but I remember going home after meeting her for coffee and telling my wife how I wish I'd thought of her idea. I rather enviously said to myself: "She's going to make millions." But she has only gone through bursts of ups and downs and never established any ongoing traction or trajectory. I see her on social media or in my inbox for a while and then months of silence.

In 2017 I coached an inspiring and immensely likable financial advisor with big goals. He exploded out of the gates and everyone in his weekly coaching group loved him. Two months later he wanted to quit. "I've figured it out now," he assured me. I told him this was unwise because his biggest presenting problem was too many peaks and valleys. For many months after that he would have a hot streak and go cold for as long. Nothing has changed since then. No big goal has been met.

Everyone rightly talks about the power of persistency. But **what gets surprisingly little airtime is the power and frequent absence of CONSISTENCY in our lives.**

Where are you inconsistent? With prospecting? Exercise? Making time for key relationships? Your financial decisions?

When I look at the 15% of biggest success stories of people I've coached, they rarely exploded out of the gates. They picked small things to work on that were effective at generating business and **did them week-in and week-out**. By year end – and several times it took 2-3 years – their results were *spectacular*: Numbers so good they sound made up. They are all millionaires now and most of them earn that every year.

To get a breakthrough and some really rewarding outcomes, it is going to involve strong habits. Big self-discipline muscles. *Consistency.*

The first one-three weeks of your mission are fairly easy, but after that is when most people start to wane and give up because:

We all-too-quickly start to talk ourselves out of it...

The unempowering hard-wired subconscious beliefs and stories have not been exposed and denounced

Our sense of worthiness is not high enough

Our hope that we'd see quicker positive results gets dented

We realize it's going to be hard work

Our grit levels are too low

We start to remember past failures as proof we are wasting our time

No one else is supporting us in our efforts to change

We may be trying to change too many big things at once instead of making small incremental change

We get demoralized by watching the news

We compare ourselves to others when scrolling through social media and feel envy at their pretend-perfect lives and 'genius'

And sometimes we just get really busy and distracted with our current lives and haven't prioritized the new direction or found a way to create a new (even small) habit around it

– and this may only be the start of the list.

How do you avoid this? Be aware of these pitfalls. **The daily battle is to make it as easy as possible to keep your thinking focused on what you want and what you're doing right to get there to keep your thinking off the above traps.**

We underestimate how much effort, strategy, planning, and how many tools this requires.

The solution for both inconsistency and learning how to change is this:

Know how to craft a tiny habit

Why? Because this teaches you how to start small and make it EASY to change. In other words: *lower the barriers to change by finding an easy way to start.*

The power of this over time is subtle and stunning.

How to Craft a Tiny Habit

This process comes from Stanford professor BJ Fogg and his 2020 bestseller, *Tiny Habits*. He has spent twenty years researching how people change and found the best way to do it is to stack the new behavior/habit you want on top of a hard-wired existing one. I was so impressed with the simplicity and effectiveness of this process that I certified as a Tiny Habits coach. His simple three-step process is this:

    a)   Current habit (e.g., pour my first cup of coffee)

    b)   Stack new desired habit (e.g., take my vitamins)

    c) Feel good

All habits are written with the same starting words:

After I… (do current habit)

I will… (add new habit)

e.g., If you're struggling to take your vitamins consistently, put them right by where you make your coffee so it's easy to remember to use and write your habit:

After I pour my first cup of coffee,

I will take my vitamins

You want to make it as easy as possible to succeed. Scale up when you're ready.

The third element and the KEY to creating a new habit is the dopamine hit right away afterwards. Fogg told me that this was the "secret sauce" to having success instilling a new habit - what he calls 'celebration'. I prefer to think of it as 'feel good'. This is making sure your brain gets a dopamine hit *immediately* after you do the right thing. Acknowledge yourself in a positive way for having done the right thing. Experiencing this feeling is *really important* so your brain feels rewarded right away and wants to do it again.

The 3 things you need for any new habit:

    a) Prompt (reminder to do it)

    b) Skill (you know how to do it)

    c) Motivation (you have the desire to do it)

Tip: EXPERIMENT until happy. This mindset helped me enormously. It's okay to try things a certain way and, if it doesn't work well, don't give up simply say 'I need to find a different approach.' Test out various ways.

You can scale up from tiny any time you want. Fogg believes that psychologically it's better to set a low bar that you hit consistently but acknowledges that not all achiever types are motivated by a low bar. You can experiment with what works for you.

Musician Miles Davis knew that great progress depended on change: "It's not about standing still and becoming safe. If anybody wants to keep creating, they have to be about change."

The key thing to understand is that you change best when you feel good, not when you feel bad. **YOU change best when you feel good, not when you feel bad**. Even if it feels like you're praising yourself for doing something too trivial, remind yourself you're on a new road to making really positive change in your life – and that is worth feeling good about: a journey of 1,000 miles begins with a single step, right?

The life changing news is to stop blaming yourself for inconsistency and erratic motivation and focus instead on the more predictable reminder and ability to get yourself in action. Find a prompt. Start small. Feel good.

BE and DO Your Change *Consistently*

CHAPTER 18

The 'Money' is Here: Power Habits

Power Habits: Leveraging the 80-20 Law with One Habit

A number of years ago, a financial advisor called Asvin came up to me after a workshop I ran at the Personal Finance Society conference in Birmingham (UK) and said: "I've been in business for 24 years. For the last seven, I've achieved Court of the Table, but I've never made it to Top of the Table. Do you think you could help me get there?"

Top of the Table is the elite level at the Million Dollar Round Table, the most revered organization in the world of life insurance. I asked him the question I ask every new client: "What type of person do you need to be to make it to TOT?" He thought about it and said: "I need to be more consistent. I have great months and then other things seem to come along and distract me."

I told him: "You need a Power Habit to prove to your brain that you're becoming increasingly consistent. A Power Habit leverages the 80-20 Law which states that you get 80% of your outcomes in any area of your life from 20% of your activities: it gets you a significantly skewed outcome for the time you put in. This is an activity you do week in and week-out whether you feel like it or not. What's the most important activity you need to be consistent with – and how can you measure it?"

He looked over his numbers in recent years and replied: "I need to increase my average number of meetings from five to seven. If I can do that, I'm sure I can make Top of the Table."

For the next twelve months, we talked every Monday for thirty minutes. Every week. The same commitment. It wasn't sexy or fascinating. It was consistent.

Most weeks he fell short of seven and sometimes it was hard to see where it was all taking him. But his consistency paid off. Even though he ended up averaging 6.5 meetings/week, he exceeded his goal by an additional 21%. More importantly, he has exceeded it for the nine years since in an *increasingly upward trajectory*.

Identify Your Power Habits

First make sure you're clear about what type of person you need to be so you can be/do/have what you want in the upcoming months. Then your next step is to decide on a Power Habit that will get you the biggest bang for your buck to help you get there. Have one or two for your professional life and one or two for your personal life.

When my coaching is focused on prospecting and referrals, the answer is always around making a certain number of specific asks per week. If you knock on enough of the right doors, sooner or later ever better opportunities will come.

I've also had clients commit to making 'stretch' asks – by their own definition an ask that gives them butterflies. These take longer to come to fruition (9 months+) but can be very powerful at helping you go bigger with your business.

If you want to be increasingly healthy, consistent workouts are going to leverage the 80-20 Law and be a great power habit. A diet of mostly veggies, protein and fruit will likely get you there too. Date nights with your partner or one of your children are also a great example of a power habit that will have a much bigger positive impact on your key relationships.

An alternate way to arrive at your power habit is to answer this question that Gary Keller wrote about in his book *The One Thing*: *"What's the one thing I can do such that by doing it everything else will be easier or unnecessary?"*

What's Your One Thing?

Keller discovered the power of this when the board of his real estate company reduced a brainstormed list of 100 ways they could grow their business all the way to down to pick their 'One Thing': Keller should write a book about how to make $1m/year selling residential real estate. The book was so popular that it catapulted the firm to #1 in the USA as Realtors from other companies jumped ship to join them believing Keller Williams could help them make $1m/year more easily.

The premise is that you will become far more successful by spending your time on fewer things and doing what you do best – as in Chapter 9: Unearth and Max Out Your Zone of Excellence.

His simple message was to time block four hours/day to do what matters most and guard that time with all your might.

What ONE THING can I do such that by doing it everything else will be easier or unnecessary?

Note: your answer should be BIG and specific (e.g. if you know your business will grow 10% each year doing what you're doing now, you would want to aim for something much grander – 25% or 100% to get you thinking beyond the obvious).

Once you have your priority established (yes, one priority not eight!), bring the question towards the present by asking yourself: Based on my goal, what's the ONE THING I can do this year?

Then, reduce this to what's the ONE THING I can do this week?

Skipping these steps makes the outrageous goal too intimidating.

Now you can look at a power habit. Is it a time allocation to work on the big goal or something you can do daily in smaller chunks?

When you can only focus on ONE thing, your answers may surprise you because you can't lean on the crutch of the laundry list of possible next steps.

What I've learned since I read this book in 2013 is that **it may take you many attempts before you really are clear about your One Thing.**

Another metaphor in the book that explains how your ONE thing adds up over time is the domino effect. Once you start with the right question, your focus and actions accumulate. Step by step these actions build MOMENTUM to create exponential results not incremental ones. And Keller did it himself by co-founding Keller Williams and building what became the largest real estate agency in the USA at the time.

Apply an extreme version of the 80-20 Law to your focus (the Pareto Principle that 80% of your results come from 20% of your activities). Whether that means spending much more time with your top 6 referral sources or top 3 clients who are most likely to refer you, stop trying to convert 80% of the people you know to refer you – it's a waste of time.

You only want 3-4 Power Habits. You want to make it easy to focus on what matters most. When your day gets thrown off by the common unexpected event, it is the Power Habit that gets priority.

A few tips about power habits:

   a) *"To live great you have to think big."*

You don't know what you are capable of unless you set an ambitious goal: Big is not bad. It may cause some fear and worthiness questions but answer this: **"Do you know what your limits are?"**

No, you don't. Keller argues that you start out by thinking BIG (5-10 years out) and then break it down to SMALL (this moment).

Be more aware of how you might be causing your own inconsistency. Then sit with your own wisdom and ask: *What is the one thing - if I did it consistently - that will make the biggest difference for my business growth?*

Come up with your answer. For more on thinking bigger, revisit Habit 4, Key 12: Elevate your Dreams and Goals.

b) **WATCH OUT! Routines can feel dull after a while but must be maintained:** It's like the Olympic swimmer who joked: "I only have to swim twice: When I feel like it and when I don't." We all have a need for the interesting and the new. **You need to quiet the voice trying to persuade you to add variety when you already have a great recipe.** We can unwittingly take our eye off the very habit that is getting us to where we want to go.

c) **WATCH OUT! Your lack of worthiness creates self-doubt:** rather like a ship starting to steer in a new direction, what's been normal and comfortable for your thinking will be challenged as you start to sense ever better results. This can prompt warning signals from your brain saying: "This direction is unfamiliar. Are you sure you know what you're doing?" (See Chapter 11 – Understand Your (Brain as a) Garden for more on this and revisit Habit 4, Key 1 for the best mindsets.

This is where you need your Inner Hero voice to chime in: "I've worked hard for this. Yes, I deserve to be on this new path."

You MUST identify your power habits. Without any doubt it is the consistent implementation of these that I have seen from past clients that leads to outstanding outcomes.

BE and DO Your Change *Consistently*

CHAPTER 19

Track Your Mining Process

Now you know how to design your own habits and identify which ones are your power habits – the most important ones – now I'd urge you to track them.

I am a HUGE fan of habit tracking.

Here are some of the benefits:

You get frequent dopamine hits so you can feel good often throughout the day.

You get proof on a very consistent basis that you are doing your best.

It helps you align with your new identities and provides proof that you are becoming this type of person.

It builds self-respect – you keep integrity with yourself that you are doing what you said you would do. And when you don't, it can make you feel incongruent for good reasons – you're letting yourself down (unless you've picked an unimportant or ill-timed new habit)

It builds self-worth. You have documented proof that you are taking positive steps consistently.

It builds confidence. You are doing things that make you feel good about yourself and are in your best long-term interest.

You get great results sooner or later (with the Journey Mindset).

Look at the picture of the Habit Tracker at the end of this chapter (p. 268).

Hopefully you'll find it fairly easy to understand.

a) Across the top, write in your top 1-2 identities.

b) Consider adding why it's so important underneath.

c) Then you'll notice the months of the year across the top and the days of the month below that.

d) The next thing I'd draw your attention to is in the bottom half of the tracker: "Power Habits." If you only write in 1-2 habits, this is the place to start and these are the most important, remember? If you're uncertain, you can't go wrong with the key 1-2 professional habits and at least one relating to exercise.

e) Returning to the top half, this is where your other 'supporting' daily habits go. I like to have these represent my whole life so include smaller health habits, work habits and ones relating to my family. In addition, I also usually have a few Daily Questions there too (See Chapter 20). Some habits you might simply put an X in if you get it done. Others might be better suited by a number score depending on whether you're measuring yourself in some way.

f) In the bottom half there is also room for weekly and monthly habits.

The first few months I used my tracker, it was a mess. I would cross various habits out either because I lost interest in them, they were too hard, or I simply was trying to change too many things at once.

The best advice I can give is to EXPERIMENT with it and **make sure it feels good to use.**

You're much better off starting with 3-5 things on your tracker and growing from there if you want to. You might want to shade out big areas, so you're not tempted to fill it all out and then get overwhelmed by trying to make too much change too fast.

If you're scared to start tracking, I do understand AND *just start*. Start tracking one thing and when you feel ready, add to your list.

One reason to have more items on your tracker is that you reference it more often which helps keep them top of mind. The more you think about them, the more congruent you will be about following through on them. Remember your goal is to normalize these behaviors to become hardwired so you can improve the quality of your life and, if you want to, go onto even more impactful change. But do remember you can only work on so many new things at a time. And you probably don't know what that number is until after you do a lot of experimenting.

Tracking is not for everyone all the time! When I trained as a Tiny Habits coach with Stanford professor BJ Fogg, he was not a strong advocate because he had seen it demoralize too many people. They would start out on a good path, but when life threw them off at some point (as it does all of us), they would stop doing the habit and would feel so dejected by this, that they would often give up – the tracker made them feel even worse about themselves as if 'proof' of failure.

Sometimes tracking isn't helpful to your progress. If you're feeling a bit fragile or that you're being tested too much by life, then tracking may well backfire. It may be one too many things. You change best when you feel good not when you feel bad.

What do you do when tracking feels like too much *right now* or you've fallen off the wagon?

Both are common occurrences. These are your options:

a) Look in the mirror. Choose your hard.

Tracking your habits and results is hard; Going too easy on yourself for fear you might feel badly about yourself (and living with mediocre outcomes) is hard.

Our egos can convince us of all sorts of nonsense and when we don't track or pay close attention to our habits and outcomes, it's scary how well we can fool ourselves into how we spend our time and the choices we make. I do it too: "Ooh. A Do-Rite Boston Cream donut – well having one of those is okay because it's a high-quality reward for all my hard work and besides, it a *luxury* donut!" But my waistline shows a less-enthused verdict.

At least be honest that it's not *all* for the best that you need a break right now from tracking.

b) Reduce your tracking. Experiment. After a hyper phase of having three pages of items to track one year (yes, a bit mad), I scaled down to two pages and then one. I've also taken breaks from tracking because I have over-done it and burned myself out. Experiment with not tracking for a while or perhaps to track just one thing.

Make it easy to succeed. Change can be challenging to adjust to. If you don't feel good about it, you're better off changing what's on it. Now. Reduce your targets and make it easy to succeed.

c) **Pause your tracking and put in a calendar reminder to revisit when to resume.**

Sometimes it is necessary and healthy to take a break because of a lifequake that demands much of your energy. I understand. I've had them too: I've lost a parent, had twins, and been immobile with back pain that required surgery. I've experienced what felt like cumulative failure.

When you've fallen off the wagon and you do check back, look in the mirror please! It's too easy to fool yourself in your comfort zone of not being accountable. Yes, life is easier but:

Are you getting the same strong results or trajectory you had when you were tracking? Perhaps if a certain habit stuck, your results are good, but otherwise it's highly unlikely.

Yes, you may have lived successfully off your old mojo for a while, but it's not a long-term plan for success and you know this. Those fumes are getting thinner.

I see this with coaching groups all the time. After we stop meeting weekly and I do a three-month check in, most people have not kept up their power habit because they no longer have to report back every week to me on their tracking of specific activity. Clearly, it's human nature to ease off, but if you want to mine your gold, be selective and wary about going easy if only because this mindset and way of being sticks. Then all you've done is dug yourself a new hole to dig out of. Again, I do it too; we all do. It's being human *so don't beat yourself up*. Use this knowledge and get back into your habits and the habit tracking game and use it to your advantage.

Should you decide to continue not tracking, set another calendar reminder. This might be the hardest step of all especially if you underestimated the effects of your lifequake.

We all do better with accountability – and this is something high achievers who are mining their gold understand better than anyone.

So HOW you think about your tracker is really important: See it as a TOOL to SERVE YOU. Nothing else. It's NOT meant to be something that makes you feel rotten about yourself.

Many people I coach do not stick with using a habit tracker for various reasons. Some people don't want to use a hard copy. Some prefer apps. Some use spreadsheets. Others use their electronic calendars and schedule their habits. Some experience early 'failure' and are wary to return to it because of negative association. Some recoil at the sight of what feels like too much structure. And I would still argue it is a priceless tool to stick with the vast majority of the time. Each of us does best with a different amount of structure. Some will help you mine your gold sooner.

It helps to understand the power of positive neurochemicals (such as dopamine) to your brain and feeling good. It's important to be personally vested in the identities you come up with. The more you want to become that type of person, the more you will want to follow through on making change.

Experiment with WHAT you put on your tracker. If you only use other people's ideas and don't really 'own' what you come up with, you will feel less affinity for the habits and less ownership. It will be easy to dismiss it as 'assignments' from an authority figure rather than personally handpicked by you and for you.

Again, see the tracker as your servant and friend: as really positive reinforcement for you doing the right thing. Do it for a few months and you will be extremely pleased with all the little things that are cumulatively getting you ever better results! Do it for a few years and you will be amazed at what becomes possible for you.

BE and DO Your Change *Consistently*

BREAKTHROUGH BOUND HABIT TRACKER

Remember:	1. The Journey Mindset. The Consistency Mindset. Go to the gym forever.
	2. "I change best when I feel good, not when I feel bad." BJ Fogg
Who I am becoming:	1. _____ 2. _____
WHY?	_____

MONTH	JAN	FEB	MAR	APR	MAY	JUN	JUL	AUG	SEP	OCT	NOV	DEC	TOTAL
HABIT	1	2	3	4	5	6	7	8	9	10	11	12	13	14	15	16	17	18	19	20	21	22	23	24	25	26	27	28	29	30	31	

MONTH	JAN	FEB	MAR	APR	MAY	JUN	JUL	AUG	SEP	OCT	NOV	DEC	TOTAL
POWER HABITS	1	2	3	4	5	6	7	8	9	10	11	12	13	14	15	16	17	18	19	20	21	22	23	24	25	26	27	28	29	30	31	
WEEKLY																																
MONTHLY																																

www.breakthroughbound.com
+001 (312) 622-3121

CHAPTER 20

Use Daily Questions - the Growth Tool for Fortune 100 CEOs

Marshall Goldsmith tells a story in his book *Triggers* about a high-performing executive at a Fortune 100 company. The CEO was getting glowing reports from his direct reports about his progress at work but was so frazzled by the end of the workday, he was getting home and spending his evenings arguing with his wife and yelling at his kids.

"How is it you get to be a consummate professional at work but an amateur at home?" needled Goldsmith. This then prompted his client to add a new daily question to his Habit Tracker: *On a scale of 1-10, did I do my best to be a loving and patient husband and father today?*

When I read this story, it hit a nerve for me. While I wasn't doing *that badly* at home, I'd be lying if I said I my patience wasn't running out 30-60 minutes *before* my children's bedtime – the time when they were most likely to drag their feet and not comply with my need for peace and no to-do items!

Daily questions like this have several benefits *especially for identities you are working on that do not have tangible targets.* They help us get better and adjust faster to change.

These questions **are Goldsmith's secret weapon with the Fortune 100 CEOs he coaches.** And *if the questions are good enough for them, they are good enough for you and me* – especially for qualitative areas that are not easy to measure. **Pick and choose which questions sound useful and experiment with them on your Habit Tracker.**

All the questions start with: **Did I do my best to...**

Here are his standard six 'foundation' questions.

On a scale of 1-10, did I do my best to...

1. Set clear goals today?
2. Make progress toward my goals today?
3. Find meaning today?
4. To be happy today?
5. Build positive relationships today?
6. Be fully engaged today?

Did I do my best to... injects personal responsibility and ownership into the questions.

It's not easy *"to face the reality of our own behavior – and our own effort level – every day."* Especially when we have told ourselves it is something important. So, either we push ourselves into action or we abandon the question.

You can come up with others that relate to Achilles Heels of your own. Here are a few commonly used by clients of mine:

"On a scale of 1-10, did I do my best to..."

*Detach emotionally from outcomes?
*Not take things personally?
*Be present and engaged at home? (no longer an amateur at home)
*Accept what I can't control?

Goldsmith adds that 90% of people rate themselves as above average, yet **within two weeks 50% will give up on Daily Questions**. I lasted 6-8 weeks the first time I tried them in 2015. I made three mistakes.

1. I didn't personalize the questions enough so at some point allowed my negative self-talk to convince me that these were (somehow) Goldsmith's priorities, not mine. I took his recipe too literally.

2. I lacked the worthiness at the time to see that the best of the best commit to these questions to get even better and that, somehow, I didn't fully deserve to play with this crowd. It was okay for me to have a 'kick around' but not actually be on the field for the big game. I forgot that nobody is better than you or me.

3. This was the big one that I quickly convinced myself I didn't need to do, and you may too:

   "The only essential element is that the scores are reported somehow – phone, email, or a voicemail – to someone every day. And that someone is the coach."

   Reading off our scores becomes a test of our commitments. That 'coach' can be one of three things:

   – Simply a scorekeeper who makes no judgement (says nothing)

   – A referee blowing the whistle if your scores are repeatedly low

   – A full-blown advisor who asks you about what you're doing and why

It's quite easy to see why you wouldn't want this level of accountability. It's confronting and forces you to step up and be counted. I feel sad that my past self didn't have the internal strength or resolve to do this. I guess I had too many other challenges at the time or perhaps had not built up enough support.

The Daily Questions provide the structure and accountability to keep top of mind your biggest priorities that are harder to quantify. Change doesn't happen fast using these questions. It gradually shifts your awareness which, when you think about it, is how most real change happens anyway – slowly. So do stick at it and the rewards will come.

However you want to make change, it is work. **Let me leave the final words on this topic with Marshall Goldsmith: "We have to go to the gym forever."** None of this is easy, I know. But it's the difference in your one life between fairly good and outstanding. And this is within your control!

BE and DO Your Change *Consistently*

CHAPTER 21

Start the Day Strong

Do you have a morning ritual to start your day out on a high?

You do it because:

a) It centers you
b) It focuses you
c) It energizes you
d) It gives you a *great confidence boost right out of the gate*
e) It is one of the few parts to your day that you can control
f) It is a well-documented high achiever best practice for a reason

(The only exception to this is I found I could not do it when my children were infants and toddlers because of all the bad nights' sleep and middle-of-the-night wake ups. So don't feel guilty if you're at this stage of life. Having said that, I regret not having re-started it sooner and found tiny ways to do something.)

Make up your own 'recipe' for a morning ritual.

I don't think it matters *what* you do so long as it empowers you and gets your day off to great start. I've tried numerous things over the decades and they all felt beneficial.

Pick one or more of these ingredients to _experiment_ with until you have a routine that fits with you and however much time is reasonable. It's always best to start small and work up:

1. **Exercise:** Some kind of movement. In his book _The 5am Club_, Robin Sharma recommends intense activity that breaks a sweat because of the physiological benefits. Other people are more than inspired by yoga or stretching. At the time of writing, I ride my bike around a lagoon. I don't cycle that hard. My inspiration comes from nature. Breathing exercises can also be powerful. Useful resources for this include Wim Hof and The Oxygen Advantage programs.

2. **Meditation or prayer:** The best benefit to meditation seems to be increased focus: slowing down the brain and quieting the chatter. On its deepest level it connects you with pure consciousness, a time to state your intentions for the day. All great things start out as ideas, and this is your opportunity to drop in the first ripple in the lake. And it discards the unhelpful self-talk.

   For the spiritual, prayer is grounding like nothing else. It can provide clarity, calm, guidance and reconnect people to their purpose.

3. **Journaling:** The best use of journaling is to increase your self-awareness, so you don't just busy your way through life never knowing your best self or deepest self or living the life best suited for you. It can be a great way to explore ideas and solve problems.

4. **Reading an inspiring passage - your voice: I'd urge you all to read something inspiring first thing in the morning.** In the past I've written out and read my goals every day at the kitchen table. I've worked out on exercise machines and listened to recordings of my voice reading through my ideal life. Currently I stop halfway on my bike ride by the shore of the lagoon and read my Inner Hero story out loud.

Do whatever works for you. It could be an inspiring passage, inspiring music, or a religious text. Reading professional or personal development content is also extremely valuable.

Richard Branson shared these five sayings on LinkedIn that he uses to feel centered and inspired starting out his days. He plants his brain garden!

a) Screw it, let's do it
b) You miss 100% of the swings you don't take
c) Only a fool never changes his mind
d) Isn't life wonderful?
e) You don't learn by following the rules. You learn by doing and by falling over.

Make it easy by starting small: Even if it's 5 or 10 minutes, do something empowering to start your day. Even if it's 10 leg squats and reading through your top 5 goals. This is where tiny habits can be very helpful as they are brief and easy and some can be scaled over time.

In the real world, you may have to wake up before your children if you want to avoid personal life interruptions! You can start with one positive activity such as meditation or exercise. Once that feels consistent, you can stack another positive habit on top such as reading for professional or personal development. There are many beneficial activities you can consider, so go easy and experiment. Clearly you only have so much time for this routine.

The most important part of a morning routine is it puts your head in a positive place rather than feeling flat, routine, or worse.

Do you have to get up earlier? I think it helps and it's gratifying to know you're accomplishing great things while others sleep. However, sleep deprivation isn't smart for long-term health and some people truly do their best work later in the day and even at night – get to know yourself better. I go to bed earlier but that's annoyed my wife – this part isn't easy.

<u>Have realistic expectations:</u> I will not claim it makes your entire day great because you can't control for every outcome. *How you manage the rest of your day is also on you.* But **it is far and away the best competitive advantage you could possibly have to start out the day powerfully.** So, if you don't have a morning routine, create one that fits you and if you do have one, ask yourself: *how could I make it more energizing or inspiring?*

BE and DO Your Change *Consistently*

CHAPTER 22

Leverage Flow State

In the quest to be more productive, do better work and enjoy it even more, you want to learn more about getting into a flow state and how to make it happen because it will significantly speed up mining your gold.

Firstly, what is flow exactly? According to *The Art of Impossible* author Steven Kotler, it's an *"altered state of consciousness, a state where every decision, every action, FLOWS seamlessly, perfectly, from the last."*

It is our peak state of focus, where what we are doing is the reward in itself. Time either slows greatly or flies by. Our sense of self vanishes, and our inner critic is quiet.

This gets you ever better results - even more productive states of mind. Living in a state of flow as often as possible is crucial to aim for because *"flow may be the biggest neurochemical cocktail of all. The state appears to blend all six of the brain's major pleasure chemicals and may be one of the few times you get all six at once."*

It's about knowing your zone of excellence (what your best work and skills are), knowing when you do your best work, when you do your best thinking and where you are most productive - what environments are the best for you to be in?

How do you find more flow?

1. **Devote at least 15-20% of your time on flow activities – what you do best and love to do - your One Thing/Power Habit**

   If your Power Habit takes more than a few minutes, you're going to have to schedule it and prioritize it. Tuesdays became my full writing day the year I wrote this book and *most* other days I would also get up early to write for two hours because I do my best thinking in the mornings.

   You may have heard about Google's Twenty Percent Time policy that allows its engineers to spend 20% of their weeks working on **passion projects**. Kotler shares: *"Over 50% of Google's largest revenue-generating products have come out of Twenty Percent Time, including Adsense, Gmail, Google Maps, Google News, Google Earth, and Gmail Labs."*

   This is a power habit for Google. 3M has 15 percent time for its engineers for the same reasons and with equally stellar results.

2. **Passionately Guard Your Time Block**

   Gary Keller put this sign on his desk: "Until my ONE Thing is done - Everything else is a distraction!" If it worked for him…

   Useful things to learn to say:

   "I'm available after 10am each day,"

   "I'm available most weeks on Monday, Wednesday and Friday between 9-4pm"

   "I'm sorry. I already have an appointment at that time."

   "If I have that done by (specific time), would that work?"

Say no to the people and things that prevent you from spending your best flow time on your highest leverage activities, **or you run the very real risk of never coming close to fulfilling your potential.** I'm not being melodramatic here. Your best work needs time and thought.

Your own need to do other things might be your biggest challenge, so brain dump anything you need to do on a list and put it out of sight. Start to enjoy the benefits of flow state.

3. **Know how to leverage your brain and body**

   To do this effectively and enjoy the powerful long-term benefits of leveraging the flow state:

   a) Get enough sleep: your brain needs to incubate on ideas. I've had to get to bed around 9pm so I can wake early to write. It used to be 10:30pm.

   b) Engage in regular exercise. Your brain and body need all the chemical benefits.

   c) Schedule flow time *when you do your best thinking*.

   For writing this book and doing my best work, coffee shops have been best with some caffeine provided. I have headphones to control the background noise if need be and not too much visual distraction. I generally do best not being able to see people walking in and out as that distracts me too much. My favorite place to write, as I mentioned earlier in the book, is the coffee shop in the atrium at the Field Museum in Chicago because it is also an inspiring environment. It lifts me up psychologically.

   You may do your best thinking later at night. Some believe that our brain has just two great hours in it per day when we are at our prime.

4. **Find the intersection between Curiosity-Passion-Purpose**

   Kotler has been studying high achievers for over 30 years and has found three areas that overlap: Curiosity is healthy and gets you started. Passion helps to sustain your motivation. Purpose puts your attention outside yourself. When you combine all of these, then you're in a powerful place to stay the course and produce great work.

5. **The Challenge-Skills Balance** – the MOST IMPORTANT for Flow!

   Your tasks must slightly exceed your skill set – what you're currently good at. Kotler came up with the concept that your new task must exceed your skills "by 4%," but he has also found this needs to be much higher than 4% for aggressive A types. Either way there needs to some uncertainty about what you're working on to keep you on enough of an edge to be highly engaged.

   Lastly, you're not going to be feel on a roll every day. There are four stages to flow and all of them count:

   a) Frustration is the first (totally normal) stage. The key is to decide to fight it.
   b) Let your problem incubate – let it go for a few hours. Kotler recommends light activity is best such as bathing, saunas, stretching, showers, or walks but not TV and beer!

   c) Flow - AVOID distractions, negative thinking, low energy, and lack of preparation. Add more flow triggers - novelty, unpredictability, or complexity!
   d) Active Recovery – recharge the battery: nutrition, sunlight, sleep. Not TV. Mindfulness, light yoga, massage, Epsom salt bath, and ice baths.

6. Avoid a fear of chaos

The world will not care about you getting into a flow state or your power habits so your list of things not yet done will still pile up. If you do everything on your to-do list, you might feel good that day, but it will not get you closer to mining your gold. I implore you to persevere and fight to find the time to stay the course. I've had to sacrifice almost all of my exercise time to get this book finished. I've put on a few pounds; it's difficult. Be prepared for other areas of your life to be less than perfect as you strive to excel for a certain period.

If reading this makes you a little anxious, it's normal. You can start to see that achieving big results and mining your gold is hard – to have the courage to stay that focused. Leonardo da Vinci knew it too: "God sells us all things at the price of labor." So stick to the time it takes!

BE and DO Your Change *Consistently*

CHAPTER 23

How to Handle Depletion and the Everyday Unexpected

Your environment is at war with you every day and it almost always takes you by surprise: Your child wakes up with a bad cold and can't go to school; your plane is delayed; it starts pouring with rain; you have a client with an urgent need or who wants to meet later, or your partner has a bad day at work and not only needs to talk about it now but needs you to make dinner. In Marshall Goldsmith's book, *Triggers,* he refers to such things as *"the high predictability of low predictability events."*

It matters because these things can easily throw you off your well-intentioned goals for the day and, longer-term, they can throw you off your gold mining.

He notes that *"**We are superior planners and inferior doers"**** because of:

a) **Unpredictable events** and how we respond to them

b) **We get depleted** as the day wears on. Our self-control and self-discipline wane like the battery on a mobile phone.

Our failure to get what we want done has many negative effects: **on our morale, on our behavior, on**

our results, and on our capacity to change. <u>That is a daunting list!</u>

1. **Handle UNPREDICTABLE EVENTS well**

   a) Pick your battles.

   Goldsmith insists: ***"Our best behavior is not random and is within our control"*** and one tool is to catch yourself before you react with what he has coined: **AIWATT** – a principle to reduce stress, conflict, debate and wasted time. Basically, you're asking yourself: Should I engage or 'let it go'? *"It is a reminder that our environment tempts us many times a day to engage in pointless skirmishes – and we don't have to take the bait."*

   Am I willing
   At this time,
   To make the investment required
   <u>To make a positive difference</u>
   On this topic?

   b) **Don't take things personally.**

   We behave more calmly when we realize that **other people's behavior is because of what's going on with them, not us**. There's a great thought from Wayne Dyer on this: *"How people treat you is their karma; how you react is yours."*

When other people set you off, remember that you only control how you behave.

Exercise: Picture someone who drives you crazy: How much sleep is that person losing over you tonight? Who is being punished here? Who is doing the punishing?

Don't get mad at people for being who they are. Just accept them.

Now, if you're over 18, you don't have to live with them or spend time with them!

Being in business development you know how hard it can be not to take it personally when people say no. Or don't get back to you. Or just don't want to do anything right now.

It's hard to get used to especially when you try your best and have those days when no one seems to be 'out there' responding at all. It can be discouraging and make you feel badly about yourself. And then when you do experience the no's, you then have to fight the feeling of looking needy because that is such a turn off to others and hinders everything you do next.

The Reality Check

I remember a throwaway line from Brian Tracy many years ago (which I'm paraphrasing) when he noted: "If you can't handle rejection – and since the vast majority of people will rarely need what you're selling right now - you've picked a pretty interesting way to make a living."

The first time I heard that I thought it was rather insensitive. I remember thinking, "Well, I love what I do. I just don't like the selling part much and I'm not very good at it."

But Tracy's right. Regardless of how passionate you are about what you "sell", and regardless of how focused you are on what you do and how you can help people, it's so easy to forget that most of the rest of the world has other more pressing priorities – in their opinion anyway – and often will: their dog can't hold down food, their daughter broke her wrist, their mother has an important hospital appointment, a pipe burst in the garage, they're moving house, they're going on holiday on Monday, their aunt is having a nervous breakdown, their spouse is working 16-hour days because of abc crisis – "the high predictability of low predictability events".

From the mundane traffic jams and 'unexpected' bad weather and flight delays to the life events from birth, illness, marriage, injury, divorce and death, there are plenty of reasons people do not get back to us THAT HAVE NOTHING TO DO WITH US!!

It's Not Personal

We all need reminding that nothing other people do is something we should take personally - EVER. If someone else is mean, negative, or sarcastic towards you, that person is the one with the problem. Our culture has normalized reacting to personal attacks as if it is healthy – even countries react to slights – but this is the collective ego reacting.

You must not take the rejection and disappointment personally. You must treat it as part of the game – the 'dance' of sales. **I score myself daily on a scale of 1-10: "Did I do my best not take anything personally today?"** I'd highly recommend it. I need the reminders because I grew up getting a lot of criticism as a child from an unhappy mother which left me with rather a thin skin. You too can make changes in this area and it may take many months. So what? It's better than living like a puppet your whole life reacting to every swing and arrow that comes your way.

Don't take anything personally. Score yourself every day.

And never give up on yourself.

 c) Three Band-Aid solutions to immediate challenges:

   iv) **Anticipate what might happen** (before you go somewhere or plan something: e.g., if you're trying to lose weight, meet somewhere you'll be less tempted to self-sabotage)

v) **Avoid some environments** so as not to bring out your worst or tempt you to get off track (e.g., there's a very busy four-way stop traffic intersection I avoid in my town because it brings out the worst in me (and quite a few other drivers!), and I fear that one day I'll get upset with a driver who turns out to be the parent of one of my children's friends)

vi) **Adjustment in your environment** (your doctor is delayed for your appointment and instead of getting angry, you say to yourself: "Now I have more time to read that book")

2. **Handle DEPLETION well**

a) **We need to plan our days differently as the day goes on because we need to manage ourselves differently as the day goes on**. We start the day with two roles – part leader and part follower and they grow apart as the day goes one. We need more step-by-step direction later in the day.

STRUCTURE is how we overcome waning motivation, self-discipline, energy, and decision fatigue. Marshall Goldsmith adds: ***"Structure provides help because we don't have to make as many decisions; we just follow the plan."***

You only have so much self-discipline each day, so plan to do your power habit/s earlier in the day rather than hoping you're going to have the energy to do crucial proactive things later in the evening.

Here is a great example from author Stephen King:

"My own schedule is pretty clear-cut. Mornings belong to whatever is new – the current composition. Afternoons are for naps and letters. Evenings are for reading, family, Red Sox games on TV, and any revisions that just cannot wait. Basically, mornings are my prime writing time."

Gary Keller dismisses the objection that King can afford to do that because he's a successful author. He asks the question: **"Does he get to do this because he's Stephen King or is he Stephen King because he does this?"**

b) **We need to practice active recovery.** Take more mini breaks during the day so your battery doesn't run down too fast. Make the time to allow your body to recharge physically with a hot bath, sauna, massage, walk or stretching (not TV and alcohol). *This is no longer a nice to have for the high achiever.* Your body can only push so hard for so long and you become less productive.

c) **Improve your self-awareness** (see Habit 4, Key 3: Elevate Your Self-Awareness)

The more you know yourself, when you are at your best and when you need to pause and re-strategize, the better.

d) **Free up mental space**

What's one thing that Steve Jobs, Albert Einstein, and Barack Obama have in common? They always wore the same outfits. Jobs always wore a black turtleneck, blue jeans, and New Balance sneakers. Einstein wore several variations of the same grey suit.

Barack Obama wore only grey or blue suits as president. When asked why, he explained: "I'm trying to pare down decisions. I don't want to make decisions about what I'm eating or wearing. Because I have too many other decisions to make."

Mark Zuckerberg typically wears a grey t-shirt and jeans. "I really want to clear my life to make it so that I have to make as few decisions as possible about anything except how to best serve this community."

What can you do re. what you wear and what you eat that you could 'automate' to reduce some decision fatigue?

e) Stack Your Habits

When I first read about this in James Clear's *Atomic Habits*, I made the mistake of thinking of habit stacking as merely a 'technique'. What I missed was that the deeper value to a good habit is for it to become *automatic* – something hardwired that requires no thought. This then **frees up more mental space** so you can focus on *even more important matters* and, if you want, go bigger.

This is where it gets really exciting.

FIRST: Learn how to create your own habits (revisit Chapter 17). That's incredibly valuable and empowering because you now know how to change effectively and be consistent (where most people fail).

For example:

After I wake up (pick something you already do habitually)
I will stretch for ten minutes (your new habit)

SECOND: Start to stack other empowering habits on top of these to build out increasingly effective routines in your life.

For example:
After I stretch for ten minutes,
I will do cardio and weights exercises for twenty minutes

What I've learned is that (surprise surprise) this takes time. You have to see the benefits to your new habits for quite some time before you are likely ready to experiment with additional ones that make sense to stack onto your current good habits. One fact that still amazes me is that BJ Fogg, the creator of the *Tiny Habits* method (outlined above), has up to 11 new, small habits on the go at any given time. What I take from this is that if you work on yourself long enough knowing the process works (that he has pioneered and tested for over two decades), *you can create positive change beyond anything you can imagine.*

The easiest times of day to habit stack (and be consistent so you reduce decision fatigue) are with:

a) Your morning routine – what you do after you wake up
b) Mealtimes
c) Workout times (keep them at the same time)
d) Work routines
e) An evening routine (pattern of positive activities leading up to bedtime)

Building a morning routine is the easiest one to start because you can avoid work-related interruptions. For more on this revisit Chapter 21: Start the Day Strong.

Start small and build up (if possible) so you don't feel failure and the temptation to give up. It's as important that you feel good about your progress because this is when we change best. As you layer on new habits, you'll get better outcomes, less mental fatigue, and more mental space for new and better priorities.

BE and DO Your Change *Consistently*

CHAPTER 24

4% Growth and Feeling Alive

Do the Uncomfortable, Leverage Flow State, and Target Big Projects

In 2019, I interviewed Will Barron for the podcast I hosted that year: *The Road Rarely Taken: How 'Ordinary' People Get Out of Their Own Way and You Can Too.*

Will is the host of the Salesman podcast, the world's largest B2B sales podcast. At the time, he averaged over 700,000 downloads/month. It was an inspiring conversation on many levels.

What struck me the most was his transparency about interviewing well-known people. I asked him: "Do you ever get intimidated by some of the big names you interview? Didn't you feel like an imposter in your early years?"

I loved his response:

"I still feel like an imposter. I think if that feeling does go away, you're not pushing hard enough."

David Goggin's book *Can't Hurt Me* included this exercise:

1. Write out all the things that you don't like doing or that make you uncomfortable that are good for you/important.
2. Decide which one to start first.

THE 5 HABITS TO MINE YOUR GOLD

Several years ago, my list included:

Cold calling
Pushing myself hard physically
Confronting people
Talking about money
Getting up early
Debt
Approaching well known people for interviews
Thinking big and following through
Tech e.g. learning how to podcast
Learning what I need to learn
Living within a budget
Learning new ways to do things
Opening up to wife and others about my feelings
Prioritizing my passions
Taking the leap
Embracing change
Accountability
Abundance thinking
Shining in the spotlight
Being assertive
Cheering on others
Being true to myself

While one advantage to being miserable is it can be easier to make changes, don't wait for such pain! The principle of doing the uncomfortable is powerful and one that most people will avoid because it sounds, well, uncomfortable! In 2019 there were so many things I was unhappy about. I was in a lot of emotional pain and there wasn't one area of my life I felt good about except my relationship with my children. I'd highly recommend the exercise.

As a result of the list, I was willing to push myself back out of my comfort zone because my life had to change and get better. I decided to learn how to produce a podcast from start to finish and I began interviewing people. The technical side of this was all out of my comfort zone. So was approaching people to interview. I also took a course about running Mastermind groups and, as soon as I could, I started my own group and then a second one This was new too. I was very open to trying new strategies.

I pursued a lot less of my former (comfortable) work in order to learn more about ways to help others get out of their own way so I could help people follow through better and get better results.

I felt a lot happier. I appreciated what I had more and was more present for it. I realized that I enjoyed my work and helping people. I love to learn. I love to exercise. I enjoy loving on my kids. I love to present to groups and be as helpful and open as I can. I enjoy writing. In other words, I was getting to do many of the things I enjoyed and was good at.

I spent little time stressing about why I wasn't making millions and making myself feel like a loser because of it. I focused on what I could control better which was finding better solutions for me and my clients to enjoy life more. I focused more on having happier clients and, while it was a slow process, I was able to point to ever more successes every year. I was more tuned into what I liked to do and felt content on the inside.

The podcast interviews showed me that 'success' is not all about achievement if it's at the expense of things I value more – such as being a good dad, being authentic to myself and others and having good health. I am deeply driven to make a difference but not at all costs.

As I did with my list, start with one item. Rather like crafting a tiny habit, ease into doing something that stretches you. It's very subjective.

As I shared previously, the concept of 4% growth comes from the work of Steven Kotler and his research on high performers and what he referred to as the "challenge/skills sweet spot". It's a stretch for you – based on your standards – but not a crazy leap.

What helps to become bolder is to do uncomfortable things in different areas of your life AND CONNECT THE DOTS: physical challenges such as a harder workout or fasting; social or emotional risks such as having a difficult conversation that you've been putting off with a key person in your life; or a mental challenge like learning something new that's quite hard for you. This helps you PROVE to your brain that you are becoming the type of person who faces down many fears.

You connect the dots by saying to yourself: "If I can do this hard physical task, then I can do this hard work task." This is not easy, but you've chosen to read about a topic that is not easy. If it were easy, everyone would do it. And I'm guessing you don't want to be like everyone.

> Remember! *"Fear screams loudest when your magic is closest."* - Robin Sharma

Miguel, one of my clients, put "4%" on a Post It note by his computer. Every day it would catch his eye and remind him to do something that required some extra courage. Whenever I'd ask him about it, he would light up and say how much good it was doing his confidence and helping him sustain a positive momentum. Truthfully, we need these actions even more so when things are not going well or we are just starting out on a venture. But the 4% concept is always a sign of growth.

I want to state too that this is not something that has to happen every day of the year. I made the typical A type mistake of over-doing it - the pace was too intense. But the concept is always worth revisiting and, more often than not, is going to serve you to help you continue to grow.

There is real joy in the 4% - Growth That Can Help You Feel Alive Again

"Some people die at 25 and aren't buried until 75" - Benjamin Franklin

"Adventure is worthwhile." - Amelia Earhart

I wasn't sure what was coming over me. Whether it was my age – 54 – and knowing my dad died not long after his 58th birthday – or whether my life cycle was whispering in my ear that there was no time to lose. (I think I've always heard a ticking clock in my head.) Or whether I knew I had so much more potential that I had a new sense of urgency. I wasn't sure.

What I did know was that I was having a ball testing myself each day with some new challenge. I felt alive again by using this question: **what would be an adventure or a small, new stretch today?** I urge you to consider doing the same.

An extra uphill run, a longer cold shower, fasting longer, holding my breath longer, calling someone outside my comfort zone, mountain biking a difficult trail, or lying in the waters of Lake Michigan at 5am; I started to become my own human guinea pig. This was so far removed from who I'd been for most of the previous 54 years, it was rather puzzling.

I started really enjoying myself again. It wasn't just the activities themselves; it was helping me see things differently: things that were just 'normal' suburban living that I'd got used to, where I was just existing and no longer truly living. It was an easy trap to fall into once I became a father of twins.

Now I was having new experiences. I was testing myself, building my self-respect more. My self-confidence grew as I saw that I had no idea what I was capable of. I started asking myself different questions: I'd listen to a great song and think: "I haven't written one of those yet. I don't know why I didn't think to start creating something like that." And I had a new respect for the people who did get off their backsides to create something because that involves taking a risk and putting themselves out there. Who cares if I didn't like it or even derided them at the time? They got in the ring and contributed something with their one life. Good for them.

Is it time for you to ask yourself more: "Does this really matter?"

"Who said this was something to value and what does my instinct or heart say?"

I decided to stop taking my medicine for acid reflux after nine years and see if I could make enough changes to my lifestyle that I didn't have to depend on it. I was more willing to acknowledge that I'd repressed too many negative emotions in my life and that this could be a reason I'd not jumped into the ring more. I was willing to acknowledge that what got me 'here' wouldn't get me to loftier peaks with better views and deeper valleys with darker nights.

Days felt fresher, routines felt uglier. I started doing Wim Hof breathing exercises and cold therapy and was shocked how much better and re-energized I felt. It's a fantastic way to quickly recharge before a meeting and feels much better than thinking that caffeine is the only solution. Oxygen – who'd have thought?

Firsts for me in those early weeks included:

Mountain biking (three times) *Enjoying* a cold shower
Breathing exercises *Enjoying* going for a run
Enjoying running up hills
Lying in the (very cold) water of a lake, staring at the stars, and doing breathing exercises
Swimming in Lake Michigan at 5am in the dark in 45F (7C) temps (then running up the hill to the street seven times and back before cycling home in just shorts and running shoes)
Biking and running without a shirt on in sub-freezing temperatures
Going on a spontaneous hike with my children
Teaching my daughter how to play with a bonfire (which we chanced on in nearby woods)

Adding a walk in the woods as a second workout for the day
Listening to a night-time meditation designed to influence my sub-conscious mind
Listening to popular 80s music and enjoying it (!) (I was too 'cool' for this at the time – in my own mind!)
Fasting 4-5 workdays/week for 15-18 hours – I'd never done that voluntarily before
Taking half a day off to 'play' and see how that helped my thinking and creativity

I suppose after 54 years I said to myself: "I know what I'll get if I keep doing what I'm doing."
Someone asked me how I was able to change my thinking after a lifetime of feeling so negatively about some of these things.

"I decided to" was my answer.

I decided to notice all the positives – and it was a process; it didn't shift overnight. It's a useful reminder that we can do this any time. We can believe anything we want. I used to drool over baked goods and desserts everywhere I went. Now I look at them and *most* days I say "urgh: sabotage" to myself. I'm not trying to be perfect here or self-righteous or hypocritical, I'm just playing with my head in a way that serves me at the moment. It's not as hard as I always 'believed'. You really can do the same especially if you treat it as a game.

Your version of feeling more alive may look very different. It doesn't matter. **The real point isn't the list of activities: It's the knock-on effect it has on every other area of your life.** You will find you start to dial it up with everything that matters. It's helped me connect the dots between facing fears in one area and saying to myself: "If I can swim in a Great Lake in 45F degree temps in the dark, I can…"

I've taken more risks in my business. I've had more fun with my kids. I've started to open my heart up more. And this is just the begin-ning (I hope!). In the midst of raising young children these past nine years, I think I was just swirling around merely existing, not truly living: chauffeuring the children between events, waiting for coffee at coffee shops, holding client meetings, watching my kids play in the park, cleaning up the kitchen and cleaning out the cat litter.

All of us has a *window* of opportunity. And, sadly, these windows close. Things we take for granted that we will do again do not always come back. The Pandemic tried to teach us this.

If nothing else, ask yourself often:

1. **What's a 4%/bigger target to aim at this week/month?**
2. **How can I follow my love more this week?**
3. **What would make today more fun?**
4. **What would make me feel more alive today?**
5. **What's a micro adventure I could go on today (or this week)?**

It's not selfish for you to do this too. Everyone wins because you are getting so many benefits. Your rising tide raises other boats. Do something today. Please! As Robin Sharma says in his outstanding book, *The Everyday Hero Manifesto*, "Ideation without execution is the sport of fools. And that making amazing dreams come true is an enormous act of self-love."

BE and DO Your Change *Consistently*!

CHAPTER 25

DO YOUR BEST and Go to the Gym Forever

A few years ago, I hired a coach because he had a peace about him that I definitely didn't feel at the time. And I wanted that peace and mindset.

One of his core messages was that the only thing you had any control over was how you decide to handle the moment right in front of you. Everything else was past or future. It helped me better understand (over time) that the *only* thing that is real is right now. The only thing to focus thoughts on is right now.

But what it ended up helping me be conscious of is whether I do my best with whatever is in front of me.

Firstly, I have to say that for about six months even with daily reminders I felt, experienced, and noticed absolutely nothing!! If my coach hadn't been so adamant about its importance every time we spoke, I would have forgotten it in seconds.

I was so hardwired to do everything the way I always had, it took me months of reminders to incredibly slowly shift my awareness of how I did things and how much effort I put into different things. It's quite shocking to 'notice' that you're not really listening to your spouse or children at certain times, or even in a client meeting you find yourself thinking about something completely unrelated.

The strange thing about this particular learning journey is you don't even notice the day when your way of thinking shifts. 'Suddenly' one day you're going about a task, and you consciously say to yourself: 'Is this your best effort?' and you realize that you've been asking yourself this for a while.

As a practical action to-do, what I recommend is to ask yourself at the end of each day:

"On a scale of 1-10, to what extent did I do my best today?"

What I've learned about how our brains work – to create new neural pathways – is the consistent repetition that it requires. And while all our brains have plasticity so are adaptable to change, I'm pretty sure there's no clear timeline for each person on how long this takes. Sorry!

However, the benefits are sensational if you're willing to persist. What I've learned is that more often than we realize, we do *not* do our best and when you start being more conscious of it, the positive changes you see – gradually of course - are increasingly satisfying and empowering.

Over time your self-respect will grow because you acknowledge yourself more. You will feel better about yourself when you do your best. After all (and forgive me for stating the obvious) – **you can't do any better than your best!**

And you start to wonder what can happen when you consistently do your best (because you admit to yourself just how often you don't give 100%). Eventually you start to see that the sky is the limit. And I'm talking about your sky. Because you also learn better what some of your limits are and where you can do your best but it's never going to be terribly good or bring you great joy. In other words, it can help you learn about your strengths and greatest skills better as well as what you truly love to do.

Since a lot of achiever types are reading this, I have to include that we as a group are usually far too critical of ourselves, so part of this experience is doing a better job of giving yourself credit for doing your best even if the outcome isn't so amazing. There is the rather silly expectation, for example, that if you do your best exercise, that it means YOU should be knocking out Ironmans, until you realize your body isn't going to respond well!

That's part of the journey: **be kinder to yourself. It really does not serve you to take two steps forward and then berate yourself for not being perfect and take two steps back.**

Over time (yes, it may be months) the rewards feel like you've built this really strong foundation of confidence and self-respect. There is a very positive domino effect as you see yourself achieving more in every area where you do your best. Whether it's business, personal relationships because you're more present and making more conscious effort, health, spiritually, and financially – all these areas are getting higher levels of effort and attention. And this is how you elevate your journey. Your positive vibration will ever better impact those around you and is only good for business. What you project out – even unwittingly – can only be good when you're doing your best.

The rewards are quite profound. You get to mine your gold.

And you have to go to the gym forever.

Lastly, it was in a Marshall Goldsmith book that I first read about the concept that you never stop needing to go to the 'gym'. On one level I can see that this idea can suck the energy out of you. To accept that there is no exotic destination that you arrive at permanently in life and live in a serene state of bliss on a sun bed by the pool in the Caribbean until your body breathes its last breath. Success is temporary.

It's certainly not an inspiring thought that the work never ends.

But **it's not work; it's your better life!**

It's growth. It's living to be your best self. It doesn't mean never taking a break. It doesn't mean not living from a place of love or not living aligned with what you value and define as success. It doesn't mean not enjoying the present and the journey.

It means handling all that life throws at you to the best of your abilities and being a shining light to others. It means trying and failing, knowing there is always a feast of enlightenment to expose yourself to from brilliant minds and beautiful artists – however they perform this. It means lifting others up and making as big a difference as you can in your small part of the planet.

French president Georges Clemenceau noted that: "A man's life is interesting primarily when he has failed – I well know. For it's a sign that he tried to surpass himself." Don't be scared! Stay on your journey and have more stories to tell your grandchildren and great-grandchildren.

William Feather reflected on persistence: "Success seems to be largely a matter of hanging on after others have let go."

BE and DO Your Change *Consistently*

Mine Your Gold

'Life isn't about finding yourself. Life is about creating yourself.' – George Bernard Shaw

What would you love to create?

When I introduced this book, I said there were three reasons I have had a lifetime urge to find solutions to and hence write a book about how to get out of your own, so you can pursue what you truly want and tap into your greatest strengths.

First, I had grown up feeling powerless to help my mother live the life she wanted. This has provided me much fuel. Yes, it stemmed from both love and pain, and as a 'must know' for myself, but over many years has driven me to make other people's journey clearer. Yes, my loftiest goal is for these five habits to be a 'recipe' through life's ups and downs to help you live your definition of success.

How can you make it your duty to commit more deeply to mining your gold?

Whether you believe God has gifted you with the tools to do it or not, to paraphrase Wayne Dyer: do not die with your music inside you. I don't know if Dyer knew he was dying of cancer when he wrote those words, but you have to be aware enough to know that time does not wait. People generally share their wisdom because they want to empower others to get the most out of their lives. Don't wait any longer. Time waits for no one including you!

At the week of my writing this, one of my boyhood hometown (Coventry) heroes, Terry Hall of the Specials, died aged 63. Despite awful sexual abuse as a child and lifelong battles with depression, he *created*. Even during the recent Pandemic – after three months of feeling completely lost and "trying not to die" - he decided to record an album of covers inspired by the Black Lives Matter movement. Called *Protest Songs*, it charted at number two in the UK. Leonardo da Vinci wrote: "What is fair in men, passes away, but not so in art." **If Terry Hall can do it after what happened to him as a child, you do not have an excuse.**

Remember: most of us want the same things and yet too often feel like we are so far from this.

If you want to feel freer to spend your time doing what you truly want, be more loving, and more purposeful, first accept where you are. **Then put your head down to make change and try to feel as good as possible on your journey.**

Revisit the sections from this book about how to fuel up, pull the weeds, elevate what you can control, and how to change. Learn to let love drive.

Then work on your consistent doing problem.

When you get stuck, you now have a clearer path out and a broader understanding of obstacles. **Your journey is not going to be a steady climb up to permanent glory.** Life doesn't work that way. There will be setbacks and lifequakes. And now you know how to handle them.

Be the courage to take steps now - even if you don't feel like you have it in you.

Second, my big dreams weren't encouraged past early childhood as my parents and most of my teachers resigned themselves to a tolerable life well below their own dreams. I felt like I grew up in a cage. Since then, I've always done my best to be a positive force for good and to encourage others to be, do and have what they really want in life. Do you need more support? And who can you support on their path?

Know that everything you need is inside you and find others who can support you - even if they are role models you don't know, or they are from history, and you can only imagine having conversations with them. That's what Napoleon Hill (author of *Think and Grow Rich*) did. He created his own board of directors full of leaders from history. Talk to God - whoever supports you. Just don't buy into the myth that you are separate and alone.

Keep your dreams of childhood alive.

Believe you can shine your light as bright as you want and as often as you want.

Third, how could anyone overcome three decades of feeling fairly worthless? Of frequent criticism, self-doubt, and low self-confidence? How could anyone replace the learned, hardwired negative self-talk from childhood to build the self-belief to make much of their life? Finding ways to help first myself and then others overcome this stubborn, at-times brutal hurdle has also driven me deeply. It's like cutting away at a tumor.

I've been there and am now cheering you on.

Keep reinforcing empowered ways to think and believe: it works slowly but surely over time. Surround yourself with the message that you can do whatever you set your mind to.

If you still feel a long way off, ask yourself: How much time have I given it?

Don't believe the past negative messages of unhappy people anymore:

You can believe whatever you want!

Believe that if others can do it, you can too if you put in the work.

It's easy to envy the fame and riches achieved by a celebrity like Queen's Freddie Mercury and think he got lucky, but he understood it as well as anyone:

I've paid my dues time after time
I've done my sentence but committed no crime
And bad mistakes, I've made a few
I've had my share of sand kicked in my face
But I've come through

And we mean to go on, and on, and on, and on

We are the champions, my friends

And we'll keep on fighting till the end
We are the champions, we are the champions

I've taken my bows and my curtain calls
You brought me fame and fortune
And everything that goes with it, I thank you all

But it's been no bed of roses, no pleasure cruise
I consider it a challenge before
The whole human race and I ain't gonna lose

And we mean to go on, and on, and on and on

Build your fuel. Purpose is certainly the most direct route as Martin Luther King knew only too well: "No one really knows why they are alive until they know what they'd die for."

Don't fear that your growing success (however you define it) will cause you to lose those around you. Your presence will liberate others who also wish to make the most of their one life.

Build your worthiness.

Build your tenacity.

Pull the weeds often: Avoid people trying to sell the quick fix or who make you feel less than.

Elevating what you can control and knowing how to be and what to do to make the change consistently all contribute to helping you put one foot in front of the other on your journey. It is virtually the only way that works. Do the work. Think longer-term and have faith in growing your circle of influence.

What I wish for you most is to keep moving. Stay in the game. Nelson Mandela understood it supremely having spent 27 years in jail protesting apartheid: "A winner is a dreamer who never gives up." That's the secret.

Whenever life allows, keep making progress - keep making small changes if something isn't working well. Make almost every day your Olympic Games.

When you have a setback and feel the inevitable discouragement, get back on your feet and do something that takes you forward again - even if you've taken multiple steps back.

I wrote this book to help set you free as it's freed me:

It sets you free from what you don't know that you need to know if you want to mine your gold.

It sets you free from the mental shackles that have held you back.

It set you free by providing a recipe and action plan to follow to mine your gold.

Let love drive.
Fuel up often.
Pull the weeds often.
Elevate your control.
BE and DO Your Change *Consistently.*

Act now, set yourself free, and make your life your art. Your art can live forever.

THE 5 HABITS TO MINE YOUR GOLD

Appendix: New Year Review Questions to Sustain Your Gold Mining

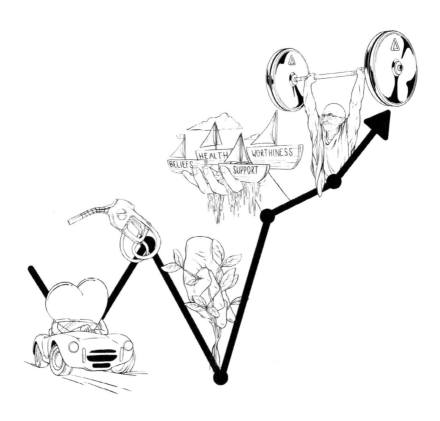

How to Kick Off Your Prep for the New Year (or Mid-Year Review)

When you are ready to reflect on your year and start planning for next year, ask yourself:

a) **How well do you learn from your past?**

b) **How effective are you at planning your upcoming year?**

I have to say I always put in quality time with the reflection part and process through lessons life tried to teach me (I won't claim I learned them all), but given what I 'know', I'm struck by how consistently my goals are wildly high every year – even after all these years.

I applaud my optimism, but at some point in the year it is demoralizing to see how far off I am from this perfect life where business is unprecedented, my relationships are all fabulous, and I look like someone who has eight hours to spend in a gym every day!!

The trick is to have something to measure that you aspire to and drives you as much as is possible.

It might be:
A goal
A habit
An identity shift: I am the type of person who is increasingly…
Your purpose
Your definition of true success

The wise target is to have an increasingly upward trajectory. The wise action over the holidays is to clarify the few key habits you want.

Almost no one lacks the desire at the start of the year. What often quickly goes wrong is a lack of identity shift (see the above question) and being inconsistent. This is why becoming clear about the most impactful habits serves you so well.

1. **Here are some of my favorite reflection questions.** TAKE YOUR PICK!

   Reflect on the REALITY of your year. What are the facts about the different areas of your life? We can be masters of deceit at times like this. Leonardo da Vinci reminds us: "The greatest deception men suffer is from their own opinions." This is not for you!

   a) Review your year and different areas of your life, then list 10 (or more) things (professional/personal) you would commend yourself for. Next to each success, write the most useful lesson you learnt and *what's to be taken from this lesson*. Is there a next step or a principle you can apply from this daily, weekly, or monthly?

   b) Knowing what you know now, if you were to start the year over again, what advice (professional/personal) would you give to yourself, one year younger? Write down at least 10 lessons life was trying to teach you (because it's naïve to think we have engrained and mastered all these lessons. Many of us make the same mistakes every year.) I also like to write down where I got the idea or who introduced me to this person. This reminds me of the richness in my world and reminds me of people who brought great value to me in ways beyond introductions. A great idea, resource, or planning tool can bring a lot of value.

   c) Who do you NOT want to be next year? (The type of person who…)

   d) What were your three biggest regrets of the year? Consider revisiting Bonnie Ware's *Top 5 Regrets of the Dying* shared in Chapter 6.

e) Don't believe your hype. Based on your *actual* outcomes this year:

    i) What are your current beliefs? (revisit Habit 4, Key 2: Elevate Your Beliefs)

I deserve and expect to be somewhat out of shape, fairly weak and inflexible

I deserve and expect my business to generate $X (not what I'd hoped for) amount

I deserve and expect few, if any, fun and wild moments

I deserve and expect to live my purpose except I'm not clear what it is

    ii) What are your intended beliefs for next year?

I deserve and expect to be fit, strong and flexible

I deserve and expect my business to generate $X (achievable and inspiring) amount

I deserve and expect ever more fun and wild moments

I deserve and expect to live my purpose fully almost every day

One odd thing that helps me with belief change is thinking about people who believe things I think are completely ridiculous or offensive. In other words, if they can brainwash themselves on something pretty far-fetched or completely whacky, why not apply the same principle for what I believe to be for the greater good of humankind?

2. **My monthly GPS system also is a useful activity at year-end.** Next year, what do you need to…

Stop (doing)?
(Do) Less?
Keep (doing)?
(Do) More?
Start (doing)?

Accept for next year? (What realities are beyond your control and/ or require significant patience?)

3. **Aspirational targets:**

   a) **What breakthrough/s do you want next year?** After you've written these down, ask: "Do *I* want these break-throughs or are these someone else's wishes for me? Which ones do I and I alone *really* want?" Make sure there are no 'should do's' on your list because they might make someone else happy or proud.

   b) **What type of person do you need to be next year for it to be a breakout year?** Preface it with the word 'increasingly' then brainstorm a list before deciding on no more than two: confident; focused; productive; healthy, present etc.

   c) **What power habit will prove that to your brain?** Only have 2-3 of these. They are your most impactful habits that get you the 80-20 Law results (80% of your results from 20% of your activity).

4. **Optional: Deep targets** (borrowed at some point from Robert Holden)

   d) What does God (pick your universal power of choice) wish for me next year?

   e) What does my soul want for me next year?

   f) How will I follow my heart next year?

From all the above questions 1-4, now you're ready to **decide on your choice of guideposts for the year:**
Goals – set these and then ask: **Are my goals worthy of me?** If setting these never works for you, focus on monthly or quarterly goals or...
Habits

An identity shift: "I am the type of person who is increasingly…" (bold, organized etc)
Your purpose
Your definition of true success

Experiment. Modify like a GPS each month (use the questions in point 2) because life will often throw the unexpected at us. Enjoying a good life requires constant slight and frequent adjustment. Maybe that's your paradigm shift: get as much clarity about what you want for the upcoming year that you can control, be inspired about that, and put touchpoints in your calendar to revisit and consider edits each month.

Wishing you an outstanding and deeply rewarding new year!